TABLE LANDS

Children's Literature Association Series

TABLE LANDS

Food in Children's Literature

Kara K. Keeling
and Scott T. Pollard

UNIVERSITY PRESS OF MISSISSIPPI / JACKSON

The University Press of Mississippi is the scholarly publishing agency of the Mississippi Institutions of Higher Learning: Alcorn State University, Delta State University, Jackson State University, Mississippi State University, Mississippi University for Women, Mississippi Valley State University, University of Mississippi, and University of Southern Mississippi.

www.upress.state.ms.us

Designed by Peter D. Halverson

The University Press of Mississippi is a member of the Association of University Presses.

Copyright © 2020 by University Press of Mississippi
All rights reserved

First printing 2020

∞

Library of Congress Cataloging-in-Publication Data

Names: Keeling, Kara K., author. | Pollard, Scott T., author.
Title: Table lands : food in children's literature / Kara K. Keeling and Scott T. Pollard.
Other titles: Children's Literature Association series.
Description: Jackson : University Press of Mississippi, 2020. | Series: Children's Literature Association series | Includes bibliographical references and index.
Identifiers: LCCN 2020006549 (print) | LCCN 2020006550 (ebook) | ISBN 9781496828347 (hardback) | ISBN 9781496828354 (trade paperback) | ISBN 9781496828361 (epub) | ISBN 9781496828378 (epub) | ISBN 9781496828385 (pdf) | ISBN 9781496828392 (pdf)
Subjects: LCSH: Food in literature. | Children's literature—History and criticism. | BISAC: LITERARY CRITICISM / Children's & Young Adult Literature
Classification: LCC PN1009.5.F66 K44 2020 (print) | LCC PN1009.5.F66 (ebook) | DDC 809.9/3564—dc23
LC record available at https://lccn.loc.gov/2020006549
LC ebook record available at https://lccn.loc.gov/2020006550

British Library Cataloging-in-Publication Data available

CONTENTS

Acknowledgments
- VII -

Chapter 1
An Invitation to the Table
The Tastes of Children's Literature
- 3 -

Chapter 2
American Children's Cookbooks as Scenes of Instruction
Tracking Historical Shifts of Work, Play, Pleasure, and Memory
- 11 -

Chapter 3
Puddings and Pies
Meat Pastries in the Tales of Beatrix Potter
- 35 -

Chapter 4
"A Little Smackerel of Something"
Food and the *Künstlerroman* in the Winnie-the-Pooh Books
- 51 -

Chapter 5
Food of the Woods and Plains
Two Visions of Food, Culture, Land, and History in Laura Ingalls Wilder's
Little House Books and Louise Erdrich's Birchbark Series
- 64 -

Contents

Chapter 6
"A Profound Love for Luscious Things"
Food as Symbolism and History in Maurice Sendak's *In the Night Kitchen*
- 90 -

Chapter 7
Dangerous Angels: The Weetzie Bat Books
Food, Place, and Sparkly Glam Slinkster Cool Vegetarianism in Los Angeles
- 106 -

Chapter 8
Ratatouille and Restaurants
A Portrait of the Artist as a Young Rat
- 122 -

Chapter 9
"Beating Eggs Never Makes the Evening News"
Politics and Kitchens in Rita Williams-Garcia's *One Crazy Summer* and Its Sequels
- 144 -

Chapter 10
Refugee Narratives, Cuisine Clash
The Case of Thanhha Lai's *Inside Out & Back Again*
- 166 -

Notes
- 179 -

Works Cited
- 189 -

Index
- 203 -

ACKNOWLEDGMENTS

This project would not have been completed without substantial contributions and help from many people. We owe first and particular thanks to Margaret Mackey, both for her helpful editorial suggestions for our first article on Sendak when she was the editor of *Children's Literature in Education* and for seeing the further applicability of the idea when she asked us for a similar take on *The Tale of Peter Rabbit* for the centenary volume she was editing. She was the one who first suggested that there was a book to be written on the subject and that we should write it. She is very much the fairy godmother of this volume.

We owe our own institution much gratitude for supporting us through this project. Dr. Jean Filetti, former chair of the Department of English; Dr. Mary Wright, the current chair; Dr. Lori Underwood, the Dean of the College of Arts and Humanities; Dr. David Doughty, the Provost; and the Faculty Senate of Christopher Newport University, all made possible the joint sabbatical we were awarded for the fall of 2017, during which we accomplished much of the work that went into researching and writing many of these chapters. Letting two professors from one department take off the same term from teaching was a stretch of institutional resources, and we are grateful to all of them but especially to Dr. Wright who had to create a departmental schedule without us that still met the needs of our students. Drs. Margarita Marinova and Kevin Shortsleeve, who stepped in to teach the courses we would normally have taught, also made that sabbatical term work. We are also grateful to the rest of our colleagues in the English Department at CNU who have listened to our various enthusiasms and supported this project in many ways over the years.

Likewise, we are thankful for the help we were given by the librarians of the Trible Library at CNU, particularly Jesse Spencer, the interlibrary loan librarian who was indefatigable in tracking down what must have seemed highly esoteric books, ranging from histories of rats to gigantic collections of early comics. He was very patient with our occasional failures to return the books to him as soon as we should have. Thanks are also due to Dr. Mary Sellen, our university librarian, who has supported growing the collection of food studies books.

We have other librarians to thank as well: Rita Smith, who was curator of the Baldwin Library of Historical Children's Literature at the University of Florida's George A. Smathers Libraries when we first started this project and was helpful during our studies there, and her successor, Suzan Alteri, who was kind and obliging on our second visit. Ellen Ruffin, curator of the de Grummond Collection at the McCain Library of the University of Southern Mississippi, was also very welcoming during our research there. Kudos to the staff of both libraries who hunted up the children's cookbooks and managed all our requests during those intensive research days when we were trying to make the most of limited time.

Many colleagues have helped our ideas evolve over the years since we first grew interested in the relationship between children and food. We owe a debt of gratitude to all the contributors to our 2008 anthology, *Critical Approaches to Food in Children's Literature*: Genny Ballard, Holly Blackford, Winnie Chan, Lan Dong, Jodie Slothower, Jan Susina, James Everett, Leona Fisher, Lisa Rowe Fraustino, Elizabeth Gargano, Robert Kachur, Jacqueline Labbe, Karen Hill McNamara, Martha Satz, Richard Vernon, Annette Wannamaker, and Jean Webb. You all opened our eyes to the myriad possibilities and approaches to the subject. We would also especially like to thank Michelle Martin, Sara Schwebel, and Dianne Johnson-Feelings for their invitation to speak on food in children's literature at the School of Library Science of the University of South Carolina; we vividly remember their warm hospitality.

Katie E. Keene and the editorial staff at the University Press of Mississippi have been encouraging, kind, efficient, and thorough throughout the process of turning a manuscript into a book, and we deeply appreciate the work they put into this volume to make it the best possible version of our work.

We are also grateful to the readers and editors of the various children's literature journals who have shepherded other aspects of this project through their venues, in particular Michelle Abate and Karen Coats for their help with our article on food in Neil Gaiman's *Coraline* in *Children's Literature*; Mavis Reimer for her work on our article on food in the novels of Polly Horvath in *Jeunesse: Young People, Texts, Culture*; Karin Westman, Naomi Wood, and David L. Russell for their aid with our article on Pamela Muñoz Ryan's *Esperanza Rising* in *The Lion and the Unicorn*; and Gitanjali G.

Shahani for soliciting our chapter on Laura Ingalls Wilder for the Cambridge anthology *Food and Literature*. Without these earlier projects where we refined our ideas and approach, this volume would not have come to fruition. We would also like to thank the many members of the Children's Literature Association who attended sessions to hear our papers that were embryonic versions of many of these chapters: your questions, suggestions, and ideas were invaluable—especially when shared over lunches and dinners between and after sessions.

Our CNU students, too, deserve a vote of thanks: the many students who have taken Scott's senior seminars on Food and Literature and his freshman seminars on Corn: Exploring New World Foods in a Global Context, and the students of Kara's Children's Literature and Adolescent Literature courses who have enthusiastically engaged with us on just what, how, and why food signifies in literature.

Finally, on a personal note, we would like to thank those who have in many ways tutored us in our own growth as cooks and eaters. Miss Vance of Lincoln Middle School in Rockford, Illinois, and Mrs. Delauter of Mango Junior High School in Sunnyvale, California, taught our school cooking classes, trying to prepare us and our classmates to be able to cook for ourselves when the time came. Above all, we remember and thank George Ackerman, proprietor of the Warwick Cheese Shoppe until his untimely passing in 2014, who introduced us to wines, cheeses, European butter, and many other good edibles and taught us how to better appreciate fine food and drink.

We owe a debt that can never be fully articulated to our families. Catherine and Florence Critch, Scott's cousins in Newfoundland, Canada, extended their hospitality to us in their beautiful home at the foot of the Tablelands of Gros Morne National Park, the magnificent mountains that gave us the idea for the title of this book. We deeply appreciate the support of our siblings and their families. Kent Keeling and Marie-Claude LaPlante, and Darcy, Alan, Liam, and Kelly MacLeod: thank you for many good meals together at your lovely homes and while out and about on adventures in farther places. Finally, we extend our enormous love and gratitude to our parents, Keith and Margie Keeling and Tom and Dodie Pollard, who fed us as we grew, taught us table manners and graces, expanded our palates, and made uncountable meals over which we could celebrate the joys of family together.

TABLE LANDS

 Chapter 1

AN INVITATION TO THE TABLE

The Tastes of Children's Literature

I feel, having set forth the principles of my theory, that it is certain that taste causes sensations of three different kinds: *direct, complete,* and *reflective.*

The *direct* sensation is the first one felt, produced from the immediate operations of the organs of the mouth, while the body under consideration is still in the fore part of the tongue.

The *complete* sensation is the one made up of this first perception plus the impression which arises when the food leaves its original position, passes to the back of the mouth, and attacks the whole organ with its taste and its aroma.

Finally, the *reflective* sensation is the opinion which one's spirit forms from the impression which has been transmitted to it by the mouth.

—JEAN ANTHELME BRILLAT-SAVARIN, THE PHYSIOLOGY OF TASTE (1825)

In the preceding quotation from the chapter "Analysis of the Sensation of Tasting," Brillat-Savarin formulates the analytical circuit that links body and mind through the act of eating. In other words, we do not taste only with the tongue, or even with the interaction between tongue and nose. Humans taste with the mind as much as with the body: the mind engages with the taste of what passes over the tongue to discern the opportunities of pleasure. An easily recognized moment of this phenomenon occurs when Lewis Carroll's Alice consumes a bottled drink just after she has fallen into Wonderland: "so Alice ventured to taste it, and finding it very nice, (it had, in fact, a sort of mixed flavour of cherry-tart, custard, pine-apple, roast turkey, toffee, and hot buttered toast,) she very soon finished it off" (11). Here, Alice performs the three components of Brillat-Savarin's principle: having cautiously sampled the contents of the bottle to check for danger, she is conscious instead of the pleasure of taste. Her mind interprets the sensations on her tongue according to previous experience so that she can recognize individual flavors within the mixture, even if they form a nonsensical grouping of sweets with savories. Despite their strange mixture, she finds pleasure in the bottled drink, both in its physiological taste on her tongue and in her ability to identify the flavors she tastes. It is this drink that transforms her and allows her passage into the adventures of Wonderland.

Carroll's text, like so much of children's literature, is filled with foods to eat—as well as voracious creatures who threaten to eat the child protagonist. The bottle Alice encounters is the first of many taste adventures in the novel. This episode serves as an emblem for our own scholarship: an entryway into an interpretive adventure with children's literature. In fact, it seems appropriate to note here that this project started over a meal. We were discussing Maurice Sendak's *Where the Wild Things Are* while eating dinner together one evening in 1995 when it occurred to us that another picture book we had recently purchased for fun, Henrik Drescher's *The Boy Who Ate Around*, offered an interesting counterexample of the ways children negotiate excessive desires, both for food and for power and agency. Out of this conversation, we produced a conference paper, which eventually turned into an article for *Children's Literature in Education*. The editor, Margaret Mackey, suggested that we take a similar approach to Beatrix Potter's *The Tale of Peter Rabbit* for a centenary anthology she was working on. In reading and teaching other texts we began to see the omnipresence of food in children's literature, leading to further conference papers and articles. We organized a special session panel on the subject, sponsored by the Children's Literature Association for the Modern Language Association's annual conference in 2004, and we were astonished at the number and breadth of submissions: we could easily have organized four panels from them. Later, we invited submissions for an anthology, *Critical Approaches to Food in Children's Literature* (Routledge, 2008), which ultimately brought together scholars who represented an array of approaches that significantly broadened the theoretical palette: archival research, cultural studies, feminism and gender studies, material culture, metaphysics, popular culture, postcolonialism, poststructuralism, ethnic and racial studies, and theology.

The development of our own scholarship on food's signification in children's literature took advantage of how the field of food studies advanced in the 1990s and 2000s, a growth which seemed to correlate with a rising interest in popular culture in both food and foodways—that is, the culturally based practices that govern the production, preparation, and consumption of food. Food studies crossed disciplinary boundaries from the social sciences into the humanities. In the social sciences, there are landmark scholarly moments, like Mary Douglas's 1972 *Daedalus* article, "Deciphering a Meal," the ongoing Oxford Symposium on Food and Cookery (founded 1978), and the Association for the Study of Food and Society (founded in 1985). In the humanities, food became a viable focus of scholarly study with Susan J. Leonardi's 1989 *PMLA* article, "Recipes for Reading: Summer Pasta, Lobster à la Riseholme, and Key Lime Pie," which was followed by important books, such as Carolyn Korsmeyer's *Making Sense of Taste: Food & Philosophy* (1999) and Denise Gigante's *Taste: A Literary History* (2005), and the multidisciplinary journal *Gastronomica: The Journal of Food and Culture* (founded in 2001). Moreover, theorists like Claude Lévi-Strauss, Roland Barthes, and Julia Kristeva provided metalevel linkages among disciplines. Even popular culture saw a boom in food histories, cookbooks, and food-related television programs such as cooking shows, competitions, and reality shows. In the field of children's literature, Wendy Katz, Jean Perrot, Maria Nikolajeva, and Lynn Vallone were important predecessors in food scholarship up to the beginnings of the twenty-first century. Since then, Carolyn Daniel, Susan Honeyman, Bridget Carrington and Jennifer Harding, and Rebecca A. Brown have made important contributions to the field.

Our own critical approach to the signification of food in children's literature has undergone a dramatic shift over the years, enabled in part by the work done in food studies. That change is reflected in this volume. In our first two articles in the 1990s and early 2000s, we focused on food as a literary trope—or, rather, as a cultural signifier that becomes a literary trope. We did some food research, though, which generally focused on food as cultural signifier. The recipe for rabbit pie, from *Mrs. Beeton's Book of Household Management*, with which we began the *Peter Rabbit* essay, indicated the usefulness of material culture as an approach to how food signifies in a sociohistorical context. In our 2008 anthology, we saw how many of our contributors fruitfully pushed beyond discussions of food as literary signifier to include a variety of other discourses. In particular, we found an interesting model in James Everett's study of oranges in nineteenth- and early twentieth-century literature for and featuring children: it shows the history and cultural significance of the orange as agricultural product and colonial import in the British and American culture of the time in a wide-ranging survey of works from Maria Edgeworth's "The Orange Man" in 1796, through the Brontë sisters' *Jane Eyre* and *Wuthering Heights* (both 1847), to Richard Wright's *Black Boy* (1937) and Patricia Polacco's *An Orange for Frankie*, published in 2004 but set in the Great Depression of the 1930s.

As for our own work in the last decade, we have approached food in each of the works we have analyzed through various and disparate material discourses. To understand the presence of frozen fish fingers in Neil Gaiman's *Coraline*, we researched British freezer technology, the history of British frozen food, fish and chips, and industrial cod fishing. To understand the construct of comfort food as nostalgic signifier in Polly Horvath's *Everything on a Waffle* and *The Canning Season*, we explored scholarship that addressed comfort food from the perspectives of the humanities, psychology, rhetoric, and sociology. To understand agriculture and farm labor in Pam Muñoz Ryan's *Esperanza Rising*, we researched the history of farming in the United States, immigrant farm labor in California, Mexican history, and the Mexican Revolution and its aftereffects. Finally, for our essay concerning Laura Ingalls Wilder's Little House series, we researched nineteenth-century Northern European immigration to the United States, pioneer food and foodways, midwestern foods, and westward expansion and its ideological father, Frederick Jackson Turner. The practice of ranging across disciplines prepared us for the challenges of *Table Lands*.

We intend *Table Lands* to be a broad survey of food's function in children's texts, showing how comprehending the sociocultural contexts of food reveals fundamental understandings of the child and children's agency and enriches the interpretation of such texts. We make no claim that our investigation is exhaustive, for such a study would be impossible to contain within a single volume: the harvest, preparation, and consumption of food is such a central human activity that it permeates literary texts at all levels. As we observed in our introduction to *Critical Approaches to Food in Children's Literature* (where we discuss this issue in greater detail), food is fundamental to life; it recurs throughout literature, and it is omnipresent as a motif in children's literature. To repeat Brillat-Savarin's oft-quoted comment, "Tell me what you eat and I will tell you who you are" (15); children's literature is, after all, full of young people seeking to find who they are. What we hope we have done in this book is to show a set of important patterns through studies of individual texts as casebooks, which may be models for further exploration by other scholars. We thus examine, in roughly chronological order, a variety of texts from historical to contemporary, noncanonical to classic, many from the Anglo American tradition but enriched by several books from multicultural traditions: Native American (Ojibwe) in our study of Louise Erdrich, Jewish American in our examination of Maurice Sendak, African American in the chapter on Rita Williams-Garcia, and immigrant Vietnamese culture in Thanhha Lai's semiautobiographical novel—even a discussion of regionalism in our look at Francesca Lia Block as a Los Angeles writer.[1] We have included a wide variety of genres, formats, and age-group audiences: realism (both historical and contemporary), fantasy, cookbooks, picture books, chapter books, young adult novels, and film.

We begin the book with a chapter on children's cookbooks in part as a nod to Susan Leonardi's 1989 article in *PMLA* on reading recipes, which was the inaugural point for the field of food and literature (food and foodways as foci for textual analysis), but, more importantly, we use the essay as a way of conceiving a culture's attitude toward and construction of the child as a being with a set of skills, capabilities, and talents (or the lack thereof). In essence, we explore what children do vis-à-vis food within the sociocultural milieu of the cookbook texts we consider. To track the historical changes from nineteenth-century household books for children to twentieth- and twenty-first-century children's cookbooks, in order to make sense of not only the texts but their materiality as well, we turn to history, cookbook scholarship, feminism, and critical theory. To that end, we chart the changing expectations and skills sets of children at key historical moments: the cookbooks show a changing set of adults' expectations of skills based on shifting ideologies of child capability.

The next four chapters are grounded in a set of four canonical children's authors (Beatrix Potter, A. A. Milne, Laura Ingalls Wilder, and Maurice Sendak) from Great Britain and the United States. We began our work on food in children's literature in the 1990s and early 2000s with articles on food in *The Tale of Peter Rabbit* and *Where the Wild Things Are*, but the essays in this volume on Potter and Sendak represent a serious refocusing and rethinking of our earlier approaches. In our first go-round, we treated food in their work primarily as literary tropes, outgrowths of literary signifiers. For Beatrix Potter in this volume, we shift away from *Peter Rabbit* to focus on her other food-oriented tales, particularly *The Tale of Mr. Tod*, *The Tale of the Pie and the Patty-Pan*, and *The Tale of Samuel Whiskers, or, the Roly-Poly Pudding*. We use period cookbooks in our analysis and research period food and foodways, nineteenth- and early twentieth-century British rural and urban cultures, the food-related problems of poverty, and period-applied social work theory. For Maurice Sendak, we focus solely on *In the Night Kitchen*. To understand Mickey's hero arc and Sendak's illustrations, we explore

Jewish immigrant history and migration patterns in the United States, Jewish American foods and foodways, period-relevant Jewish American cookbooks, food manufacturing in the first half of the twentieth century, and roadside/programmatic architecture, all of which provide a rich cultural background that reveals Sendak's story as both quintessentially Jewish and deeply American in how it situates Mickey's nighttime adventure.

Honey and its constant presence as plot device make *Winnie-the-Pooh* and its sequel *The House at Pooh Corner* an obvious choice for study, especially given that honey—and the bees that produce it—feature in pastoral idylls going back to Virgil's *Georgics*. We treat Pooh's story as a *Künstlerroman* and use the history of honey and bees, as well as Mary Douglas's semiotic analysis in "Deciphering a Meal," to demonstrate the deep structure that links food as literary trope to the real structure of a meal, allowing us to see Pooh as a poet who sings of his desire for honey, celebrating food through his art.

We begin chapter 5 with Laura Ingalls Wilder's Little House books, but the purpose of the chapter is comparative: Louise Erdrich's Birchbark series invites us to remember that other people, with other foodways, lived in the prairies and woods in which Wilder famously set her novels, both long before and during the Ingalls family's incursion. We have considered food in Wilder's work elsewhere. In another recently published essay on the Little House books that we wrote for Gitanjali G. Shahani's anthology *Food and Literature* (2018), we looked at the foods detailed in Wilder's series as a lens to understand and critique how New Western history highlights the exclusive, European American discourse of westward expansion. The essay for this volume contrasts the foodways of Wilder's and Erdrich's narratives as a way to showcase the competing cultural values of the two nineteenth-century families in the stories as well as those of their twentieth-century writers. Wilder chronicles the transplantation of European methods of agriculture into the American Midwest with its attendant restructuring of the environment. Erdrich's Birchbark series, on the other hand, works as a challenging counterhistory to Wilder's colonialist affirmation and depicts a people whose foodways have long worked in concert with their local ecology, as our research into Ojibwe practices of cultivating wild rice, harvesting maple syrup, berrying, and hunting buffalo made clear. We explore how the Ojibwe family's forced western trek takes them away from familiar foods and foodways, as well as how Erdrich remaps the region, recreating it as it was before the invasion of European agriculture and husbandry. Within her novels, Erdrich champions Ojibwe culture and its food and food practices; understanding them more fully thus creates a richer comprehension of the region's food and foodways than Wilder's books alone can ever offer.

The chapter on the Birchbark series also functions as a transition to the volume's final four chapters on contemporary children's books, in which we focus on the intersections of geography, history, and food in works from the 1980s through the two decades after the turn of the millennium. Francesca Lia Block's Dangerous Angels books are full of food—all of it significantly shaping the series's narrative arc and character development. To explore the links among food, setting, and culture, we turn to Los Angeles: its geography, architecture, and the urban history of Hollywood and the foothills (especially Laurel Canyon) dominate the novels; a well-documented food culture (restaurant histories, farmers markets, contemporary food writing) marks the region. We follow a similar course for Disney•Pixar's *Ratatouille* but focus on the postrevolutionary history of haute cuisine, French food, chefs, and Parisian restaurants—as well as scholarship on rats—to situate this story of alterity, talent, opportunity, and self-actualization.

The final two chapters parallel our discussion of Wilder and Erdrich, as we turn to stories of migration and how food and foodways both reflect and influence narratives shaped by mobility. In *One Crazy Summer* and its two sequels, *P.S. Be Eleven* and *Gone Crazy in Alabama*, Rita Williams-Garcia tracks the twentieth-century African American internal diasporas from the South to the Northeast and the West. We situate that movement within southern food and foodways, soul food, African American cookbooks, the Black Power movement, and the Black Panthers' breakfast program in Oakland, by tracing how the protagonist, Delphine, matures through her experiences with both the radically revised foodways of her urban worlds but also through coming to understand the deeper, slower, traditional foodways of her rural family's past. In the last chapter, we look at Thanhha Lai's *Inside Out & Back Again*, which depicts one family's struggles as Vietnamese boat people who are resettled in Alabama in 1975. We examine the novel through the lenses of refugee studies, Vietnamese studies, Vietnamese food and foodways, and contemporary Vietnamese American cookbooks to show how food is a primary signifier of the difficulties posed by forced migration, cultural clashes, and assimilation into a foreign environment with vastly different foodways. Forming a new personal and cultural identity by fusing her past and present lives requires Hà, the protagonist, to work toward finding some kind of equilibrium, signified by her continuing pleasure in the comfort of traditional Vietnamese dishes and her adaptation to the strangeness of American cuisine.

* * *

To conclude, in *Alice's Adventures in Wonderland*, when Alice drinks from the bottle at the bottom of the rabbit hole she enacts an analytical circuit that depends on the necessary and intimate connection of mind and body, which reflects Brillat-Savarin's conception of taste. In *Making Sense of Taste: Food and Philosophy*, Carolyn Korsmeyer argues against the historical devaluing of the senses related to taste (taste, smell, touch) and argues for the reassessment of taste and the mind-body link entailed with it. For Korsmeyer, the knowledge produced by that link is worth investigating not only because of the pleasures of its savory results but also because "a study of taste and its proper activities thus takes us into territory involving perception and cognition, symbolic function and social values" (4). Additionally, she argues "that much of the importance of food is cognitive; that is to say, it has a symbolic function that extends beyond even the most sophisticated savoring" (103). In this volume we attempt to chart a similarly sweeping signifying function of food. By turning to the many discourses and disciplines that we do, following Brillat-Savarin we discern the authors' sensitivity to the savor of food within literature, and, following Korsmeyer, we become more sensitive to the multifarious symbolic systems within which food is embedded and creates meaning. Our chosen texts—culinary, filmic, literary—then become metonymies reflecting the milieus that inform them. Food and foodways are rich with interpretive possibilities. In this volume, we touch on a few of the synergies that exist among food, culture, and children's texts, but there remains much more to be said in this ever-opening and developing field. Given the omnipresence of food, cooking, and eating in children's literature, the worlds within texts for children are indeed table lands, and children's literature invites us as scholars to the table to taste, chew, and discuss the stories.

 *Chapter 2*

AMERICAN CHILDREN'S COOKBOOKS AS SCENES OF INSTRUCTION

Tracking Historical Shifts of Work, Play, Pleasure, and Memory

> How do we in America teach our children about cooking, about food and the pleasures of the table? How do we transmit our culinary heritage?
> —JAN LONGONE, "'AS WORTHLESS AS SAVORLESS SALT'? TEACHING CHILDREN TO COOK, CLEAN AND (OFTENTIMES) CONFORM" (2003)

When thinking of children's literature, most people are unlikely to think first of cookbooks for children. Such texts occupy a small niche in children's culture, but they offer a window through which one can see how the culture shapes its ideological assumptions about children. Cookbooks are the most literal expression of texts constructed for children's consumption, and they most directly address the relationship between children and food. In children's cookbooks, food is not a mediating signifier between the child and culture; rather, food is meant to be the product of a real child's efforts in the real world, a test of how the child has internalized and acted upon the cultural values inherent in the cookbook. However, cookbooks in general are not merely lists of recipes organized by meal, type of ingredient, or social function. In her pioneering *PMLA* article, Susan Leonardi argues that the term "recipe" itself in its Latin root (*recipere*) "implies an exchange, a giver and a receiver. Like a story, a recipe needs a recommendation, a context, a point, a reason to be. A recipe is, then, an embedded discourse" (340). Cookbooks are an outgrowth of recipes; they, too, make use of narrative structures as organizational methods that are "akin to literary discourse" (342). Such narrative structures are thus inherent to the cookbook genre, as Leonardi makes clear, opening it up to literary analysis that treats cookbooks as literary objects. Replete with narratives, cookbooks for children are also literary objects, worthy of analysis as children's literature. Just as the narrative strategies of cookbooks allow us to follow signifying chains to the cultural and historical contexts that produced them, so, too, as Sherrie Inness notes, do "juvenile cookbooks . . . demonstrate to boys and girls the attitudes that society expects them to adopt toward cooking and cooking-related tasks" (38). In short, cookbooks for children are as complex in their ideological underpinnings as any other type of text for children.

Although Leonardi's 1988 article led to a boom in narratological analyses of cookbooks—an MLA search for "cookbooks" yields seventy-one entries, all published within the last three decades—a similar search produces only one entry for "children's cookbooks." Other fields have also done little with children's cookbooks: only three scholarly treatments have looked at the history of children's cookbooks within gender studies, food studies, or studies in children's culture. The first was the above-cited chapter in Sherrie Inness's feminist analysis of American cookbooks in *Dinner Roles: American Women and Culinary Culture* (2001), in which she explored the inherent gender orientation of cookbooks for children, primarily in twentieth-century cookbooks aimed at girls or at boys. In "'As Worthless as Savorless Salt'? Teaching Children to Cook, Clean and (Oftentimes) Conform," Jan Longone targeted her study of nineteenth-century children's cookbooks for a food studies audience in *Gastronomica* (2003). Carol Fisher offered a brief appraisal of nineteenth- and twentieth-century children's cookbooks in *The American Cookbook: A History* (2006), as part of a chapter titled "Cookbooks for Special Audiences." She reviewed twelve cookbooks from the late nineteenth to the late twentieth century, spending most of her time on two from the nineteenth (*Six Little Cooks* and *The Mary Frances Cook Book*) and two from the twentieth (*Betty Crocker's Cookbook for Boys and Girls* and *The Better Homes and Gardens Junior Cookbook*). Jodie Slothower and Jan Susina wrote the one literary study of children's cookbooks, focusing specifically on ones linked with popular literary texts (such as Georgeanne Brennan's *Green Eggs and Ham Cookbook: Recipes Inspired by Dr. Seuss* or Barbara M. Walker's *The Little House Cookbook: Frontier Foods from Laura Ingalls Wilder's Classic Stories*). They identified an astonishing number and assortment of books with recipes for fans of particular children's novels and picture books.

All of these sources offer useful surveys of the cookbooks that have been produced for American children; Longone and Fisher review several key texts worthy of further investigation. Slowthower and Susina's chapter offers a well-done, comprehensive, and literature-based examination of a particular (and popular) type of cookbook, each example of which is aimed at a relatively small audience: fans of a book or author who are also interested in cooking. But the cookbooks that are aimed at teaching children how to cook in a systematic and wide-ranging manner need further examination. Longone notes the wider implications of such books: "American publications . . . offer insight into how we decide to feed our children and how we have taught them about cooking, food, and the pleasures of the table. But much more than practical cookery lies within the covers of children's cookbooks" (110). Longone's comments suggest that children's cookbooks offer a particular intersection of discourses about both children and food, ripe for inquiry. Such analysis would fit Warren Belasco's argument for the broader applications of any serious food study, which he makes in *Appetite for Change: How the Counterculture Took on the Food Industry* (2007): "It does seem that many food studies thus begin not out of intrinsic interest in the food but in what food can tell us about something else—gender, labor relations, class, ethnic identity, imperialism . . ." (x). This chapter will assess the ideological assumptions underlying children's cookbooks—assumptions about both the nature of food and the nature of children as potential cooks—to reveal the complex social forces that create the child as an agent possessing skills and purpose. If recipes are embedded discourses, then analyzing the larger discourses that inform the books in which they are embedded reveals much about adult beliefs in children's abilities and agency—or the lack thereof.

Nineteenth-century American cookbooks produced for children were an outgrowth of a literate middle class with few (if any) servants but sufficient economic means to purchase some books for children—and cookbooks offered some practical outcomes. A child who could cook had an independent skill that could help adults with a chore that occupied many hours of daily domestic labor. This fits the pattern noted by Jessamyn Neuhaus, in *Manly Meals and Mom's Home Cooking: Cookbooks and Gender in Modern America*, that cookbooks grew in popularity because as "many families migrated west, the population became more widely dispersed. Consequently, fewer women could turn to mothers and grandmothers for advice and instruction about cookery" (16). Cookbooks for children could fill in for absent relatives or provide lessons for girls whose mothers lacked time to give them close instruction. Neuhaus also observes that "private collections of recipes, or 'receipt books'" were popular at this time and provided a creative outlet for women (16).

Elizabeth Stansbury Kirkland's *Six Little Cooks, or, Aunt Jane's Cooking Class*, the first American cookbook published for children (Longone 107, Fisher 162), follows both patterns that Neuhaus identifies: it depicts six neighborhood girls (some of them cousins) who ask an older female relative (the eponymous Aunt Jane) to teach them to cook; she provides not only practical lessons but insists that each girl write down every recipe in a blank book to keep for her future use (Kirkland 8). The book consists of fourteen chapters that run through a variety of different cooking scenarios, from cooking each of the three normal daily meals, to preparing medicinal dishes for a mother who isn't feeling well one day, to improvising desserts as hospitality for unexpected guests. Aunt Jane sets up a particular cooking challenge for the girls to meet each day; the story does not merely provide the sample recipes that she gives them but also demonstrates the procedures in the various stages of preparing each dish; thus, it also shows their difficulties and triumphs as they work through the process, guided gently by Aunt Jane through conversation, anecdote, and advice. It thus models for its readers the kinds of instruction that older women traditionally provided for girls in the kitchen—albeit with an idealized, patient adult teacher who never loses her temper when the cooking goes wrong.

To create these scenes of instruction, Kirkland uses a series of narrative frames. The outermost frame is told by a heterodiegetic narrator, who speaks in the first person and tells the story of the girls and their aunt, commenting on the girls' motivations and actions. Within this frame, Aunt Jane often tells stories to the girls as they cook—frequently based on her own experience, sometimes even illustrative tales about mistakes that she made as a girl learning to cook—in order to caution them about proper kitchen procedures. The recipes are embedded within Aunt Jane's instruction: she dictates all 207 of them to the girls, apparently from a very capacious memory since no book of her own is mentioned. The book thus provides its readers with a set of recipes, detailed instructions, and advice that they can try if they are stimulated by the book to try cooking on their own. Such inspiration is what Kirkland claims in her "Afterthought" that she wants: "My object is only to excite such an interest in the pursuit of it as may induce little people of ten or twelve years old to make some playful attempts at a beginning, with the hope that in future years they may be inclined to follow it up in serious earnest" (232).

Kirkland represents such inspiration dramatically at the very beginning of her book with Grace, the oldest of the six girls and the first to become interested in cooking: "'Oh, Aunt Jane,' said Grace, looking up quickly from the story-book she was reading. 'I wish you would teach us all how to cook.' . . . Grace was reading about a wonderful little girl who made such remarkable things in the way of cakes and puddings, that our young person was seized with a desire to do likewise without delay" (Kirkland 5–6). The little girl in the story fires Grace's ambition; Grace admires her practical culinary skills, perhaps especially because of the girl's ability to produce desserts. Less obviously but more importantly, the young cook of the storybook implicitly embodies the domestic ideology so popular in nineteenth-century America: her competence at baking suggests she is a young "angel of the house," and Kirkland uses the storybook heroine to embed a larger cultural narrative within her cookbook. Kirkland's intent, as stated in her afterword and implied in her characters' enthusiasm for learning cooking, mirrors Catherine Beecher's ideology in her popular *Mrs. Beecher's Domestic Receipt Book* (1846), which "directly linked the activity of cooking to the glorified role of homemaker, insisting that the tedious and worrisome aspects of housekeeping paled in comparison to the rewards reaped by devoted homemakers" (Neuhaus 15). Kirkland portrays her six girls as inspired by the task of learning reasonably complex cooking procedures: they start relatively simply (baking easy fruit cake, custard, and popovers), gradually learn to cook more complicated dishes, and acquire a stock of recipes to draw on in the future. Aunt Jane helps them prepare a culminating tea party for their families, serving tea biscuits, tea cakes, Sally Lunns, breakfast puffs, baking powder biscuits, Dover cake with fruit, chocolate cake, sponge cake, macaroons, jelly cake, wine jelly, and chocolate meringue. As the girls choose the menu, Aunt Jane stresses the proper attitude toward cooking as a service: "To enjoy cooking you must never think of your own satisfaction in eating what you make, but of the pleasures you are going to give others" (224). The book somewhat undercuts this homily by providing a preponderance of sweet recipes—exactly what captured Grace's imagination in the beginning. The desserts serve as a lure to the kitchen, where the girls initially want to please themselves but also come to understand the larger purpose of the skills they develop: serving others. Kirkland defines the "others" to be pleased as "our fathers and mothers and brothers" (224)—properly angelic service to the patriarchal structure of the family is thus clearly delineated for the girls. The story ends with adult approbation of the girls' efforts and the long-term usefulness of the lessons:

> You can imagine for yourselves that it was a proud and happy day for the mothers and fathers of our little friends when they had such convincing

proof of their children's progress as was afforded by the excellent supper prepared by them, and that the young people themselves, when they shall put in practice in future years the lessons of that happy time, will always look back with pleasure and gratification to the summer in which they were members of Aunt Jane's Cooking Class. (231)

In portraying the development of six young cooks, Kirkland addresses Longone's questions, cited as the epigraph for this chapter: how Americans pass on their cultural traditions of food between generations and the values that underlie that heritage. Kirkland creates a benevolent pedagogy that passes on complex knowledge and skills, situates the girls in the kitchen and dining room of the family home, gives them an incipient mastery of those spaces, and (through the receipt books that they begin to fill) sets them up as future housewives who will, like Aunt Jane, pass on their knowledge to their daughters, female relatives, and neighbors. One answer to Longone's second question from this chapter's epigraph is that America's culinary heritage in the nineteenth century was passed on through all the cookbooks authored by women; however, a better answer would ground itself in the everyday practice of women and girls of the period writing down recipes in their own receipt books, which they would pass on in turn. Given this multigenerational teaching tradition, such texts construct the girl child as a nascent autonomous being who has internalized women's skills and roles and then can act on them.

As Sherrie Inness notes, instructional cookbooks like *Six Little Cooks* "became more prevalent in the twentieth century, when the rising importance of the juvenile cookbook business helped ensure that children's cookbooks were broadly published and distributed" (38). An early twentieth-century example of such an instructional text is Clara Ingram Judson's *Cooking without Mother's Help* (1920), which embodies the desire to develop agency in its very title. Ten-year-old Alice tells her mother of her wish to cook independently: "Helping is helping, but it isn't cooking. I want to learn to cook all by my very self, with you not even in the kitchen to tell me when things are done,—that's what I want to do" (7), a plea seconded by her younger sister Mary. Like Kirkland's girl characters, Alice and Mary learn first to cook individual dishes and after a series of twelve lessons prepare a "graduation" dinner for the family and two guests. Like Aunt Jane, Alice's mother emphasizes cooking as service to others, warning her daughter that as a cook she must think beyond her own preferences: "a good cook has to consider many things,—the tastes of her family and the needs of their bodies,—besides her own notions" (55). The angel of the house remains alive and well in this 1920s text.

Judson's book has a homodiegetic narrator: there is no overt narratorial intervention. In contrast to Grace, whose desire to learn how to cook is catalyzed by the book she reads, Alice is inspired directly by watching her mother cook. The mother agrees to provide lessons, as long as Alice and her sister Mary "are willing to be careful and painstaking so that the food is not wasted" (8). Thus the mother begins her lessons by articulating the virtue of frugality.[1] Unlike *Six Little Cooks*, where the girls clamor for sweet dishes, the sisters in *Cooking without Mother's Help* seem more mature, requesting instruction in the preparation of primarily savory dishes, with the mother offering just a few sweet dishes for special occasions, such as picnics in chapter 5, and to balance a meal plan at the "graduation" dinner in chapter 12. Judson is focused far more on practical cookery than Kirkland is. At the beginning of the book, the girls seem to have already internalized the traditional meal pattern of the middle-class American household. These idealized girls are not much interested in sweets, unlike Kirkland's more believable apprentice cooks, nor do they need a storybook inspiration to motivate their mastery of kitchen and household skills—such desire seems built into them. Moreover, unlike Kirkland in her "Afterthought," Judson does not intrude overtly into the narrative to tell readers her intentions. The "angel in the house" standard is simply a given, and thus essentially covert, like Judson's narrator.

Despite the more than forty-year difference in the publishing dates of these two books, Aunt Jane and Mother both require the girls to begin their careers as cooks by fetching blank books that become the recipe books the girls themselves will author by collecting recipes as they learn them. Learning to cook is closely tied to the scribing of recipes in a personalized cookbook that reflects each girl's cooking training. The act of writing connects those skills to a personal and family history that is handed down to them from their older female relatives; the books mark the girls' entrance into an authorial community that extends across generations. The girls' authorship within the story perfectly illustrates Janet Theophano's observation in *Eating My Words: Reading Women's Lives through the Cookbooks They Wrote*: in the nineteenth century the acts of writing and cooking were intimately intertwined. At a time when women's public writing was often carefully circumscribed, cookbooks were a place where ordinary women could record their subjectivity and network it with other women in their families and communities to produce an alternative historical record. Theophano discusses her search for such texts, noting how she privileged texts that "had been written out in longhand," with particular focus on those in which "the creative process reflected more of a collage, with women creating their books out of bits and pieces assembled from various sources" (5)—in other words, texts just like Aunt Jane's mother's receipt book and those young Grace and Alice are beginning to construct. These books are valued as the repositories of generational memory and knowledge and are lovingly preserved across the generations. Aunt Jane shows the girls her mother's "receipt book," from which the girls copy one of the oldest and most elaborate recipes, for a "cheese-cake." In becoming cooks with their own hand-copied recipe books, the girls in *Six Little Cooks* and *Cooking without Mother's Help* go through a rite of passage to take their place as writer-cooks who preserve and pass on the family cooking traditions through skills and practice in service.

The differences between the two books in the style and nature of the dictation/writing relationship is worth noting. In *Six Little Cooks*, Aunt Jane is present in the kitchen throughout the lessons. The recipes she dictates are relatively short—usually just lists of ingredients. After the girls have finished writing them down, and they choose which recipes to prepare, Aunt Jane proceeds orally with further, often lengthy instructions and advice about cooking techniques, so that the girls can commit it all (and there is much) to memory. For example, near the end of the book, Aunt Jane dictates this recipe for a small sponge cake: "One teacup powdered sugar, one of flour, three eggs, half a teaspoonful cream tartar, a quarter of a teaspoonful soda" (176–77). In conversation with the girls, she follows the recipe with over two pages of further interactive instruction (177–79). In contrast, in *Cooking without Mother's Help*, the ratio of dictation/oral instruction is reversed. Reflecting the book's title and exemplifying its thesis, the mother's interactions with her daughters are far more textual and much less verbal. While both Aunt Jane and the mother dictate recipes for their apprentices to copy down, the mother's recipes are longer, more detailed, precise, and instructive, resembling the layout of recipes in contemporary cookbooks. After the recipes are written down, the mother asks her daughters if they have any questions, and after a few further oral instructions and clarifications the mother leaves the kitchen to her daughters. In a parallel example, from near the end of *Cooking without Mother's Help*, the mother dictates a sponge cake recipe, which fills two pages in very small type. As with all the recipes in the book, this one is broken into three sections (utensils needed, ingredients needed, methods of work), the last of which includes lengthy instructions and advice (90–92); the recipe is followed by a half page, in larger type, of a few questions and clarifications. Because their mother leaves the kitchen, the information Alice and Mary write down needs to be more complete in order for them to have the autonomy and agency they want. In both books, the expectations of mastery are similar, but the scenes of instruction differ. Both illuminate Longone's questions, demonstrating how children are taught cooking and the pleasures as well as the transmission and preservation of a culinary heritage.

This American culinary legacy changed significantly after World War II, for a variety of reasons that had a significant impact on cookbooks designed for adults, as well as those for children. According to Laura Shapiro, in *Something from the Oven: Reinventing Dinner in 1950s America*, the food industry during the war had invested deeply in technology to produce field rations for soldiers on the front lines, food that could be easily transported, accessed, and consumed, and that required little or no skill to prepare. Not surprisingly, they wanted a further return on that investment "to create a peacetime market for wartime foods" (8). Thus arose a culture of marketing that was intended to "persuade millions of Americans to develop a lasting taste for meals that were a lot like field rations" (8). Foods were dried, powdered, and boxed (mixes for cakes, biscuits, and other baked goods); frozen (orange juice, fish sticks, vegetables) to be stored in newly manufactured appliances such as deep freezes; and canned (meats like Spam, in addition to the long-established tradition of canned vegetables). According to Shapiro, food manufacturers envisioned "a day when all contact between the cook and the raw makings of dinner would be obsolete" (xvi-xvii). These changes began to sever longstanding American cooking traditions, particularly in urban and suburban areas, and the availability of industrialized foods fed a growing appetite for convenience. Old traditions did not die entirely or immediately, by any means: the women who had lived through the Depression and the war knew how to cook from scratch to manage a household frugally as well as to cook and bake social food (for parties and church dinners, for example) to demonstrate skills and impress family, friends, and neighbors. The period saw an explosion of cookbook publishing, first in reprints of older cookbooks from before World War II, representing the legacy of older traditions; second in new cookbooks that catered to the new foodways developing around the convenience foods being pushed by large-scale food corporations; and finally in a set of gourmet cookbooks by authors desiring to save older traditions (such as James Beard) or to expand horizons by introducing complex foods from other cultural traditions (such as Julia Child) (Shapiro 28–29, 222–25; Inness 166–67).

Just as the postwar food industry endeavored to modify the skills and agency of the adult homemaker, so was a parallel modification attempted with children. Neuhaus notes that "with the birth rate at an all time high, cookbooks turned renewed attention on the child eater" (173). Given that "throughout the twentieth century, cookbooks for children have mirrored the categories of adult offerings" (Fisher 166), one would expect that the same three kinds of cookbooks would have been marketed to children in the postwar era: traditional, convenience, and gourmet. But as Neuhaus claims, with the exception of just a few cookbooks like Irma Rombauer's *Cooking for Boys and Girls* (1946, 1952), "the recipes in 1950s children's cookbooks presented more novelty foods than real meals. In keeping with the overall trend in cookbook publishing for adults, juvenile cookery instruction tended to focus on combining or heating up canned, processed, and frozen ingredients" (174).[2] Rather than producing cookbooks designed to pass on the traditional knowledge of American cuisine and teach the skills of cooking it, publishers instead chose short, simple texts that emphasized convenience cooking, calibrating it as "fun food" for children and adolescents. Older cookbooks for children, like *Six Little Cooks* and *Cooking without Mother's Help*, were about memory, training, skill development, and the preservation of familial/historical continuity through the dictation and writing of recipes. Those motivating ideas were lost in the postwar period, however, and replaced with the more socially isolating idea of a child or children simply having fun with food.

Annie North Bedford's *Susie's New Stove: The Little Chef's Cookbook* (1950) is an exemplary text for the period. It is a Little Golden Book, and because of its low cost (25 cents, as were all Little Golden Books according to the website) and wide distribution it reached a broad audience. Although not explicitly an advertiser's or manufacturer's cookbook, like *Betty Crocker's Cookbook for Boys and Girls* (1957) or the *Better Homes and Gardens Junior Cookbook: For the Hostess and Host of Tomorrow* (1955), *Susie's New Stove* is marked by product placement. The title's ambiguous reference hides this, but only slightly: although "The Little Chef" could refer to Susie, it is actually the name of the toy stove made by the Tacoma Metal Products company.[3] Susie cooks actual food with her "really-truly" toy electric oven and stove whose elements heat up enough to warm up liquids on the burners and heat small items in the oven; she uses the miniature utensils that come with it to produce child-sized portions that fit child-sized plates and bowls. The "toy" thus surpasses most children's playthings: it is not for merely imaginative play but allows the child to do "real" cooking in the sense of combining some ingredients and heating them up to actually eat.

Although written thirty years after Judson's and over seventy years after Kirkland's cookbooks for girls, *Susie's New Stove* shares with them a similar narrative structure. Bedford organizes the book around catalyzing scenes of instruction: Susie wants to learn to cook, and her mother volunteers to teach her; the lessons progress, leading to a culminating cooking experience that involves responsibility for a "complete" meal (preparing her father's birthday dinner); the story is set within the house; and the recipes are detailed similarly to those in *Cooking without Mother's Help* (equipment, ingredients, method). Like Grace and Alice, Susie experiences a moment of motivation to learn to cook as the story opens: "Susie likes to play house. She has a family of dolls. She has a little table and chairs. She has a set of little dishes. And she has a really-truly little electric stove, with a set of little pots and pans! 'Now I must learn to cook,' said Susie the first time she saw her new little stove" (Bedford). The narrative introduces Susie as a girl embedded in a constellation of domestic toys: the stove, with its accessories, is the culmination of the list; possession of the stove is what motivates Susie to learn to cook. Susie cooks first for herself and Mike (her brother), then for her friend Carol, who comes over to visit, then for her family (mother, father,. and Mike) at the end.

One significant difference between *Susie's New Stove* and the two earlier texts is how it develops the scenes of instruction and their narrative arc, and the relationship suggested between the adult woman who instructs and the girls she teaches. The interactions in *Six Little Cooks* and *Cooking without Mother's Help* are rich with conversation and advice; Janet Theophano's feminist lens suggests the process of writing recipes empowers the incipient cooks by positioning them within a discourse among women in the family across generations—a conversation to which they are now adding just as the adult women in their family have and which is further enriched by interactions with the teaching aunt or mother figure while preparing the dish. In *Susie's New Stove*, the mother does not dictate the recipes she shares, and Susie does not write, does not preserve those recipes, perhaps because they are too generic and embody no family history. Consequently, the relationship between mother and daughter seems hollow. Susie's mother says she will teach her what to do, but for the most part their only interaction is the recipe directions, with no extra elaboration on cooking techniques. Only once in the book does the mother actually teach technique to Susie, and then it is only about timing: "'First,' said Mother, when Susie and Carol were both in aprons, ready to work, 'we will fix the cold things. It will not hurt them to stand a while. Then when the soup is hot, and the crackers are toasted, you will be all ready to sit down and enjoy them. This is how we start'" (n.p.) For most of the lessons, the mother just says, "This is how" (or similar phrase), which Bedford follows with recipe directions. Bedford portrays this mother as very hands off, showing only minimal instruction and minimal generational interactions. The book also has a covert narrative voice that offers occasionally heterodiegetic commentary within the recipes. At the end of the recipe for cooking frozen mixed vegetables, the narrator intrudes parenthetically to comment on the mother's actions: "Step 8. Serve half the vegetables and half the frankfurter on each plate. (Mother had second helpings ready for Susie and Mike.)" This comment clearly comes from an intrusive narrator—not the mother who is supposedly giving the recipe. Furthermore, this moment undermines whatever agency Susie might achieve by cooking: the comment makes clear that Susie can't prepare the full meal on her toy stove and must be rescued by her mother. The concluding celebration meal undercuts Susie's agency even further because the mother clarifies that Susie will have the opportunity to use the adult stove "just this once." Susie may have become a "good enough" cook to be allowed to work on it, but clearly, she is not going to be contributing to the household meals regularly—unlike the girl protagonists of the earlier cookbooks.

Also, when the mother grants permission for Susie to use the big stove to cook the big meal, she once again acknowledges the limits of the toy stove. Given the commercial tie-in with the Little Chef stove, *Susie's New Stove* is less a guide for the maturing girl child and more a promotion of the Little Chef. The book is an instructional guide for the toy stove and oven, not a girl's guide to mastering household duties. Because of the small amount of heat the toy stove produces, it takes twenty minutes or more to cook three tablespoons of frozen mixed vegetables in a toy-sized pot; the long preparation time and the child-sized servings may work fine in Susie's play world, but they do not make for efficient domestic planning. Yet, even given the limited aims of the book, it reflects the reduced agency inherent in both adult and juvenile cookbooks in the postwar era, as noted by both Inness and Neuhaus. In keeping with the children's cookbooks of the era, Susie does have fun with food. To return to Longone's questions: while *Susie's Little Stove* may teach a little about the pleasures of food, it does much less to preserve culinary heritage. Granted, she is younger than the girl protagonists of the earlier books; the Little Golden Books are aimed at a preschool to early elementary audience. But even given the age difference, and the difference in abilities that it inherently entails, *Susie's New Stove* undercuts its protagonist's abilities in ways that mirror other assumptions about children and women in the 1950s—ideological beliefs about women and food in general that underlie cookbooks for adults.

From its opening pages, the story perfectly fits the gender pattern of most postwar juvenile cookbooks, according to Inness: "The dominance of illustrations of girls cooking, not boys, conveyed one underlying message of these books: girls were the cooks and boys were the consumers. Girls and boys carried these messages into adulthood, assuring that the majority of women prepared and served food to men" (40–41). Mike supposedly helps Susie; however, he only "cooks" one item himself (lemonade—thus he never uses the toy stove), and he is never shown in the illustrations actually doing the cooking (although he does set the table at one point). Instead, Mike is usually depicted eating the food or sitting at the table waiting for apron-covered Susie to serve it to him. More insidiously, Bedford casts Mike rather than Susie as the idea man: he is the one who most frequently suggests what he wants to eat (for example, initiating the cocoa that is their first project, and having food rather than just cocoa for their second project); he is also the one who suggests the final birthday dinner for their father. Bedford also makes Mike the approver-in-chief: he is always the one who first endorses Mother's decisions about the menu, after which Susie chimes in her agreement. Thus, despite suggesting that a boy can be involved in cooking, the visual narrative carefully excludes Mike from active kitchen roles, casting him as diner rather than cook. *Susie's New Stove* thus epitomizes Inness's argument (quoted above) that cookbooks for children model for readers the gender-based roles that society expects them to play (37). The verbal and visual depiction of Mike, in particular, demonstrates Inness's point that "[t]he first and most important lesson for boys was that cooking was *not* their responsibility" (46). While the girls in *Six Little Cooks* and *Cooking without Mother's Help* learn cooking skills that are, on one level, intended to teach them to serve households generally headed by men, these skills also give the girls a sense of competence and independence, providing them entrance to the kitchen where women have traditionally exercised power within the family and community. Susie, however, only learns to *play* at such skills. The book overtly suggests that she develops agency by learning to cook, but since she cooks on a toy stove rather than a real one, and cooks recipes that generally require only a modicum of mixing and heating prepackaged convenience foods, the book covertly undercuts the agency she is supposedly developing—especially when compared with what the girls of the earlier generations achieved in their stories.

Jerrold Beim's *The First Book of Boys' Cooking* (1957), one of the rare cookbooks aimed specifically at boys, seems to suggest a desire to create gender equity in the kitchen, a particularly surprising approach in a cookbook from the 1950s. The dust jacket informs the readers that "Jerrold Beim and his two sons, Andy and Seth, run a completely masculine household, often without the help of a housekeeper. They had to learn to cook and, in the process, they learned how enjoyable it can be." This book clearly grows out of the experience of a single-parent male household in the 1950s. The book's rhetoric constantly reassures the boy reader and potential cook that cooking is an appropriately masculine activity: it equates the kitchen with a workshop full of tools and chooses "recipes . . . for the kinds of things boys like to eat most. No frills or fuss—just down-to-earth cooking with some fun ideas for good measure" (1). If the boy cook lacks "a man-type apron" he should just "get a clean dish towel and tuck it in the front of [his] belt" (6). In her discussion of *The First Book of Boys' Cooking*, Inness notes that Beim distinguishes the special preparations (salad) and places (outdoors) that are marked in the book as appropriately masculine. In her general assessment of this small subgenre of children's cookbooks, she notes that, "Clearly, the few boys' cookbooks that did exist conveyed to young men that cooking was a pursuit only in the right circumstances" (47). Thus, a boy cooking is not conceived of as a regular presence in the domestic order and is thus as disempowered and delimited—lacking agency—as much as a girl cook like Susie.

The same postwar ideology of convenience functions as much in *The First Book of Boys' Cooking* as much as it does in *Susie's New Stove*, for Beim freely recommends "frozen foods, ready mixes, all the modern methods of cooking" (1); thus many of the recipes depend on convenience foods—such as "Jiffy Stew," which requires boiling canned condensed vegetable soup, water, and half a pound of chopped beef. The book does teach basic skills, but the food preparation is kept simple. There is no progression toward a culminating meal, nor does the book imply a need to serve others, as the three girls' cookbooks suggest. This difference may result from the book's organization as a conventional cookbook rather than as a narrative about a child learning to cook: instead of providing a story of a child building skills and then using them in preparing a special meal, the book divides its recipes into conventional cookbook categories (beverages, bread and sandwiches, main dishes, vegetables and salads, desserts). Beim does constantly address his boy readers, unlike the other texts, as a kind of substitution for the narratives that dominated the earlier story cookbooks: the book is self-consciously chatty in explaining techniques, often throwing in gender reassurance. This overt narrator parallels the "lively" narrator of the original edition of *The Joy of Cooking*, whose discourse Leonardi praises for creating a community of cooks across generations, classes, and races (342–43); in this case, however, the gender connection is inverted to welcome boys into a newly forming community of masculine cookery. The narrator does move the recipes toward some culminating complexity in the last chapter of the book, when the boys escape the female domestic sphere for outside: "Outdoors is where a man can really shine as a cook! When you cook inside, you have usually borrowed the use of the kitchen from your mother. But with outside cooking, boys or men take over completely. The world around you is your kitchen" (63). Here the boy is taught to build three different kinds of fires for different cooking purposes; additionally, he can scour the woods for natural ingredients to make wild salads of "dandelions, clover, deer grass, oxeye daisies, thistle, sorrel, and pepper grass" (79). In the initial illustration of the boy in the kitchen, he looks confused, although he later displays self-confidence in the illustrations as he becomes more competent. Outdoors, however, the boy's supposedly instinctual interests in and knowledge of the natural world come to the fore to make him a fine and skilled cook, using natural resources in the proper masculine manner. Beim pushes the boys out of the kitchen (culturally considered a woman's "natural" place, Inness notes [44]), to hone their skills and find themselves in the natural world outside, perhaps suggesting the value of masculine woodcraft from earlier generations. However, in so doing he ultimately deprecates the feminized domestic sphere. Add this to the rising influence of industrially made convenience food of the 1950s, and this book too joins in creating further cultural erosion of long-prized kitchen knowledge and skills.

Part of the attrition these two cookbooks show stems from their orientation toward play, rather than work. While Kirkland's and Judson's girl protagonists do find pleasure in their work, Bedford and Beim's protagonists construct their cooking activities as play: they cook for their own pleasure. If in the two earlier books the pedagogy teaches girls to focus on service to others (family, friends, community), these two postwar books are much more focused on individual gratification and the creation of favorite foods for personal consumption. These books teach children to focus on egoistic pleasure; they treat children as insular beings who look only to pleasing themselves, rather than pleasurably integrating them into a community with responsibilities for others. While individual pleasure in food remains important in turn-of-the-millennium cookbooks for children, contemporary chefs Molly Katzen's and Alice Waters's cookbooks for children offer a significant paradigm shift from the fifties' era cookbooks: a resurfacing of complexity, an increased valuation of child agency, and an ideology of fresh, sustainable, organic, healthy foods that are defined as attractive to children. Katzen's series of three books (*Pretend Soup and Other Real Recipes* [1994], *Salad People and More Real Recipes* [2005], *Honest Pretzels and 64 Other Amazing Recipes for Kids Who Love to Cook* [2009]) and Waters's two books (*Fanny at Chez Panisse* [1992], *Fanny in France* [2016]), restore both knowledge and capacity to child cooks.

Gourmet cooks and cookbook writers of the immediate postwar era, such as James Beard or Julia Child, neither addressed a child audience nor wrote cookbooks for children. But gourmet cooks of the next generation—who came out of what Warren Belasco calls the "countercuisine" (4)—have chosen to write cookbooks for children, perhaps because they see children as a viable audience for their visions of food and its power to achieve social justice. Alice Waters is the founder and owner of Chez Panisse, a globally famous restaurant in Berkeley, California; she is also a national and international activist who advocates for people's engagement with and access to local and organic foods. Mollie Katzen was the founder of the Moosewood Restaurant and author of the influential vegetarian *Moosewood Cookbook* (1977). Like Waters, she has spent her life as an activist for access to local, organic foods and their ability to change both the physical and social landscape. Belasco notes that both Waters and Katzen are acutely aware of community and believe that food is inexorably part of it. From the Chez Panisse Foundation, Alice Waters initiated the Edible Schoolyard project "to expose public school children to the edible dynamic of community gardening" (249). Katzen's community mindfulness initially developed through the Moosewood Restaurant, which was run as a "collective operation" in which all the employees participated and saw themselves as part of a "vital link in alternative food" (95); Katzen's involvement with the Harvard School of Public Health as a charter member of the Nutrition Roundtable is also indicative of her focus on community (Ireland). Finally, her three cookbooks for children were developed in concert with her own children's preschool teacher and fellow students.

Katzen's and Waters's contemporary, collective, hands-on engagement with food can best be illustrated by Luce Giard in *The Practice of Everyday*

Life, Volume 2: Living and Cooking (1998). Giard believes the traditional family-centered generational bestowal of cooking knowledge ceased to function in the late twentieth century:

> In the past, one learned the recipes of one's mother or grandmother. Throughout the years my mother carefully preserved the manuscript notebook of recipes that her mother had written down for her at the time of her wedding; neither my mother nor I found it useful to continue this when my own wedding day came around. Times had changed and my sources for culinary information were more often in the media (recipes written in women's magazines, or explained on radio or TV shows) or my friends. (178)

And now in the second decade of the twenty-first century, such a network would include all the burgeoning social media sites and apps that give people access to cooking knowledge and practices. In such a rhizomatic knowledge matrix, Giard replaces family recipes with the act of *doing-cooking*:

> I learned the anticipated joy of anticipated hospitality, when one prepares a meal to share with friends in the same way that one composes a party tune or draws: with moving hands, careful fingers, the whole body inhabited by the rhythm of working, and the mind awakening, freed from its ponderousness, flitting from idea to memory. . . . Thus, surreptitiously, and without suspecting it, I had been invested with the secret, tenacious pleasure of *doing-cooking* . . . [which] is the medium for a basic, humble and persistent practice that is repeated in time and space, rooted in the fabric of relationships to others and to one's self, marked by the "family saga" and the history of each, bound to childhood memory just like rhythms and seasons. (153, 157)

Giard uses "*doing-cooking*"—a creative, networking aesthetic that focuses on the joy of food preparation for oneself and others—to enrich a more linear, generational dissemination of cooking knowledge, as in *Six Little Cooks* and *Cooking without Mother's Help*. Katzen's and Waters's cookbooks are interesting, because they are neither about convenience nor tradition, neither easy self-satisfaction nor serving others, but the aesthetics of the food and its preparation. In the process, Katzen and Waters recover for children the kinds of abilities, skills and judgment overlooked by the postwar Bedford and Beim but fundamental to Judson and Kirkland. The difference between

Katzen and Waters is that the former's community is essentially local while the latter writes to a global stage.

Having made her reputation as a vegetarian cookbook writer in the 1970s and 1980s, Molly Katzen refocused her writing on children's cookbooks, discovering, one might say, her inner Aunt Jane when she realized how deeply interested her own son was in preparing food in his preschool class. As described in the "Greeting" at the beginning of *Pretend Soup and Other Real Recipes: A Cookbook for Preschoolers & Up*, Katzen worked in cooperation with his teacher, Ann Henderson, and the other children of the class to develop a series of recipes for them to make at school and at home. One striking feature of her cookbooks for children is their overt double address: some sections offer advice for adults, others for children. While Katzen speaks to adults and children, given the communal ethos that motivates these books, she also includes the voices of the children with whom she is working and cooking. In each book, next to a page of Safety Tips, there is a page entitled "Kids' Own Rules," with gems such as "Never touch a cookie when it is in the oven.—Nathan" (*Pretend Soup* 17), and preceding each recipe is set of comments from the children who made and tested the recipe, such as "I made the green bean into nine green beans with my knife—Charley" (*Salad People* 44). Taking into account as well everyone whom Katzen thanks in the Acknowledgments (the schools, teachers, children and parents involved in the project; Katzen's family; and editors and publishers), these books are in a broad sense coauthored; at the very least, they encompass a multiplicity of voices. These books are born out of a local community, and Katzen remains true to her communal ethos.

Katzen's initial motives are personal and familial, reminiscent of Theophano's discussion of recipes as touchstones of family history, tradition, and memory. In the preface to *Salad People*, Katzen discusses the special recipe her mother made, called "Faces," which was "a cheerful montage of cheese, fruit, and vegetables arranged to look like little people, one per plate.... Looking back, I now realize that it sparked my first realization of the visual and emotional power of colorful, fresh, lovingly prepared food" (10). This awakening is reminiscent of Grace's inspiring storybook in *Six Little Cooks* or Alice's appreciation of her mother's kitchen skills in *Cooking without Mother's Help*. Katzen, though, wants to empower children because of their "willingness . . . to approach cooking with an open mind and with the goodwill to effect something real" (*Salad People* 9), but without the familial, gender, and domestic value arcs that shaped those earlier books. Katzen makes clear her ideology and the connection between child agency and cooking in the pedagogy, which she bullets explicitly at the beginning of each book. This pedagogy is both experiential and integrative: reading and math skills, aesthetics, motor skills, personal and emotional development, food literacy, community and working with others, learning as a lifelong habit of mind. She envisions cooking as a heuristic to teach children a broad set of skills which allow them to function more autonomously and knowledgeably in a larger community (*Pretend Soup* 12, *Salad People* 13, *Honest Pretzels* x). In keeping with her dedication to vegetarian cuisine, Katzen also notes in *Pretend Soup*, "we didn't want to fill the book with recipes for desserts or gimmicky 'kid food.' Instead, we hoped to get children downright excited about healthy 'real' food—food they might not have touched with a ten-foot pole if they hadn't prepared it themselves. Judging from the responses (see 'The Critics Rave' section in each recipe), we have accomplished this goal, and we are thrilled!" (11). Katzen's food ideology permeates her cookbook, but her thoroughly kid-tested recipe choices argue convincingly against the prevailing American cultural focus on convenience foods that are all too often full of fat and sugar. One key ingredient, as she sets up her argument, is giving even quite young children autonomy: choosing which recipes in the book to make and preparing the foods they have chosen.

Given Katzen's language, community is not necessarily centered in or bounded by family: "We designed this book precisely for this purpose: to enable very young children to cook as independently as possible under the gentle guidance of an adult 'partner.' The traditional roles of adult-as-main-cook and child-as-miniature-sidekick are reversed. Your child, as head chef, gets to 'read' a pictorial version of a real recipe and do much of the preparation, with you, the attendant grown-up, as helper" (*Pretend Soup* 11). Note that Katzen does not use "parent," much less "mother," in this introduction. Nor is Katzen like Aunt Jane; she does not pursue the "angelic" domestic values that Kirkland and Judson, and even Bedford, did. In essence, Katzen reflects and manifests Giard's philosophy of *doing-cooking*, when the preparation of food is a physical, emotional, intellectual, and communal act that will inevitably produce larger repercussions. In *Pretend Soup*, Katzen addresses "A Few Final Thoughts" to the adult audience: "As your child becomes more attuned to food and cooking, everything that goes on in and around the kitchen will become more interesting, including grocery shopping, setting the table, cleaning up, etc. . . . This might be a good time to look for some picture books about fruits and vegetables, to make field trips to bakeries and farmers' markets, or to plant or visit a garden" (15). Katzen here explicitly urges the adult readers to engage with the children in their local community: notably, she suggests local, independent vendors rather than supermarket chains. Further, the suggestion implies the importance of expanding the young cooks' knowledge of their community institutions, and she makes clear how learning in the domestic context can (and should) beget learning in a community context. Yet, at the end of the introduction of *Honest Pretzels*, Katzen does advocate for individual textual understanding of cooking on the part of young cooks:

- Buy your child a blank, bound journal so she can record her responses to the recipes, new ideas, and more. This can be the beginning of her own personal cookbook!

- Give your child a special pad of paper to make his own shopping lists, and give him a folder to store these in. He can keep track of what he's cooked and can refer to his own "files" the next time around. (xiv)

Like Aunt Jane or Alice's mother of a hundred years ago, Katzen believes that personal writing is important as a means of preserving cooking knowledge or the experience of cooking—now, however, for either gender, as her equal-opportunity pronouns reveal. However, children are not bound by the dictating voice of adult authority in her books but are free to write and reflect, create and preserve through their own agency. In fact, to give child cooks freer rein, Katzen reverses the traditional authority structure of adults and children: "the child is the executive chef and the adult is the sous chef" (*Honest Pretzels* xiv). In these three cookbooks, Mollie Katzen defines herself as a teacher of children, one who would facilitate children learning about the pleasures of cooking and the community and culinary heritage that make such pleasures possible. She provides answers to Longone's questions about how to teach children culinary pleasure and skills, answers which are not bound by domestic family history but which depend on engaged communities and on the intrinsic agency and curiosity of children.

As an outgrowth of her long career as restaurateur and international activist for local, organic cuisine, Alice Waters has written two children's books—*Fanny at Chez Panisse* (1992) and *Fanny in France* (2016)—using a fictional representative of her daughter Fanny as the protagonist and narrator. In the first book, Fanny absorbs her mother's food ideology (local, organically grown food; produce eaten only in season) while growing up in her mother's famous restaurant. Throughout the text Fanny is involved in many of the aspects of food production, from picking bugs out of the zucchini flowers before stuffing them, to creating an olive pizza in the shape of an olive oil bottle, to making a compost "cake" out of the leftover food scraps from the restaurant that will nourish the garden. But her most signal insight into the nature of food involves the restaurant's extemporaneous menu choices depending on the availability of ingredients. Fanny notes that when their fish man cannot provide the expected halibut and offers crabs instead, or when beans are available but the mushroom man has no mushrooms because of lack of rain, the menu changes from the original plan, and she illustrates the creative nature of food preparation:

> All the cooks—Paul, Jeff, Michael, Jerome, Alan, and Seen—change everything. They put the fresh crab in the pasta instead of the soup, and they put the beans in the soup instead of the salad, and they put the cheese in the salad where the beans were supposed to be. It gets really crazy but I like it this way because every dinner turns out to be a surprise. (14)

Fanny's flexible attitude toward food may strike some adults as unlikely, but it is perfectly natural in a child who has developed a wide palate because she has been brought up with a wide range of menu selections, rather than boiled hot dogs and pudding made from a mix, à la Susie in the 1950s.[4] Fanny shows the possibilities for children who are defined as food capable, just as the children were in *Six Little Cooks* and *Cooking Without Mother's Help* a century and more ago.

The difference between *Fanny* and the earlier books is that it is not designed to be instructional: that is, with the expectation, real or otherwise, that Fanny is being prepared for domestic work. The book is not organized as a set of cumulative lessons. Rather, the book splits between an initial narrative section, which is then followed by a set of culinary practices and then recipes. The narrative section is organized as autobiographical and exploratory. Fanny narrates a series of experiences—being at the restaurant, driving around town with her mother, visiting one of the local farms that supplies Chez Panisse—all of which illustrate how she is enmeshed in the extended local community that centers on the restaurant. From the very beginning of the story, when her mother picks her up at school and then takes her around town on a series of restaurant errands, Fanny demonstrates how everyone around her is *doing* food, that food is at the center of everyone's life. In essence, Fanny is learning just by being in this world—partaking and participating in it. She does not have to experience discrete lessons. Rather, she accumulates knowledge osmotically. Unlike the earlier books, where the girl characters all cook, Fanny, as a singular cooking agent, does not. Rather, she is simply an active part of a large and dynamic food community and has the freedom to explore that community from within; unlike Grace or Alice or even Susie, Fanny is not someone who is being trained for a specific social role. The recipes are a result of that accrued experience, included for the pleasures they give rather than as knowledge necessary for a woman to be a successful housewife.

Alice Waters organizes her second Fanny book, *Fanny in France*, in a similar way: a narrative section followed by a set of food rules and recipes. The book documents trips Fanny took to France as a child. Like *Fanny at Chez Panisse*, the narrative of this book is organized experientially around the many foods, meals, and people Fanny encounters in her travels. In essence, to travel in France—to be with people in France—is to always be doing something with food, *doing cooking*. If in *Fanny at Chez Panisse* Fanny explores local food networks, in *Fanny in France* she experiences national food networks. Again, Fanny does not function as a singular cooking agent tasked with mastering a set of defined skills, but with every episode she becomes part of a community of people—men, women, girls, and boys (basically, everyone in each episode)—who prepare and eat food. Everywhere she goes in France, life centers on food. Inescapably involved and engaged by the world around her, Fanny opens up to new experiences (cleaning octopus, milking goats, making cheese). The narrative section does end with a cumulative experience, a national picnic, during which the mayor of Paris proclaims, "In France, eating is togetherness" (85).[5] The recipes that follow are included for no other reason than the pleasure they afford Fanny. The two Alice Waters books use many of the same elements of the earlier books (utensils, ingredients, methods of preparation; setting the table; manners), but they lack scenes of instruction and the pedagogical intention to produce a woman who can manage a household. Rather, in both books, Fanny's agency is developed through the pleasures of communities who cook and eat together. The way Waters structures Fanny's experiences in the two books reflects what Warren Belasco notes about the countercuisine: "In the hip pastorale, there was a middle ground that might be reached at once—a way to have fun and live conscientiously. . . . And the place to begin, [Gary] Snyder suggested, was the food" (66). To return to Longone's questions once again, in these two books Fanny learns about food, the pleasures of the table, and a complex culinary heritage, and she does so without feeling constrained by conventional gender roles and expectations. For Alice Waters, a child's experience and knowledge of food is about liberation and an enriching cultural and culinary landscape.

Children's cookbooks stand apart from other genres of texts for children because they are part of a small group of texts that intend for the children who read them to act on that reading in the real world and produce actual physical objects (in this case prepared food).[6] Cookbooks thus have a directed, practical performative end and, as a result, possess a more complex relationship among the various entities (author/narrator, child reader/narratee, adult reader/narratee) which compose the reading/performance nexus. Like many other texts for children, they are overtly didactic, but their didacticism differs from books meant to enact a simple authority and teach correct moral behavior. The reading/performance nexus of children's cookbooks reflects a complex relationship between the actions taught and the values and ideology which inform that teaching *and* are meant for the child reader/narratee (and even the adult reader/narratee) to internalize. The text embodies social values in its descriptions of and prescriptions for acts of cooking and food and meal preparation, as well as in its address to both children and adults; ideological tenets underlie ingredient choice and sourcing, as well as methods of serving and consuming the food produced. This chapter has analyzed cookbooks espousing three distinct sets of values—female domestic service (Kirkland, Judson), consumerist (Bedford, Beim), and communal (Katzen, Waters)—each of which is grounded in particular historical moments. Despite the differences between them, one distinguishing trait that unifies all these cookbooks as a genre is their use of double address,[7] for the author of each writes to both child and adult readers. Adults have traditionally been gatekeepers of children's literature, controlling children's access to books, but they also safeguard the kitchen, which is full of dangers to the inexperienced child. Thus, the writers of children's cookbooks are constantly aware of the adult readers who will be looking over their children's shoulders as the children move into the kitchen to follow the recipes and make snacks or meals. These adults will inevitably stand in as teachers, guides, and authority figures to direct and facilitate the children's actions, in order to coordinate the instructional ends of the cookbook. Sometimes such adult address is overt. Kirkland writes an "Afterthought" which is aimed, she says, "not to my readers, precisely—but to their mothers and aunts" (232). Katzen specifically addresses the "Owner's Manual" sections of *Pretend Soup* and *Salad People* to adults, and each recipe begins with a section labeled "To the Grown-ups." Although the latter disappears in *Honest Pretzels*, because of its older child audience, the book still includes an extensive section of advice titled "To the Adult" that follows the introductory "Hi Kids!" (viii-xiv). Other authors make the adult address more covert. Judson speaks through the mother figure, as a mask in which she embeds adult authority and voice, thus assuring adult readers that all the proper advice for child kitchen technique will be provided. Bedford offers covert clues to the mother-facilitators on how to make child-play more fulfilling and realistic—a "tiny" simulacrum of domestic bliss. Beim creates an adult male narrative voice who uses the language of an adult male to reassure boy readers that they can cook and still remain masculine. More radically, and in keeping with her broad sense of community, Waters decenters adult authority among a host of Fanny's grownup acquaintances: farmers who provide produce for Chez Panisse, chefs who cook at the restaurant, family friends in France who host Fanny's family for meals. All of them provide knowledge and instruction as Fanny helps them create the different dishes that she describes for readers.

Double address is genre-defining for children's cookbooks and structures what Leonardi would characterize as their "embedded discourse." Thus, the writers of cookbooks consciously construct narrators who embed the discourse of recipes (the directions of how to manufacture dishes at home) within a set of narratives (tidbits of story, anecdote, advice) in order to situate the recipes within a context that creates meaning for the readers. Within the sample texts examined above, Kirkland's and Judson's narrators discuss recipes as a means to teach the ideals of female domestic service to young girls through the authority of the adult women characters who instruct the girls in the kitchen; Bedford shifts cooking from work to play in her excessively simple recipes that simultaneously reinforce her readers' attachment to the shortcuts of industrialized convenience foods; Beim uses "man-talk" to create a masculine space in and outside the kitchen where boys can feel comfortable about conventionally domestic food preparation; Katzen and Waters intend for their recipes to empower children in the kitchen and connect them to a larger local and global community that cooks together. To return to Jan Longone one last time: Americans have taught our children about cooking and the pleasures of the table in an amazing variety of ways over time, and children's cookbooks have formed an important part of the discourse through which we have taught them. While some such texts have isolated child reader/cooks from their food heritage, most have more interestingly grappled with ways to empower children in the kitchen and beyond through teaching knowledge of ingredients, skills at the stove, and American culinary heritage as it has evolved through time.

 Chapter 3

PUDDINGS AND PIES

Meat Pastries in the Tales of Beatrix Potter

Food is frequently a fraught signifier in Beatrix Potter's stories, and beginning in 1902 with her first story for children, *The Tale of Peter Rabbit*, Potter regularly uses food to motivate and shape her tales' conflicts. Most obviously, Potter's tales parallel many traditional folktales and rhymes which influenced her and formed a substantial part of literature for children in the nineteenth century; her animal characters desire to eat various kinds of foods or are threatened with being eaten—a difference between acting or being acted upon. These complementary motifs blur the distinction between subject and object, but they also give Potter the chance to explore how food can serve as a form of social critique. Peter Rabbit, Benjamin Bunny, and the Flopsy Bunnies, in their titular tales, trespass into Mr. McGregor's garden in search of dangerous and forbidden vegetables, where they are themselves threatened with being caught by the farmer and killed as garden pests, then eaten as Peter's father was in a meat pie. The Flopsy Bunnies in *The Tale of Mr. Tod* again face being eaten, this time by their natural predator, Tommy Brock the badger. In their stories, Tom Kitten and Jemima Puddle-Duck wind up in similar situations when rats or a fox, respectively, wish to cook and eat them. Jeremy Fisher goes fishing for minnows for his dinner party but is nearly eaten by a trout; giving up on his original plan, he fixes a roasted grasshopper with ladybird sauce for his guests—although his friend Mr. Alderman Ptolemy Tortoise, a vegetarian, brings salad to eat instead. Jeremy Fisher is considerate of his guests' tastes, not minding that his friend (who won't or can't eat the meat he is fixing) brings a dish more in line with his own tastes. The civility with which this is handled contrasts with the dog Duchess's comic mixup of the mouse and bacon pie that Ribby the cat is serving at a tea party; Duchess secretly tries to substitute her own veal and ham pie in *The Tale of the Pie and the Patty-Pan*. The utmost incivility occurs in *The Tale of Squirrel Nutkin*, where the young squirrel nearly ruins the detente his fellow squirrels have carefully negotiated with Mr. Brown, the owl who oversees the island on which they gather nuts; Nutkin's rudeness is also not only uncivil but it begins to blur the distinction between subject and object as Nutkin almost becomes prey to the angered owl—a perilous state for an animal protagonist.

These brief examples demonstrate the rich complexity of food-related issues that underlie Potter's narratives, which offer multiple vectors for exploration. At the core of all these tales, though, is prepared food, usually cooked. None of the animal characters eat raw meat on stage. Even the predators usually want their game prepared, conforming to cultural culinary traditions similar to those practiced by Potter and her readers. Within Lévi-Strauss's canonical classifications of the raw and cooked, those who are portrayed eating in Beatrix Potter's tales most often want prepared foods, reinforcing their identity as civilized beings, whether they be animal or human.[1] Even though Potter writes animal fantasy, she nonetheless grounds many of her stories in realistic depictions of place[2]—and in foodways: she uses the food which the animals in her tales desire or consume to characterize them as properly British middle-class denizens of the Victorian and Edwardian eras, portrayals which reflect standards of decorum set by cookbooks such as *Mrs. Beeton's Book of Household Management*.[3]

In order to provide material substantiation that rabbit was a well-developed part of the English diet, we began our 2002 article about *The Tale of Peter Rabbit*, "In Search of his Father's Garden,"[4] with a recipe for rabbit pie, one of the nineteen recipes for cooking rabbit in *Mrs. Beeton's*: thus, Peter's father's end is realistic, and consequently the threat of becoming rabbit pie is present and foreboding as long as Peter remains in the garden. From that moment of historical and textual grounding, we shifted focus to the narrative, exploring the symbolic nature of food in the tale. Treating Peter as a hero on an epic journey away from home, into a savage world and back again, the essay saw the tale's narrative arc as permeated by food and investigated how that food in its myriad cultural significations shaped the narrative. Contrasting the allure of the dangerous vegetables of Mr. McGregor's forbidden garden with the decorous, respressive foods of home, we interpreted Peter's experience in the garden as initially based in his selfish desire to satiate taste (bodily desire) at the expense of safety, and the necessity of using his head to escape the mortal danger of the garden.

That is the space where the tables get turned on him, and instead of being the bold consumer of vegetables and fulfilling his father's adventurous spirit Peter nearly follows his father's example of being caught as a garden pest[5] and turned (with farmhouse thrift) into rabbit pie—the eater becoming the eaten. The story seems on the surface to be a cautionary tale, with Peter's penitent return home to be put to bed and dosed with chamomile tea while his compliant sisters are rewarded with the berries they have gathered and the buns their mother has bought. However, the ending of the story is subverted from its beginning. The front plate illustration shows Peter hiding under the covers, resisting his mother's medicinal ministrations. The apparently didactic ending is thus disrupted by Peter's continued refusal of proper domestic food, which subliminally suggests the continued desirability of the food associated with his rebellion.

The paradigm of the conflicted and irresolvable nature of food as narrative and cultural signifier operates not only in *Peter Rabbit* but also in many of Potter's other tales as well. For some of these tales—*The Tale of Benjamin Bunny, The Tale of the Flopsy Bunnies, The Tale of Jemima Puddle-Duck*—there is no actual cooking work but only the threat that an animal could be cooked. In *The Tale of Samuel Whiskers, or the Roly-Poly Pudding, The Tale of Mr. Tod,* and *The Tale of the Pie and the Patty-Pan,* the same threat is present, but these stories possess many more culinary markers. To be more precise, by incorporating in these tales the kitchens and cooking utensils and complex preparations of iconic British meat puddings and pies—as well as including the tables, tableware, and accessories for the serving of said pastries—Potter offers a much fuller sense of how these stories fit within the Victorian and Edwardian worlds in which she wrote. In "Cooking Culture: Situating Food and Drink in the Nineteenth Century," Suzanne Daley and Ross D. Forman, citing central food moments in Victorian literature (such as Oliver Twist's request for more), claim that "food is a sometimes-benign marker of social position, but it gestures at the grimmer reality that social status often determines who lives and dies" (365). Potter mirrors Daley and Forman's claim, extending it to the antagonistic relationships inherent in the interactions between the animals in her fantasy stories. In *The Tale of the Pie and Patty-Pan*—except for the undifferentiated pork, veal, and mouse of the pie fillings—the story's two pies are the benign markers of social position that express the unacknowledged and repressed conflicts between Ribby the cat and Duchess the dog. In *The Tale of Samuel Whiskers* and *The Tale of Mr. Tod,* Potter puts her animal child characters in the position in which they may be caught, cooked, and eaten as food, gesturing toward that fate of their real-life species comrades, yet she extracts her protagonists from that dangerous edible fate, so that there is no tragedy of either a successfully realized kitten pudding or bunny pie.

PUDDING

A pudding, in the British sense, is a broad and complex category of dish, difficult to define because of its many variations, but heavily tied to British national identity. Puddings may be either savory or sweet; they may be made with a pastry crust and then boiled, steamed, or baked; or made with breadcrumbs combined with other ingredients and baked in a mold.[6] In *Modern Cookery for Private Families* (1860), Eliza Acton argues the value of savory puddings across class lines:

> The perfect manner in which the nutriment and flavor of an infinite variety of viands may be preserved by enclosing and boiling them in paste, is a great recommendation of this purely English class of dishes, . . . If really well made, these savoury puddings are worthy of a place on *any* table; though the decrees of fashion . . . have confined them almost entirely to the simple family dinners of the middle class. (399)

Heather A. Evans, in her article "Kittens and Kitchens: Food, Gender, and 'The Tale of Samuel Whiskers,'" offers an invaluable feminist analysis of Potter's use of food in that story. She argues that the tale parallels the rise of women's general social power in the late nineteenth century through the conventionally female space of the kitchen, which engendered both cooking skills and the ability to produce texts (cookbooks and instruction manuals such as *Mrs. Beeton's*) that gained extraordinary cultural currency. In addition to using important Potter biographers (e.g., Linda Lear) and scholars (e.g., Margaret Mackey), Evans turns to a variety of primary source Victorian food and foodways texts to chart the rising power and frequency of nineteenth-century women writing about food, showing that Potter is one node in a well-developed network of such writings. For Evans, Potter "demonstrated the spirit of resistance and subverted the authority of convention and the constructions of gender prevalent in late nineteenth-century food writing for women" (612). Also, "through her tales, Potter introduces young readers—both boys and girls—to epicurean themes and concerns that were features of contemporary adult literature" (613). To ground her argument,

Evans performs a close reading of the rat couple's preparation of Tom Kitten as a roly-poly pudding—that is, enacting and negotiating the recipe (a pastry made of breadcrumbs or butter and dough)—while linking the scene to the importance of roly-poly puddings in Victorian culture, particularly for children. Advancing her point about gender, Evans then demonstrates how Potter showcases the skills of Anna Maria, "who proves herself to be an expert on the intricacies of baking a quintessentially English dish" (616) and who "demonstrates the principles of economical cookery that constituted a primary component of a fin-de-siècle education in the culinary arts and domestic science" (615). In other words, through her cooking skills Anna Maria Whiskers shows herself to be an exemplar of the ambitious, capable, and advancing nineteenth-century British middle-class woman.

While Evans's feminist reading is important because, in part, it resonates with what other food studies scholars have claimed about the power that women achieved in the nineteenth century through cooking skills and food writing,[7] we are curious to look at British puddings as a culinary currency that may be essentially identified with the middle class, as Eliza Acton points out in the quotation cited above. Puddings also have great mobility and can be found up and down the class register, because they "are worthy of a place on *any* table" (Acton 399). For *The Tale of Samuel Whiskers*, an understanding of the rats' access to a kitchen and the ingredients they use for their pudding is crucial to perceive the blurred class position Potter creates for the Whiskers family. Anna Maria faces a number of the same problems in cooking puddings that real women of the Victorian and Edwardian eras likewise dealt with.

Puddings, both savory and sweet, were enormously popular at the upper end of the Victorian social spectrum. In his analysis of *Mrs. Beeton's Book of Household Management*, Colin Spencer notes that Mrs. Beeton includes "over 100 different puddings" and highlights how her recipes reveal the growing love for sweet puddings: "It is no wonder when one reads the emphasis on dessert that Britain, with twice the per capita consumption, used almost half of the sugar beet consumed in Europe, as well as by far the greater part of the cane sugar imported into Europe" (275). In *Fruits of Empire: Exotic Produce and British Taste, 1660–1800*, James Walvin offers corroborating evidence, noting that "it was however for their desserts that the English reserved their most lavish additions of sugar" (121). With growing sugar imports, sweet puddings became a sign for the rising affluence of the British middle class, manifested textually in the plethora of recipes in cookbooks like *Mrs. Beeton's* or Acton's *Modern Cookery*.

For the lower end of the social spectrum, puddings were desirable as a filling dish in food-insecure households, although cooking them presented challenges to the poorest housewives. In "Loaves and Fishes: Food in Poor Households in Late Nineteenth-Century London," Anna Davin explains the role that puddings played in the diet of the urban poor: "[S]ome mothers made steamed suet puddings (sweet or savoury), which were tasty and filling. . . . Such puddings were enthusiastically recommended by apostles of domesticity. But they required skill, preparation time and long cooking, often beyond available domestic resources" (170–71). Cooking a pudding in a London tenement where the families may have had only an open fire and limited cooking utensils proved difficult if not impossible for such lower-class women. One of the "apostles of decency" to which Davin refers was the St. Pancras School for Mothers, a charitable organization that included among its services teaching poor mothers how to cook (Davies n.p.). The organization's publication, *The Pudding Lady: A New Departure in Social Work* (1910, 1916), provided household management advice (such as recipes, menus, cooking instruction, shopping lists) as well as case studies and pedagogical discussions. The core of the society's cooking instruction was suet puddings "made under conditions as much as possible like those obtaining in the homes in Somers Town" (Bibby 23). The case studies documented the excruciating poverty in which the mothers attempted to manage their homes, most obviously manifested by a significant lack of kitchen facilities and cooking equipment.[8] By the second edition (1916), the author recognized that instructing the mothers at the school had not changed their domestic behavior: too many of the mothers who had learned how to make suet pudding at the school had not made it at home because they were unable to translate the instruction into their own kitchen circumstances. So social workers began going out and doing in-home instruction to help the women overcome the obstacles they faced when trying to cook at home. Ironically, given that the school's pedagogy was based in pudding, there are only two pudding recipes in the book, one savory and one sweet; both recipes are simple, require few ingredients, and are economical and adaptable; the sweet pudding does not even require sugar, rather using dates for sweetness.[9] Even so, spartan pudding recipes designed for the poor were too "often beyond available domestic resources" (Davin 171). In other words, the pudding—which defined "the simple family dinners of the middle class" (Acton 399) and even Britishness itself, according to Samuel Johnson—did not translate down the English social scale very easily or effectively.

The pudding that Samuel Whiskers and Anna Maria attempt to make out of Tom Kitten is peculiar both in its ingredients and method: its strangeness reveals both the poverty and the middle-class aspirations that motivate the rats. Roly-poly pudding, a classic British dessert pudding, traditionally consists of a suet pastry crust, rolled out flat and covered with jam, then rolled up, fastened together at the ends, tied in a floured cloth, and boiled (Beeton 651). Although most frequently sweet, some versions with savory fillings (such as bacon) also exist.[10] Tom's inclusion as a meat filling for the rolled pudding makes it savory (although the pudding may also blur the savory/sweet dividing line, given that kittens, like small children, are frequently described as "sweet"). Presumably, the original Edwardian child audience would have been both amused and horrified at the substitution of kitten for jam in a favorite nursery dessert. A further confusion of ingredients comes in the debate between Samuel Whiskers and Anna Maria: he wants the pudding made of breadcrumbs while she insists on butter and dough. The breadcrumbs,[11] however, would not work for a rolled pudding, which requires a paste dough to roll. As noted above, Evans argues that this moment showcases Anna Maria's skills as a cook: she knows the correct ingredients for the roly-poly pudding.

Anna Maria's cooking knowledge suggests middle-class tastes; the illustrations likewise show her and Samuel Whiskers wearing clothes that suggest middle-class aspirations (a good dress with an apron for her; breeches, a waistcoat, and a coat for him).[12] These class markers are at odds with their living situation, however. Like real rats, Potter's rat characters live in the walls of the house.[13] Given their "very small, fusty room, with boards, and rafters, and cobwebs, and lath and plaster" (Potter 49), in a deserted space below the attic floor, Samuel Whiskers and Anna Maria seem to be analogous to the tenement dwellers of the British urban poor. They inhabit a space without adequate kitchen facilities (no kitchen at all), like so many of the tenements in the case studies in *The Pudding Lady*. In other words, Samuel Whiskers and Anna Maria live in circumstances where they cannot cook, so they usually steal from the kitchen instead, and yet Samuel Whiskers's first impulse is not to *eat* Tom Kitten immediately like a real rat might but to *cook* him: to make him into a dish. Both rats are willing to delay gratification, to act in a civilized manner by cooking their meal. Their choice to cook is an example of what Stephen Mennell calls the civilizing of the appetite: "The sense of delicacy and pressures toward self-control are . . . closely interwoven. In eating, it is the developing sense of delicacy which first becomes apparent, but that eventually becomes entangled with restraint" (328). Rats are naturally rapacious. Samuel Whiskers and Anna Maria do not need to make Tom Kitten into anything: they could simply start to eat him. Instead, however, they aspire to make him into that most quintessential of British foods, a pudding. In constrained circumstances, the rats put on the airs of middle-class civility rather than give in to their rat nature. Like the intrepid mothers in the case studies of *The Pudding Lady* or those in the testimonies quoted by Davin, Samuel Whiskers and Anna Maria attempt to pull off an extraordinarily frugal version of a signature piece of British culture, an attempt that would satisfy both the needs of the body and the intellectual aspiration to a more civilized existence. As the St. Pancras School for Mothers used the pudding as a class-based salvation for London's poor, so too do the rats turn to a middle-class solution to their hunger.

For Heather Evans, Anna Maria "embodies the spirit of an informed and educated cook" who "demonstrates the principles of economical cookery that constituted an education in the fin-de-siècle culinary arts and domestic science" (615). She then uses Victorian cookery principles to effectively link the rat with the two adult cats: "By salvaging the dumpling pastry after Tom Kitten's rescue, and making it into a bag pudding (65) [Warne edition p. 71], Mrs. Ribby and Tabitha Twitchit similarly exhibit good economical cookery practice" (615). But the shared value of "good economical cookery" hides the economic gulf between the rats and the cats. Tabitha Twitchit has a well-stocked kitchen and a large cooking range inserted into the fireplace, and she has the means to achieve Mrs. Beeton's dictum that households be free of "discomfort and suffering" (Beeton 3)—even if she must be thrifty enough to reuse the pudding Tom was rolled in, adding currants to hide the soot that rubbed off him.[14] On the other hand, Anna Maria has no kitchen or cooking range, and she must steal the rolling pin and the ingredients for the pudding; moreover, as she and Samuel Whiskers flee the attic space and the house, she recovers mutton bones and "half a smoked ham hidden in the chimney" to take with them. To cook, Anna Maria must steal; motivated by the instinct to survive, she is also the epitome of frugality and economy. She extemporizes a pudding out of aspirational desire rather than comfortable habit. In this case, the food in Potter's supposedly cozy world reflects the actual class divides of the real world of Edwardian England.

* * *

PIE

Although the earliest known reference to "pie" in English came in the late fourteenth century, Alan Davidson indicates that the earliest known pies were Egyptian and that evidence of "proto-pies" extends back to the classical period. Pies have a long presence in British culinary history. In British folk myth, "pie" is short for magpie, because, like the bird that "collects a variety of things," a pie contains "a variety of ingredients" (603). With the rising use of wheat flour in the fourteenth century, pies became more ubiquitous and, as Colin Spencer notes, "the rural pie was born" (93). At its simplest, a pie is "a mixture of ingredients encased and cooked in pastry" (Davidson 603), although the presence or absence of top layers or bottom layers varies, and fillings may be either savory or sweet—or even, in the medieval period, a mixture of both (thus the original mincemeat pie). *Mrs. Beeton's* offers twenty recipes for savory pies and two for sweet pies (apple and mince). Like puddings, pies are highly malleable and adaptable, materially and culturally.

Pie is the most frequently mentioned dish in Potter's work, starting in her first book with the rabbit pie into which Peter Rabbit's father "was put" by Mrs. McGregor; it is also mentioned again in *The Tale of Mr. Tod*, in which the badger Tommy Brock plans to make pie out of the rabbit babies he has kidnapped. Pies (mouse and bacon vs. veal and ham) are also a point of contention in *The Tale of the Pie and the Patty-Pan*. Potter's use of savory meat pie within her stories reflects its importance in British cooking in general but also the particular emphasis on "rural pie" in the diet of northern England, which includes the Lake District and other holiday homes where she set her stories. Like pudding, pie is malleable in both content and function: its symbolism varies among the three rabbit stories, which are grounded in the realities of farm life, and *The Tale of the Pie and the Patty-Pan*, which showcases the social expectations of village life. In both sets of examples, however, pie serves as the means by which Potter reveals the characters' essential animal natures, which do not change no matter what charming clothes they may wear or picturesque houses they may live in; conversely, through pie the characters reveal Potter's commentary on the social world which the animals reflect. Pie may serve as either as an expression of the predator/prey relationship or as a measure of sociability.

* * *

All cooking disguises the inherent violence of the act of eating. While carnivorous animals eat their recently killed prey raw, humans usually transform a once-living organism into a much less recognizable version of its original form via butchering, culinary preparation, and cooking. The process of making pie serves as a particularly effective means of disguising meat consumption: the meat is generally deboned, chopped, and hidden within a pastry shell, so that it bears little resemblance to the animal muscle or organ of its origin. Potter's stories, so often stereotyped as cozy, hide their violence the way pies hide meat, wrapping the violence in the pie shell of civilized cooking. As Evans notes, "the most violent moments in Potter's corpus revolve around food" (603): the intrinsic violence of food consumption, of killing and dismemberment to create meat, lurks under the animals' plans to eat each other, despite their "civilized" means of preparing and cooking the dishes that they intend to create out of each other's bodies.

Pie as an ultimate fatal end hangs as a threat over Potter's bunny tales in particular. Although only Peter's father actually gets cooked in a pie by the McGregors, Peter's mother uses her husband's fate to warn Peter about what will happen if he disobeys her. Although rabbit pie is not explicitly mentioned in *The Tale of Benjamin Bunny* and *The Tale of the Flopsy Bunnies*, Mr. McGregor is an implicit threat to the little rabbits' survival in both stories. The little Flopsy Bunnies, in their eponymously titled tale, are small and tender enough to warrant being eaten in a pie once captured by Mr. McGregor and taken to his wife in the kitchen: *Mrs. Beeton's* explicitly recommends that rabbit for pies "should be young" (480). Thus, readers of *Peter Rabbit* (who is a minor character in both of the later stories) might well have intertextually imported the threat that the McGregors might eat them in pie as they did Peter's father, especially given that Mr. McGregor dwells on how fat the Flopsy Bunnies are, and Mrs. McGregor worries that they may be too old and thus "not fit to eat" (49–50). In the tales of *Peter Rabbit* and *The Flopsy Bunnies*, this violence of the pie is inherent in the human/animal interactions, reflecting humans' position as apex predators, particularly of animals they regard as pests and competitors for their own food resources.

In *The Tale of Mr. Tod*, the food violence occurs between animal characters, as Potter reproduces the predator/prey relationship of wild animals despite their civilized clothes and cooking habits. Like real badgers, which eat small mammals, Tommy Brock intends to feast upon the baby bunnies he has kidnapped from Benjamin and Flopsy Bunny. Unlike real badgers, however, he intends to cook them in a pie. The story makes much of his rude and outlaw habits (in addition to kidnapping, he breaks into Mr. Tod's house and sleeps in his bed with his boots on), but he apparently intends to cook the baby bunnies in a civilized fashion. He takes out not only a blue willow pattern pie dish[15] but also "a large carving knife and fork, and a chopper," clearly with the express intent of butchering the baby rabbits he has stolen to use as the filling for his dinner pie (30). Thus—despite his boorish and criminal actions towards both the rabbits and his fellow predator, Mr. Tod the fox—in terms of food preparation, Tommy Brock aspires to behave as a middle-class, cultured animal.[16] In choosing pie, he plans a dish that demands from him complex cooking techniques to create. He plans to eat the bunnies, once he has baked them, in a civilized manner, for he has also put at one end of the table a "tablecloth, a plate, a tumbler, a knife and fork, salt-cellar, mustard and a chair—in short, preparations for one person's supper" (30). In other words, in order to eat his rabbit pie, Tommy Brock plans to set a proper table that even includes seasonings and condiments. Thus, Tommy Brock, while acting the role of predator, reenacts the human/animal relationship—that is, the civilized attitude toward masking animal prey once it becomes food. In making pie, the McGregors define their position as civilized; Tommy Brock would also make a claim that he is refined, or at least possesses a civilized and anthropomorphized animal nature, first by desiring to make the bunnies into a pie and then by putting off the realization of that desire until morning (per Stephen Mennell).

Again, food in Potter is fraught, a paradoxical signifier. Tommy Brock is initially treated with civility by old Mr. Bouncer, Flopsy's father and Benjamin Bunny's father-in-law. Hungry after waking from a winter's hibernation and having difficulty finding something to eat, Tommy Brock complains to Mr. Bouncer that he can find no pheasant's eggs (because of Mr. Tod) or frogs (because of otters). Mr. Bouncer hospitably invites Tommy Brock in for seed cake and cowslip wine. Tommy Brock accepts "with alacrity" (14), but he then violates the laws of hospitality by kidnapping his host's infant grandchildren. Peter Rabbit theorizes that the stolen bunnies are safe, however, because Mr. Bouncer acted as a good host in offering food to Tommy Brock. Peter believes that, having broken his fast with the seed cake, Tommy Brock is no longer voraciously hungry: "Your family is alive and kicking; and Tommy Brock has had refreshment. He will probably go to sleep, and keep them for breakfast" (24). Peter's comment implies that Tommy Brock's actions are no longer simply opportunistic but highly premeditated: with the edge taken off his hunger by the seed cake, he has stolen the baby bunnies because what he wants at this point is a *cooked* meal. Tommy Brock violates civility again when he breaks into Mr. Tod's house (a regular habit, according to the narrator at the beginning of the story); he has a plan to steal a cultured experience that his lack of a regular household seems to deny him. Tommy Brock's plan to cook his food does not, however, redeem his social errors, and he never gets to eat his pie because he delays its preparation. Potter ends this anthropomorphizing arc by exploiting the two predators' natural conflicts: Benjamin Bunny and Peter Rabbit rescue the rabbit babies while the fox and the badger are distracted by fighting each other.

Tommy Brock parallels Samuel Whiskers and Anna Maria in his aspirations to middle-class dining, but he lacks the domestic wherewithal to produce it. All three desire complexly prepared, cooked food that requires a kitchen with an oven to bake it. All three take significant steps toward the realization of a dish: Samuel Whiskers and Maria gather the ingredients and prepare the roly-poly pudding but, lacking a kitchen of their own or opportunity to use Tabatha Twtchit's oven before John Joiner saves the day, they never get to eat it. By stealing the baby bunnies and taking over Mr. Tod's house, Tommy Brock creates both the ingredients and opportunity to bake his pie: he has the utensils and the oven for cooking it, and the tableware with which to properly eat it. Yet by yielding to the temptation to sleep, he loses his chance when Mr. Tod reclaims his home. Tommy Brock thus comes closer to achieving a cultivated, cooked meal than the two rats, yet again Potter prevents it. While some of Potter's animals do eat others as food (see below), the potential food never occupies a subject position. The overlay of a civilized pie or pudding cannot hide the potential death of innocent subjects, who serve in the stories as analogs for children and the child readers; actually turning them into food would be far too terrifying a reminder of mortality. The conventions of children's literature usually demand the escape of the endangered child. Potter uses her rapacious would-be predators to threaten her child characters, but undermines their ability to harm them by depriving them of kitchens and the ability to cook in a way that uncomfortably mimics the deprivations of the underclasses of her own period—nor does she seem to challenge the social order that results in such deprivation. If in the wider world, as demonstrated in *The Pudding Lady*, knowledge of good middle-class fare does not provide clear access to an economically stable, food secure, and civilized existence, neither does such fare provide a similar solution to the animal aspirants of Potter's tales. Rather, food and the complex of beliefs, behaviors, and customs that surround it remain fraught and function to illustrate the irresolvable and irreconcilable motives that Potter uses to create her characters and build her plots.

* * *

In *The Pie and the Patty Pan*, Potter shifts her focus from the underlying prey/predator plot of the countryside to a village story of social niceties and good intentions gone awry. Unlike the other pie tales, where the blurred line between eater and eaten is frequently highlighted as focus and plot motive, here Potter does not introduce, or even allude to, the subject positions of the meat fillings (mouse, calf, pig) of the tale's two pies. By deftly avoiding the topic of the particular beings who inhabit the pie, she allows the tale to focus on the social blunders that result from the tensions of consideration and disgust acted out by the tale's main characters, a dog and a cat. Although the species are traditionally antagonistic, they are both domesticated and frequently live peaceably together within human households. Ribby, the tabby cat, invites Duchess, the Pomeranian dog, for tea; she plans to serve a choice meal, but Duchess worries that she will not like the food that Ribby will offer. The plot turns on the conflicts created by the demands of manners, social anxieties, and matters of taste, all of which center neatly on the pie from the title.

Potter sets the tale around the important British meal of tea. The drink itself acted "as a marker of middle-class social civility and an index of polite society" (Miller 420), and taking tea embodied the "idealized notions of English social practice, such as social charm, personal grace, and lively but polite discourse" (Fromer 533). The social events surrounding the drink "crop up over and over again in English fiction and diaries from the mid-19th to the early 20th centuries; the constants are abundance and variety of food, the presence of ham or pie, salad, the choice of baked goods, preserves, and a fine display of tableware" (Davidson 381). Through sharing this display of abundance and conviviality, Ribby the Cat and Duchess the Dog intend to reinforce their cross-species friendship. Tea should be a sociable moment of coming together to strengthen emotional ties—"a mark of caring, of relationships, of giving time to another, to listen and share; a social activity that promotes a sense of togetherness and community" (Lavelle 585)—but the distinct tastes of the characters, particularly of the dog, get in the way and magnify their differences rather than smooth them over. Of all the abundance, pie is at the comestible center of the tale's plot, source of both consideration and disgust.

As the attentive hostess, Ribby works hard to prepare for the tea party. She shops for delicacies to serve her guest, cleans the house, and sets the table with "a very clean white table-cloth, and set[s] out her best china tea-set" (20). Her inclusion of a meat pie indicates she is serving a high tea, a common rural meal (Davidson 381–82). She chooses to serve "a pie of the most delicate and tender mouse minced up with bacon" (18), clearly a favorite of her own since she promises Duchess, "You never tasted anything so good" (11). As a considerate hostess, though, she heroically sacrifices her own favorite dish in favor of her guest, telling Duchess "*you* shall eat it all! I will eat muffins" (11–12). She even works to rid the mouse meat of bones as she prepares the pie, because she worries that Duchess might choke (18). Duchess, however, is worried that Ribby will serve mouse pie, which the little dog finds utterly distasteful. Here, Duchess's physical aversion to the mouse pie trumps the social function the pie is supposed to serve, initiating the amusing plot complication of Duchess sneaking into Ribby's house to put her own veal and ham pie in the oven so that she can eat something that she finds palatable for the occasion without hurting her hostess's feelings.

Disgust over food is closely tied to a sense of taste: a dish that one person enjoys is horrific to another. Sometimes aversions are tied to cultural food preferences (insect protein is enjoyed in many cultures but disgusting in others, for example), but aversions may be individual as well (a family member who loves broccoli vs. one who will not touch it). Duchess feels enormous aversion for mouse pie, as she expresses when worrying over the mere possibility that Ribby may be planning to serve it: "I really couldn't, *couldn't* eat mouse pie. And I shall have to eat it, because it is to be a party" (14). As Julia Kristeva notes in *Powers of Horror: An Essay on Abjection*, "Food loathing is perhaps the most elementary and most archaic form of abjection" (3). So, caught between the conflict of personal taste and social duty, Duchess is willing to go to considerable lengths to avoid the food that disgusts her, to the point of slipping her own ham and veal pie (in an identical pie dish) into Ribby's oven. She creates an elaborate scheme to avoid the food she fears, yet her work is not enough, because inherent to Duchess's aversion is "the inability to assume with sufficient strength the imperative act of excluding" (Bataille, quoted in Kristeva 64). Abjection is a weak form of prohibition, as Kristeva recognizes when she here invokes George Bataille's essay, "L'abjection et les formes misérables." Thus, when Duchess begins to realize that she has eaten mouse despite her plan, she has a moment of abject food loathing and loses all rationality, insisting in the face of the evidence that she has eaten a tin patty pan (a baking device to hold up the center of a pie crust) that she used in her own pie, rather than admitting to herself that she has eaten mouse. Thus, in her "dark revolts of being" against "the possible, the tolerable, the thinkable" (Kristeva 2), Duchess breaks with civility and consideration, repressing the initial delight that she takes in the pie she has eaten: she has found it "toothsome and eaten four helpings before realizing she has been eating the wrong pie" (40–41). At this point she begins distracting herself and Ribby with the hysterical and imaginary fear that she has swallowed her own patty pan.

This moment of "oblivion and thunder" (Kristeva 9) allows Duchess to defer the realization of what happened and what she has eaten, after which she acts to save face and recover from the faux pas of her disgust. But her involuntary performance has ruined the tea and its civility. The arrival of Dr. Maggotty, the magpie, only creates more distraction and disorder, providing Duchess with an exit but not a fix for the hospitality that she has violated. In the end, Duchess abandons in Ribby's yard her tastier ham and veal pie, which is eaten by the magpie and his jackdaw friends. They smash the pie plate, although Dr. Maggotty does leave the patty pan "considerably . . . under the pump" (60).[17] Still, when Ribby discovers the pie plate and patty pan, neither of which is hers, she realizes that she has been duped: "Did you ever see the like! So there really *was* a patty-pan. . . . But *my* patty-pans are all in the kitchen cupboard. . . . Well I never did!" (60). The slight to her cooking, her pie, is clear, and whatever was left of "togetherness and community" (Lavelle 585) is lost to Duchess's implicit criticism of Ribby's culinary and social skills.

CONCLUSION

So why does Beatrix Potter write tales of failed meat pastries, failed either in execution (*Samuel Whiskers, Mr. Tod*) or intention (*The Pie and the Patty-Pan*)? In the predator/prey narrative of *Mr. Tod*, the failed pie signifies both the disturbance of the pretension to middle-class civility—because it exposes the "red in tooth and claw" reality of how a rabbit pie filling happens—and the predator/prey hierarchy, since the tale ends with the two predators in conflict and the pie filling escaping to live another day. The ending of *The Tale of Samuel Whiskers, or the Roly Poly Pudding* likewise signals the threat of rats to kittens—but although the kitten is saved from being eaten as pudding filling, the rats escape and remain at large, a more distant threat but not an exterminated one.[18] In *The Pie and the Patty-Pan*, Potter uses the pies to undercut the sociability of a high tea, exposing the hypocrisy and duplicity of Duchess while undercutting the sincere intentions of Ribby the cat and foiling whatever gentle aspirations she might have had to ameliorate the differences between her and the dog. In the face of the failed tea, Ribby resolves to stick with her own kind: "Next time I give a party—I will invite cousin Tabatha Twitchit"—a cat like herself (60). Just as the pudding is a fraught signifier, so is the pie.

The range of responses to Beatrix Potter and her tales is broad, to say the least. Commercial and fan websites employ romanticized language meant to capture a sentimental, nostalgic audience,[19] and literary critics distance themselves from such coziness to see Potter as more disruptive and radical—integral to a larger and analytical cultural tradition that casts a critical eye on the world it represents.[20] Potter's take on food in her tales is not like Maurice Sendak's in *Where the Wild Things Are*, which uses the "still hot" plate of mother's food at the end to draw Max away from his wildness back to soporific conformity and to solve the emotional family problem. Sendak's attitude toward the warm plate of food parallels Eliza Acton's attitude toward pudding, for both see food as a social unifier. Sendak's attitude is also akin to the first edition of *The Pudding Lady*, which believed an answer to social problems lay in how mothers fed their children. Beatrix Potter is perhaps more akin to the second edition of *The Pudding Lady*, which begins to grapple with the failures of its initial project and to realize the impossibility of fixing hunger through the simple solution of a good British pudding.

Beatrix Potter sites her characters squarely in a world that is full of food but in which food provides no answers, resolutions, or stable access to middle-class comfort. Instead, Potter's world is one in which food is strategic, a way of asserting power or disrupting power, a world where young characters must be alert to the constantly changing ways that food shapes the social landscape, whether real or imaginary. Rather than telling stories that offer idyllic solutions to simple problems, as adults often assume books for young children should, Potter uses food to show the complexities of the real world within her stories: she acknowledges the hidden violence of social relations, the less-than-genteel poverty of some parts of the population, and the threats that the powerful exercise over those with less power: gardeners over rabbits, badgers over baby bunnies, dogs over cats, rats over kittens, adults over children—although she does let the children survive in the end.

Chapter 4

"A LITTLE SMACKEREL OF SOMETHING"

Food and the *Künstlerroman* in the Winnie-the-Pooh Books

> Bears are greedy plunderers of honeycomb. From fictional Baloo to Winnie the Pooh, from brown bears to the sloth bears and sun bears known as honey bears, they relish the sweet wealth of energy this delicious food provides, liking both the honey and the protein-rich developing brood. (524)
>
> —HATTIE ELLIS, SWEETNESS AND LIGHT:
> THE MYSTERIOUS HISTORY OF HONEYBEES (2004)

Honey and bees have held a significant place in human foodways since the Paleolithic Era as evidenced by rock art from around the world (Crittenden 259). Virgil addresses their centrality to agriculture, dedicating the entirety of Book 4 of the *Georgics* (29 BCE) to beekeeping, including the lengthy retelling of the myth of Aristaeus, the god who introduced beekeeping to humankind. A variety of other animals (honeyguides, apes, and bears) have competed with humans for the rich resource of honey. And as Hattie Ellis makes clear in the quotation above, bears' love of honey is both a biological fact and a literary trope. Bears' love of food, especially honey, is a repeated trope in children's literature. Baloo in Rudyard Kipling's *The Jungle Book* (1894) "eats only nuts and roots and honey" (19). Laura Ingalls Wilder depicts a bear stripping honey from a beehive in *Little House in the Big Woods* (1932); Pa drives it off to gather the honey himself. Other bears seeking honey in children's literature include the Berenstain Bears in the book that launched the series, *The Big Honey Hunt* (1962). Finally, some literary bears have a similar taste for sweetness, if not exactly for honey, including Lynd Ward's *The Biggest Bear* (1952), in which the bear is attracted to maple sugar, and Michael Bond's Paddington Bear, who adores marmalade sandwiches (*A Bear Called Paddington*, 1960, and sequels).

Thus, when A. A. Milne make honey Pooh's favorite foodstuff in *Winnie-the-Pooh* (1926) and *The House at Pooh Corner* (1928), he taps into a long tradition of authors who use honey as foodstuff and cultural signifier. In fact, a brief survey of the two books reveals food's pervasiveness throughout Pooh's adventures. *Winnie-the-Pooh* begins with Pooh's unsuccessful hunt for honey from the bees and continues in the next chapter with his overindulgence in honey and condensed milk at Rabbit's. Pooh later gets stuck in the honey pot in the Heffalump trap, and he eats the honey he originally intended as Eeyore's birthday present. During the flood, Pooh is trapped on a branch eating through his many pots of honey as the rain falls and the waters rise. In the "Expotition to the North Pole," the procession rests to eat their provisions. In the first chapter of *The House at Pooh Corner*, Pooh returns home at five to eleven (according to his broken clock) for a little something; in the next chapter, he and Tigger hunt throughout the morning for an appropriate breakfast for Tigger, which they finally find at Kanga's house. In successive chapters, Pooh counts his pots of honey, eats Tigger's and Roo's lunches while they are stuck up in a tree, and remembers packing "an ordinary biggish sort of basket, full of" honey for breakfast with Christopher Robin (*HPC* 84). Additionally, Christopher Robin gives Pooh a pot of honey after Pooh spends a day lost in the mist. Even when honey is not the specific object of Pooh's food focus, he still looks forward to eating with his friends. Food is the main object of social interaction the day that Pooh and Piglet visit Kanga for lunch, then Rabbit for a little something, then Christopher Robin for a Very Nearly tea, before planning to end at Owl's for a Proper Tea. These are only the major food-inspired episodes: the books are filled with frequent brief references to food in the characters' conversations and songs. Food thus plays a part in many scenes, either initiating, advancing, or resolving the action.

Milne scholars, thus, have rightly taken up the topic of food and found it a multivalent signifier. In *Recovering Arcadia*, Paula T. Connolly makes the point that food in the two books defines the comfort zone of Pooh's home: "Comfort is the central defining feature of Pooh's house, and that is shown particularly by the importance of food here. Whenever Pooh returns home, it is usually with the intention of eating, and here Pooh's clock has stopped at five minutes to eleven, making it always 'nearly time for a little smackerel of something' (*HPC* 5)" (63–64). Moreover, Connolly points to the fact that for Pooh food is not simply the satiation of hunger: "Pooh is clearly driven by his appetite.... But his concern with food is not simply greed. He associates it with social activity" (81). In "A Taste of Nostalgia: Children's Books from the Golden Age—Carroll, Grahame, and Milne," Robert Hemmings argues for food as a safe expression of children's desire: "Books from the golden age prohibit sexuality in their nostalgic construction of childhood, but desire is irrepressibly present through the attention to acts of consumption" (59). And for Pooh, appetite "is desire unbridled. Pooh's taste for honey, on the surface so quaint and adorable, persistently threatens to unsettle the harmony of Hundred Acre Wood" (74). For Connolly, food is part of the narrative architecture, essentially signifying the stability of the pastoral setting and the characters who inhabit it, while for Hemmings food functions as a mask for an imperfectly repressed desire that has the potential to destabilize Milne's *locus amoenus* (beautiful, perfect place). For this fragile nostalgia of the imaginary landscape of an idealized childhood, food is malleable: it serves as material for a productive creativity that aids in the transformation of Pooh from ostensible hero to poet, what Connolly calls Pooh's "creative thought process" (81). That the connection between food and creativity is integral to the novels' pastoral setting is reinforced by Susan Snyder's definition of pastoral, which "hold[s] up the ideal of human beings living at ease in a natural setting that benignly supplies their material and aesthetic needs" (1). In the "ease" of the Hundred Acre Wood,[1] the combined narratives of the two Pooh novels serve collectively as a *Künstlerroman*—a narrative about an artist's growth—and Pooh's development as poet is structured around three nodes: food, sociability, and poetry. Although Pooh's obsession with food, specifically honey, may look like mere greed at first glance, his consumption of—or at times even desire for—food in company is frequently linked to his practice and performance of poetry.

These three nodes bridge sociocultural and literary approaches. To understand that crossing, British social anthropologist Mary Douglas's essay, "Deciphering a Meal," offers a useful analytical frame, because she believes in treating "the meal as a poem" (70). As a structuralist, Douglas sees food as a code, and "the message it encodes will be found in the pattern of social relations being expressed.... The message [will be] about different degrees of hierarchy, inclusion and exclusion, boundaries and transactions across boundaries" (61). Unlike Claude Lévi-Strauss, whom she criticizes for looking for a "universal food meaning common to all mankind," Douglas works from the ground up, treating meals as "small scale social relations" and focusing on the particulars of a meal to "discover the social boundaries which the food meanings encode" (62). In other words, any meal in company inherently divides into small groups within which people interact as they eat; in sharing food together, they practice the underlying cultural customs that shape their interactions and allow them to eat together. Thus, the foods chosen and consumed with particular sets of manners come to represent the customs diners have in common. To demonstrate the relationship between the syntagmatic and the paradigmatic, Douglas moves to poetics: "from coding we are led to a more appropriate comparison for the interpretation of a meal, that is, versification" (70). She adopts the literary trope of metonymy to understand meals as syntagmatic events—or as she puts it, "minute" metonyms (69)—along a temporal chain, producing a larger paradigmatic frame. For *Winnie-the-Pooh* and *The House at Pooh Corner*, this fusion of the social and the literary on a small scale, as described by Douglas, helps to show the connections among the food events, the company in which they are shared, and Pooh's artistic trajectory.

For Douglas, a meal is a highly structured event, whose boundary "distinguishes order, bounds it, and separates it from disorder" (70). The one formal, large-scale meal that best demonstrates Douglas's point here is Christopher Robin's celebratory banquet for Pooh at the end of the first book; the major characters are included at the table, while Rabbit's "friends and relations" are excluded: they "spread themselves about on the grass, and waited hopefully in case anyone spoke to them, or dropped anything, or asked them the time" (WP 153). The illustration of the banquet reinforces their lack of inclusion: Ernest Shepard depicts a number of small animals scattered on the grass around and near the table, including several rabbits of varying sizes, a squirrel, a hedgehog, a few mice, and a beetle (perhaps the forerunner of Alexander Beetle in *Now We Are Six* and Small in *The House at Pooh Corner*). The separation of banquet participants from nonparticipants suggests a highly structured event where boundaries of inclusion and exclusion are formally set. The table with its place settings serves as the means by which the number of banquet guests is set—a defining function of all tables with place settings.

Milne's text gives the places the guests occupy at the table: "Christopher Robin sat at one end, and Pooh sat at the other, and between them on one side were Owl and Eeyore and Piglet, and between them on the other side were Rabbit, and Roo and Kanga" (WP 153). This organization gives primacy to Christopher Robin and Pooh, who sit at the head and foot of the table, respectively, the positions of greatest rank and power; the other animals and toys occupy the lesser positions at the sides. The table seatings thus also structure the meal. Shepard's visual depiction of the banquet follows Milne's text exactly in the placement of the characters; however, in a number of places Milne's text and Shepard's illustration elaborate on and even contradict each other in their depiction of the meal. Notably, Milne describes the origin of the table: "Christopher Robin had made a long table out of some long pieces of wood, and they all sat around it" (WP 153). Milne's phrasing suggests a play table, unevenly cobbled together by the child out of available materials. Shepard, however, shows a formal table with a tablecloth, which Milne never mentions. He also depicts the chairs: mismatched chairs for most of the animals, with Piglet on a four-legged stool topped with a pillow (in obvious deference to his size) and an infant's high chair for Roo—none of which Milne mentions. Plates and cups sit before most of them (Eeyore has no cup, but it may be hidden by his head), but the place settings lack silverware of any kind. Before beginning his speech, Christopher Robin "banged on the table with his spoon" (WP 155)—but the illustration shows no spoon in his hand, although he is standing to speak. The curious mixture of unspoken but visually depicted table refinements, contrasted with the verbally jerry-rigged table and visually slapdash collection of chairs, creates what Perry Nodelman terms "the third story, the one told by the words and pictures together" in which visual and verbal texts may each "conflict with and even undermine" the information provided by the other (295).

One potential meta implication of the elaborations and contradictions between Milne's verbal and Shepard's visual texts is that the episode represents the play of an imaginative child: Christopher Robin is sophisticated enough to replicate the structure of meals in his pretending but is fuzzy on details. The characters are described as having eaten, rather than actually portrayed as consuming: Christopher Robin begins his speech "[w]hen they had all eaten nearly enough" (WP 155). The illustration shows the possibilities the boy can imagine: a fancy table rather than planks, cups and plates but no silverware—or food. Ernest Shepard illustrates the banquet after everyone has finished eating. There is no longer food on table or the plates, the plates and glasses are in some disarray, and the celebratory speeches are being given. As Robert Hemmings says about the scene, "It is as if food is not the point of the party" (75). Instead, the event focuses on the verbal interactions among the guests: Roo's greetings to each guest, Owl's verbose story to Christopher Robin, Kanga's advice on manners to Roo (who drinks milk, the only food actually mentioned). The banquet is capped by speeches: Christopher Robin's introduction, Eeyore's mistaken acceptance speech, the presentation of the gift of recognition to Pooh.

The three nodes that structure the two books—food, sociability, creativity—are present in this scene. Hemmings is right that the scene does not focus on food per se, but the power of the banquet setting gives the scene meaning: Christopher Robin draws on the ancient tradition of feasting and speeches to celebrate Pooh as hero. The scene is as much about what comes out of the mouth (dialogue, conversation, speeches) as what goes in (food). Pooh's mixed role as both hero and bard confuses him: he does not know how to be both the celebrant and the celebrator. He composes a poem before the banquet, the "Anxious Pooh Poem," which articulates his deep desire that his heroism be recognized—as well as his fear that it will be overlooked. His fear is nearly realized when Eeyore hijacks the banquet speech, but Christopher Robin sets the record straight by bestowing his gift of appreciation for Pooh. The gift saves Pooh's modesty: he does not need to recite a poem at the public banquet that celebrates his own achievement, allowing him to keep the roles of hero and poet separate. This scene foreshadows Pooh's epic poem at the climax of *The House at Pooh Corner*, when Pooh as bard can celebrate Piglet as hero with no muddling of the two roles.

In contrast to the single formal banquet scene, the books are full of more casual teas, snacks, and other incidental opportunities to eat "a little something," from the first chapter onwards. Although Pooh never gets the opportunity to consume the honey he tries to collect from the bee tree in the first chapter, his desire to eat it drives him throughout the story—and inspires the three songs he composes in the course of his struggles. In his initial attempt to climb the tree, he sings about how bears like honey, celebrating his favorite food. As he tires in his venture, he switches to a "complaining song" in which he wishes that bee nests were at the bottoms of trees for bears' convenience in harvesting honey.[2] He composes the third, a faintly Wordsworthian verse, as he dangles from the balloon, pretending to be a cloud:

> How sweet to be a Cloud
>   Floating in the Blue!
> Every little cloud
> *Always* sings aloud.

> "How sweet to be a Cloud
>   Floating in the Blue!"
> It makes him very proud
> To be a little cloud. (WP 17)

Pooh sings this song for Christopher Robin, the friend whom he has recruited to help him in his endeavor, and for the bees, who are intended to be his primary audience. As poetry, this song is the most complex and successful of the three songs, but the bees are neither impressed by the verse nor friendly to Pooh's aims, and he gets stung. The bees lack the named subjectivity of the other animals in the forest and provide no sociable connection with him; the only slight personification of them suggests just the opposite relationship, in fact, when they are described as "suspicious" (*WP* 15–17). The bees have good reason to suspect Pooh because he is in fact intending to steal their honey, which he regards proprietarily as his own ("the only reason for making honey is so *I* can eat it" (*WP* 6)), and he overtly intends to "deceive" them in order to obtain it (*WP* 13, 16). Such deception violates the social contract: no honey for Pooh in this chapter. Despite Pooh not achieving his desire in this opening chapter, Milne nonetheless establishes it as one of the bear's prime motivators. That desire spurs Pooh to action, to poetry, and ultimately to working with a friend instead of acting in isolation. Additionally, it promotes social connection when he seeks aid from Christopher Robin. Food, sociability, and poetry function as narrative architecture: Milne reworks them again and again throughout Pooh's adventures over the course of the two books. In subsequent scenes, Milne deploys these elements to more fully involve the Hundred Acre Wood and its denizens.

While Pooh gets no honey in the first chapter of *Winnie-the-Pooh*, he famously overindulges in the next chapter—probably the most famous of food events in the two novels—when he visits Rabbit and gets stuck after eating too much. This chapter offers a more complex rendering of the food, sociability, and creativity paradigm. Notably, Pooh's social call occurs late in the morning, after Pooh has composed "a hum": he is poetically inspired while doing his "Stoutness Exercises" and after breakfast he "learn[s] it off by heart" before he goes for a walk to practice it (*WP* 22). Composition and poetry are here inspired when he is hungry and practiced once he has eaten. Once Pooh has finished his new hum, he performs it while walking, but he finds a solitary performance unsatisfactory once he sees Rabbit's home: "Rabbit means Company . . . and Company means Food and Listening-to-Me-Humming and such like" (*WP* 24). Here, when Pooh connects audience, performance, and a meal, he explicitly links the metonymic triad of creativity, sociability, and food.

Rabbit hospitably offers "a mouthful of something" and gets "out the plates and mugs" once Pooh has come into his home, and Pooh is glad to accept, particularly because he "always liked a little something at eleven o'clock in the morning" (*WP* 26). The two friends here share a traditional British refreshment of "elevenses," a late morning light refreshment that first became common in the late eighteenth century and remains popular today (Davidson 272). Although the timing and foods consumed are variable, elevenses is encoded as part of the "ordered pattern" of British "food of the day" (Douglas 62). In this syntagmatic chain, Pooh behaves in a civilized manner, attracted to the convention of a second breakfast. Although Pooh's search to satiate his hunger may look opportunistic and improvised, Pooh's desire is actually structured and predictable. Moreover, Rabbit reenacts a conventionally structured tea (the meal, rather than the drink) when he offers tea, bread, and a sweet (honey or condensed milk). Conversely, while Pooh would like to eat everything on offer (and more), he attempts to demonstrate polite restraint by choosing both sweets but refusing the bread. However, in so doing Pooh upends convention (bread + one sweet), and as a result the socially coded moment of elevenses breaks down. Thus the syntagmatic food chain of the novel gets stuck as Pooh gets stuck in Rabbit's hole because he has eaten too much sweet; this physically manifested moral comeuppance for breaking the meal code also functions as a lynchpin for the plot, and it thus reveals the larger social structure (food, creativity, sociability) of the narrative at work.[3]

Pooh initially visited Rabbit for an audience for his new "hum" as much as for a snack. Once Pooh gets stuck in Rabbit's doorway, he shows no desire to "hum," however: physical discomfort seems to derail his creativity. Nor is food allowed: Christopher Robin permits no meals "because of getting thin quicker" (*WP* 30), but Rabbit promises that they will read to him instead. Pooh sees the nourishment of social connection and the art of reading as almost a substitute for food, requesting a "sustaining Book, such as would help and comfort a Wedged Bear in Great Tightness" (*WP* 30). Here all three nodes seem to condense into a single act: Pooh's friend Christopher Robin spends time with the bear as a sociable act, reading books as a replacement for the forbidden food. Shepard further plays with the story-as-food idea in his illustration as well, portraying Christopher Robin sitting in front of Pooh reading from an alphabet book opened to the letter J, which is followed by "Jam" underneath it.[4] If Pooh can't eat the sweet, he can at least listen to his friend read about the nursery favorite; if he is not inspired to perform, he can at least listen to a friend read another's "sustaining" words. Although Pooh's visit does not end as planned, nonetheless food, creativity, and sociability still structure the scene even after Pooh's appetite "unsettle[s] the harmony" (Hemmings 74) of Rabbit's den.

Milne's paradigmatic triad functions as well in his second Pooh book, *The House at Pooh Corner*, as it does in the first. In chapter 2, "In Which Tigger Comes to the Forest and Has Breakfast," Milne uses Tigger and the search for his meal to reintroduce the full cast of characters and the landscape of The Hundred Acre Wood. Neither Pooh nor Tigger himself knows who or what Tigger is; in this chapter, which is blatantly concerned with the question of identity, the two animals base their attempt to define Tigger on discovering the food he wants to consume: they thus pursue a series of breakfasts at the homes of various other denizens of the Hundred Acre Wood. Tigger initially offers an unsubstantiated assertion that Tiggers like everything. This has two implications: the overt suggestion that Tiggers are omnivorous gourmands with a broad palate and that Tigger is incapable of making any distinction between his species and himself as an individual member of that species. But both Pooh and Tigger find that Tigger is a far more finicky eater than he initially presented himself to be. Throughout the morning Tigger and Pooh work practically and experientially to discover what Tigger does like and will eat for breakfast.

After Tigger finds unacceptable Pooh's honey, Piglet's "haycorns," and Eeyore's thistles—raising the possibility that Tigger will not find something to eat in this pastoral setting—Pooh is inspired to compose a poem as they walk on to Kanga's:

> What shall we do about poor little Tigger?
> If he never eats nothing he'll never get bigger.
> He doesn't like honey and haycorns and thistles
> Because of the taste and because of the bristles.
> And all the good things which an animal likes
> Have the wrong sort of swallow or too many spikes. (32)

The poem efficiently encapsulates the reason for the search and its relevant concerns, worrying whether Tigger can find a food—like "all the good things which an animal likes"—that would allow him to stay and integrate into the Hundred Acre Wood and become a character for whom the pastoral setting provides. Only after rejecting the other foods in Kanga's cupboard does Tigger discover what he really likes (and immediately attributes this liking to all Tiggers): the one thing that nobody else wants, especially Roo—that is,

Roo's medicine, Extract of Malt. Pooh's poem functions structurally in the chapter to link food, character, and the social landscape, articulating the problem of belonging and pointing to the nature of the solution, realized in Kanga's discovery that he likes extract of malt.

The breakfasts—or each attempted breakfast—are small, structured meal events, or, per Mary Douglas, "minute metonym[s]" (69). As the other characters are in some way identified with a particular food, so eventually is Tigger, thus alleviating Pooh's confusion that he so evidently feels over what Tigger is at the beginning of the chapter. In essence, the chapter progresses through a set of recursive breakfasts, where at each a different food (honey, haycorns, thistles, extract of malt) organizes both the search for Tigger's identity and his introduction to the other characters around the Wood. These breakfasts are links in a syntagmatic chain, leading to a paradigmatic whole. As Tigger discovers his food identity, so are the other characters' food identities rehearsed and clarified (Pooh = honey, Piglet = haycorns, Eeyore = thistles). Milne ends the chapter reinforcing the link between food and an individual character's subjectivity as a dominant organizational trope of the novels. Like the other characters, Tigger is the food he eats. This chapter is an intense condensation of what Milne does again and again in the two books. Tigger and Pooh's search for food becomes a search for identity. That search reinforces the metonymic power of food across the Hundred Acre Wood, and it serves not only to introduce Tigger to the denizens of the woods but also to integrate him into their social milieu.

In the last several scenes of the books, the same metonymic structure motivates Pooh's actions. Just as his desire for food and company prompted Pooh to visit Rabbit, in chapter 8, "In Which Piglet Does a Very Grand Thing," Pooh sets off with Piglet with the same aim in mind: "'Let's go and see *everybody*,' said Pooh. 'Because when you've been walking in the wind for miles, and you suddenly go into somebody's house, and he says, "Hallo, Pooh, you're just in time for a little smackerel of something," and you are, then it's what I call a Friendly Day'" (*HPC* 129). Visiting means hospitality, a term that has equated companionship and sharing a small meal across cultures for millennia. Pooh and Piglet's social round encompasses all the characters that live in the Hundred Acre Wood and meals with several of them: they have lunch with Kanga and Roo, stop by Rabbit's place, then have a "Very Nearly tea, which is one you forget about afterwards" with Christopher Robin before "hurry[ing] on to Pooh Corner, so as to see Eeyore before it was too late to have a Proper Tea with Owl" (*HPC* 131). Rather than the formal banquet at the end of *Winnie-the-Pooh* to gather all the characters and celebrate Pooh's heroism, it is Pooh's desire for "a little something" that produces a grand perambulation—a set of small visits—around the forest, a buildup which ends with the disaster of Owl's tree, about which Pooh composes a lengthy epic poem on Piglet's heroism in saving Pooh and Owl. Pooh later recites the poem first privately to Piglet and then publicly to everyone while they all work together to recover Owl's possessions from his downed home. The novel culminates with acts of food, sociability, and poetry.

The Hundred Acre Wood is fertile ground for Pooh's poetry. Between the daily social rounds and the adventures[5]—all shaped by a little desire for "something"—Pooh has experiences that inspire him to compose many poems and many types of poetry (sound poetry, Romantic lyrics, occasional poems, heroic verse). The pastoral setting provides Pooh an experimental and experiential workshop for his art. Moreover, if there is a developmental arc to the poetry, it culminates with the heroic seven-verse epic about Piglet. Throughout the books, Pooh has had dual identities as hero and poet. Christopher Robin sees Pooh as hero for saving Piglet from the flood (WP 149, 155), and Pooh wants to be a hero. He struggles, however, to produce heroic verse about himself because, as the questions embedded in "Anxious Pooh Poem" at the end of *Winnie-the Pooh* make clear, Pooh has doubts about himself as hero. But at the end of *The House at Pooh Corner*, Pooh settles easily into his vocation as poet. Throughout the books, Piglet has also wanted to be a hero, envying Pooh on multiple occasions. Pooh is aware of Piglet's desire, and in the midst of the disaster of Owl's toppled tree Pooh puts his role as hero figure aside to spur Piglet to action by offering to compose a poem about Piglet's heroic acts. After Piglet has rescued Owl and Pooh, the poem comes easily to Pooh, and it unequivocally celebrates Piglet as hero. While throughout the books the audiences for Pooh's poems have been at best quite small, here, once he has read the poem privately for Piglet, he repeats it publicly for everyone in the Hundred Acre Wood: an epic performance. Within the social milieu of the books, Pooh has come into his role as poet, and the *Künstlerroman* arc finishes.

Milne creates a precarious balance of the epic and the pastoral here at the conclusion of his stories, two genres that have traditionally been defined as opposites: the epic with action, the pastoral with restfulness and peace. The world of the Pooh novels fits Susan Snyder's definition of pastoral because it "benignly" supplies the characters' "material and aesthetic needs" (1). Paula Connolly agrees and notably connects the pastoral with the supply of food in the Hundred Acre Wood: "Pooh's supply of honey seems endless, and he never has to go to work to get it. Indeed, there is no sense that these characters must ever struggle or even work for food or survival. Their needs are met, food is plentiful, life not hard.... It is leisure that reigns supreme in the forest" (102). Such pastoral leisure enables generosity: none of characters need to compete for resources in the gentle landscape. The penultimate episode of *The House at Pooh Corner* particularly demonstrates this point as well as Connolly's insight into the overarching ethos of the Hundred Acre Wood as offering "ready help and generosity . . . this is a world in which caring is the ultimate value" (108). Pooh's sacrifice of his role as hero to Piglet is unselfish and in turn inspires Piglet's own generosity in giving his house to Owl after the storm has destroyed Owl's original home—an offer which also allows Eeyore to save face. The characters can give ungrudgingly perhaps because they lack the adult world's ambition, which is unneeded in this protected space. Pooh especially exhibits the pastoral trait of *otium*, "the contented acceptance of what one is given that precludes restless striving" (Snyder 4). Steven Marx views the pastoral as particularly child focused because the pastoral excludes adulthood with its worldly concerns for "procreation, custodianship, ambition, wealth and power" (9). Marx elaborates on his view of the pastoral as essentially about youth when he notes that the "pastoral of youth represents the shepherd as *puer eternus*—the eternal boy" who is endowed "with special artistic and spiritual gifts" (11)—a phrase that irresistibly calls Peter Pan to mind but that also suggests the issues with which Milne wrestles in the final chapter of *The House at Pooh Corner*. Milne ends the book by presenting Christopher Robin and Pooh as eternal children in the final line of the book: "in that enchanted place on the top of the Forest, a little boy and his Bear will always be playing" (*HPC* 180). The romanticized eternal youth that Milne invokes here, which Christopher Robin celebrates as "doing Nothing" (178), perfectly fit Marx's discussion of the presexual pastoral of childhood: it draws on the Renaissance "ideal of the life of pleasure . . . [which] represented an alternative to the life of action.... [T]he life of pleasure was often symbolized in images of youthful frolics in fields and groves" (11–12), just as Christopher Robin, Pooh, and their friends play throughout the two Pooh books.

Despite its apparent separateness from the life of action, into which Christopher Robin is being drawn, willy-nilly, at the end of the books, food serves as a bridge between the real world and Milne's pastoral world of pleasure. As Hattie Ellis suggests in the epigraph to this chapter, for both real and literary bears and their love of honey, food connects the literary and the real: it organizes and carries signifying meaning in both. One of the tropes of the pastoral is that despite its timeless setting, heroes who visit it for rest eventually must leave for the epic world where events can go tragically wrong. Despite the carnage of World War I, less than a decade afterward Milne brilliantly creates a twentieth-century pastoral (a genre that had basically died two centuries earlier) by drawing on the genre's conventional association with youth. He gives his narrative focus, plot, and purpose in how he connects so many of the characters' adventures there with food, which sustains and provides physical and emotional pleasures. In Milne's pastoral, food is extraordinarily powerful in the way that desire for it pushes Pooh to act, to leave home, and to find company with whom he can share the pleasures of the table. Chief among those gratifications is another pleasure of the mouth, the enjoyment of language through conversation and poetry. In braiding the three elements together (food, companionship, poetry) throughout the novels, Milne highlights how each nourishes the others—and by extension, his characters who indulge in them as well.

Chapter 5

FOOD OF THE WOODS AND PLAINS

Two Visions of Food, Culture, Land, and History in Laura Ingalls Wilder's Little House Books and Louise Erdrich's Birchbark Series

> This is the anti–*Little House on the Prairie*! Of course, *Little House on the Prairie* is foundational literature. Everyone refers to it. But the series has an appalling view of how the American settlers went into an empty world: There was no one there, so Pa set out his claim. The Indians are always slinking off and Ma's holding her nose. But I do love the parts about making sausage. (161)
>
> —LOUISE ERDRICH, IN AN INTERVIEW WITH LISA HALLIDAY (2010)

In this interview, Louise Erdrich acknowledges Laura Ingalls Wilder's Little House books as cultural touchstones in contemporary American culture. Wilder's series of novels gives a fictionalized version of her childhood growing up on the edge of the American frontier as it expanded westward, from her birth in Wisconsin, through her childhood in Kansas and Minnesota, to her adolescence in eastern South Dakota. From *Little House in the Big Woods*, the first novel in the series, through the following seven novels published in her lifetime, food plays a central role in the stories—because, of course, it was a central preoccupation of all the pioneers, who had to be largely self-sufficient in hunting, gathering, and raising their own meat and crops. The sausages that loom so large in Erdrich's memory of the series suggest how memorable readers find the food that dominates the books. It is no wonder, then, that in 1979 Barbara Walker produced *The Little House Cookbook: Frontier Food from Laura Ingalls Wilder's Classic Stories*, capitalizing on young (and older) readers' nostalgic interest in the foodways of the pioneer past.

In a previously published essay, "Utilizing Food Studies with Children's Literature and Its Scholarship: Laura Ingalls Wilder's Little House Books as Case Study," we have noted that Wilder portrays the foodways of her youth with a particular ideological slant in mind: she understood her life story as representing a fundamental American experience. In describing the genesis of her stories, she said, "I realized that I had seen and lived it all—all the successive phases of the frontier, first the frontiersman, then the pioneer, then the farmers and the towns. Then I understood that in my own life I represented a whole period of American history" (Spaeth 23). The framing of Wilder's comment here suggests she did not recognize the cultural erasure that her family's ventures were based on: the Ingalls family's homesteading depended on the American government's removal of the people that occupied the land before them.[1] Louise Erdrich calls Wilder to account for such views in the above quotation—she finds them "appalling" even while admitting that the novels are also appealing, particularly in their vivid portrayal of family life and daily activities of the past. Erdrich notes that her own Birchbark series of novels, based loosely on the trajectory of her family's forced removal from their ancestral lands a few decades before the Ingalls family homesteaded on the Great Plains, was intended to show the other side of the cultural equation of pioneering: the people whose lives and lands were forcibly subtracted by the addition of European settlers from the east. She writes,

> I thought I would write about the other side, the people who were in that "empty" space, the people who were forced ahead of the settlers and what happened to them. The path taken by these people in the Birchbark books roughly mirrors the path the Ojibwe side of my family took crossing from Madeline Island, over what is now Minnesota, up to Lake of the Woods and over to the Turtle Mountains. (Halliday 161)

Taken together, the Little House books and the Birchbark series present complementary journey narratives of expansion and displacement: the creation, loss/movement, and recreation of home(s). To portray these opposing journeys of settlement and displacement, Wilder and Erdrich detail them through the extensive use of pioneer and Ojibwe food and foodways.

In both Wilder's Little House series and Erdrich's Birchbark series, three interrelated patterns shape the function and signification of food's structuring power.[2] First, both series depict food in ways that reflect the material lives of two competing cultures inhabiting nineteenth-century midwestern North America; the authors' preoccupations with food likewise show their sense that the recovery of historical foodways is important for their modern audience. Second, both sets of books depict how the daily process of gathering raw food from the land, preparing it, and eating it serves as a central structuring activity through which families enact traditions that manifest their cultural values. Third, the types and preparations of food reveal the distinct contemporary cultural values of both authors, as is common in historical fiction. Frederick Jackson Turner's theories of westward expansion underpin Wilder's interpretation of her childhood experiences on the frontier, with all the entitlement to supposedly "empty" lands that such land grabs were based on. Erdrich is much influenced by (and is herself a member of) the writers of the Native American Renaissance "whose mission is to rediscover their historical roots and cultural heritage . . . [and] inscribe their history, particularly the period of encroachment and colonization by whites, from a Native American perspective"; they also seek to "[represent] their history and culture both to their own descendants and to non-Native Americans" (Chang 133–34). Erdrich thus self-consciously illustrates through the family saga of her series the dignity and cultural richness of some of the peoples the Ingalls family displaced—a culture deeply rooted in a circuit of places that structure their lives seasonally. Portraying these families through the years over a series of books and changing geographical settings allows both Wilder and Erdrich to show the impacts of time and place on both sets of foodways and thus on the families too. As the Ingalls family moves west, they adapt the land to their needs, doing their best to master nature and impose Western agricultural practices. The family of the Birchbark series, on the other hand, adapts to the land itself, literally changing what they eat based on what is regionally available as they are forced to move from their ancestral lands on an island in Lake Superior westward to the plains, shifting from a largely vegetarian diet supplemented by game to a fundamentally meat-based diet with occasional vegetables. The foods that structure Wilder's series remain pervasive as the series progresses, thus demonstrating the mastery of the plains by traditional American foodways, whereas the foods that initially structure Erdrich's series diminish in later books of the series, reflecting the impact of displacement from their traditional home and the physical and cultural threats the Ojibwe faced from Euro American western expansion.[3]

Food dominates both the Little House and the Birchbark series to such a large degree in part because both families spend so much of their time involved in activities necessary to its production, preservation, and consumption. Both families live in geographical localities at a time that demand they be largely self-sufficient: if they do not produce enough food through the seasons, they will go hungry—perhaps even starve. Thus, to understand food in both sets of books, it is necessary to understand the full complex of behaviors to which both families dedicate a huge amount of time, as well as understand how geography and culture shape the range of foods available to them. For both series, it is not enough only to follow Brillat-Savarin's famous axiom from his 1825 *The Physiology of Taste*, "Dis moi ce que tu manges, je te dirai qui tu es" (Tell me what you eat, and I'll tell you who you are) (13): that is, to truly understand a culture it is not enough simply to explore how its people prepare and consume food. Rather, it is equally important to explore how they produce their food, because, as Wendell Berry puts it, "eating [is] an agricultural act" (227)—or a hunting and gathering act, when cultural mores depend on those methods of production.[4]

* * *

In Wilder's books, the family derives their foods from a variety of practices, from hunting and gathering to the agricultural production of grain, vegetables, poultry, and meat. Notably, though, hunting as a food source occurs only when the family is living in relatively unsettled land. As the lands the family lives on transition to more densely settled territory, the game Pa hunts declines and the protein in the family diet comes from either preserved meat or husbanded stock—poultry, cattle, and pigs. The available game in Wisconsin, Kansas, and the family's initial settlement in the Dakotas is often rich in variety: primarily deer and bear in Wisconsin, usually prairie chicken and rabbit in Kansas (although Pa mentions antelope, squirrels, birds, and fish, and provides turkeys and ducks near Thanksgiving), and geese and ducks in Dakota when they first arrive in *By the Shores of Silver Lake*. But as the supply of game runs out, Pa's wanderlust always kicks in: his dislike of the more populated woods is cited as a reason to move to Kansas (*LHP* 2), and he mourns the disappearance of the wild geese in Dakota (*BSSL* 245). Laura understands how settlement impacts their diet in *Little Town on the Prairie*: "This was settled country now, hardly any game was left, and they must buy meat or raise it" (29). Even when fresh game is readily available in Kansas, the family has a taste for domesticated meats: Pa asks for a cut of beef when the cowboys bring the cattle through their land (*LHP* 164), and Ma misses salt pork and asks Pa to get some when he takes a trip to Independence for supplies: "A little salt pork would taste good after all this wild game" (*LHP* 206). As the claim in South Dakota develops into a farm, as chronicled in *Little Town on the Prairie* and *These Happy Golden Years*, a major improvement is the presence of chickens for eggs and meat, and the raising of cattle for milk.

Gathering occurs only rarely and for very specific foods: honey, nuts, berries, and maple sugar. (Pa's harvest of naturally growing prairie grass as hay for his stock might also count as gathering, although it is fodder for their animals, not a direct food source for people.) Its sparse place as a means of food sourcing for the Ingalls family comes partly from the decreasing availability of wild foods (paralleling the gradual decline in Pa's hunting). Moreover, by the nineteenth century, gathering played only a small part in European-derived foodways in America. Pa finds a honey tree, scares off a bear that is eating the honey, and gathers it all himself, but this is only a one-time, serendipitous event in the Big Woods of Wisconsin (*LHBW* 194–98). Laura and Mary help their mother to gather walnuts, hickory nuts, and hazelnuts in the fall in Wisconsin (*LHBW* 215–16), but such gathering is left behind when the family moves to the treeless plains. Although the mention of a dried berry pie in Wisconsin suggests that the family engages in berrying there (*LHBW* 226), the only portrayal of such gathering occurs in Kansas, when the family finds blackberries in the creek bottom. Laura helps Ma gather them (eating many of them), but they dry pails full of berries each day, which then get stewed in the winter (*LHP* 182–83; 252). The other important gathered food is a community event: the annual Wisconsin harvest of maple sap, which is processed into maple syrup and maple sugar. We will address this event in greater detail below, in comparison with Ojibwe maple sugaring practices.

In *An Edible History of Humanity*, Tom Standage notes the telos of human societies inexorably becoming agricultural while marginalizing the hunter-gatherer, but the transformation was slow, and the two forms remained—and remain—entangled (22). In the section entitled "Food and Social Structure," Standage makes claims for how food fundamentally organizes both agricultural and hunter/gatherer societies: that is, foods manifest cultural traditions which quite literally structure family behavior and work (food production, preparation, and consumption). As "ancient egalitarians," "hunter-gatherers may only have to spend two days a week foraging for things to eat, but their lives were nonetheless ruled by food" (33); foraging and hunting thus necessitated a group's mobility, the absence of wealth and material accumulation, and their communal cooperation and sharing. Conversely, agricultural societies are stratified. Farmers devote significantly more time and energy to raising food than hunter-gatherer societies spend gleaning, but that division of labor produces inequality: "[Farmers'] surplus production was appropriated by a ruling elite . . . which redistributed some of it and consumed the rest. . . . With agriculture, people settle down; with intensification, they divide into rich and poor, rulers and farmers" (32). In the Little House books, the Ingalls family embody this historical telos and its entanglements. Out on the frontier, the family must utilize hunting and gathering, yet their ties to the urban east, its values and markets, have indoctrinated them to inevitably cultivate the land and colonize it through planting. Thus, although foods that are hunted and gathered play occasional roles in the family's diet—sometimes greater, sometimes less, depending on season and location—their truly structuring foods are agriculturally based: for example, grain crops (primarily wheat, but corn too), dairy from cattle, and garden produce (especially root vegetables).

Pa is determined to grow wheat everywhere he lives: the family harvests wheat in Wisconsin; plans a future wheat crop in Kansas but is forced to move before the broken sod is ready for planting the grain; plants two years' worth of wheat crops in Minnesota, both of which (along with the family's finances) are destroyed by the grasshopper plague; he finally gets wheat sown and successfully harvested in South Dakota. Pa's desire to grow wheat and his expectation that it will not only provide food for his family but also be a cash crop reflects the common attitude of farmers in the American agricultural tradition, beginning with the colonial period and following their westward expansion. In *Food in History*, Reay Tannahill notes that wheat was one of the Old World seed stocks that "British settlers introduced . . . to North America" (242). In *Why We Thrive: A History of American Farming, 1607–1972*, John T. Schlebecker observes that wheat became the focal crop because it fed the European bread-based diet: it was consumed by European-descended Americans in larger and larger quantities as that population grew (82), and, carrying on the pattern begun in colonial times, could be exported to Europe to meet demand for wheat and bread there (26–27). For Great Plains agriculture, the importation of the Turkey Red variety by Russian-German Mennonite immigrants made the expansion of wheat in the Midwest possible because it fit the climate better (Schlebecker 265; Toussaint Samat 151)— and thus also made possible the expansion of European peoples across the Great Plains. Pa's obsession with wheat, particularly in *On the Banks of Plum Creek*, where he is counting on it as a cash crop with which to improve the farm, demonstrates the centrality of wheat to European Americans' ways of thinking about food: "We can sell every grain of wheat we raise!" he exclaims exuberantly (*OBPC* 82). Wilder even identified wheat as the major theme of that novel (Miller, *BLIW* 225). In *The Legacy of Conquest: The Unbroken Past of the American West*, Patricia Nelson Limerick points out that settlers came to the west with an agricultural agenda: they "would uproot the useless native plants and replace them with valuable crops, transforming wilderness to garden" (43). "Breaking sod" to sow wheat was difficult: the family rejoices in South Dakota when Pa takes advantage of new technology and gets a plow that was especially designed to break sod:

> Pa had a new plow, a breaking plow. It was wonderful for breaking the prairie sod. It had a sharp-edged wheel, called a rolling coulter, that ran rolling and cutting through the sod ahead of the plowshare. The sharp steel plowshare followed it, slicing underneath the matted grass roots, and the moldboard lifted the long, straight-edged strip of sod and turned it upside down.... They were all so happy about that new plow.... Sam and David [the horses] ... were not being worn down, sad and gaunt by breaking sod that spring. And at supper, Pa was not too tired to joke. (*LTP* 9)

Wilder's careful description of Pa's plow reflects the improvements in plow technology in the second half of the nineteenth century, which allowed plows to move more quickly and easily through the soil, particularly in the virgin sod of the prairie (Schlebecker 102–3, 174–75).

Wheat, therefore, is a primary structuring food for the Ingalls family, particularly in its potential as a cash crop. For this reason, it serves as their connection to global food networks; although they raise wheat, they buy the flour they use on a daily basis, except during the hard winter when they grind wheat (*LW* 193) to make bread. It is also worth noting that wheat ties the Ingalls family culinarily to the deep structure of Western history and civilization. In the introductory essay to *Food: A Culinary History*, "Food Systems and Models of Civilization," Massimo Montanari makes the point that in the ancient world bread was "the symbol of civilization" (71). And although bread can be made from other grains (barley, millet, rye), over the course of Western history wheat has become the privileged, preferred, and dominant grain from which bread is made. In his discussion of the link between the two in *Near a Thousand Tables: A History of Food*, Fernández-Armesto notes, "The success of wheat ... suggests that the critical product—if there was one—was bread" (96). Throughout the Little House series bread and wheat are constants, particularly in *The Long Winter*. During the winter famine, the family grinds wheat into flour in the family coffee mill so that they can make leavened bread with Ma's sourdough starter, even though they could turn it into porridge, as Pa initially suggests when all he can purchase is grain, not flour (196). Thus, bread is the civilized food that allows the family to survive intense hunger and near starvation until the train service resumes when spring finally arrives. Wheat thus bridges the local and global, subsistence and the larger economic and symbolic functions of a particular food. Correlative to wheat, the other two food types around which the family structures their labor are dairying and gardening, both of which function locally to provide foods that they themselves consume. Because the Ingallses frequently live on the frontier, well away from towns and cities, most of their dairy products and garden produce would spoil before reaching a market; thus, these foods are part of their subsistence farming. Yet, clearly, they enjoy the variety that these foods create in their diet.

The Ingalls family makes dairy products a central part of their meals as often as possible. They own or obtain cows in Wisconsin, Kansas, Minnesota, and (eventually) South Dakota, where they settle long enough to develop a small herd of six cows and heifers, one of which Pa gives to Laura and Almanzo as a much-appreciated wedding gift (*THGY* 198, 275–76). Milking is a frequently mentioned chore; winter, when the cows go dry, means no milking, but also no milk. The girls drink fresh milk when it is available, even as near adults: Mary praises the taste of home milk over what she gets at the school for the blind (*THGY* 129). It is such a treat, and regarded so highly, that when the family acquires a cow and calf in Kansas and Laura milks it for the first time,

> Pa and Ma and Mary and Laura all agreed to give the milk to Baby Carrie. They watched her drink it. . . . Gulp by gulp, she swallowed all that good milk. Then she licked the foam from her lip with her red tongue, and laughed. . . . And everyone was happy because now there would be milk to drink, and perhaps even butter for cornbread. (*LHP* 171)

Wilder's concentration on the physical delight that the youngest member of the family experiences suggests a vicarious longing in Laura, which she sublimates in thinking of the milk they will all have, now that they once again own a cow. Home-processed dairy foods are frequently mentioned as well. Wilder describes in great detail the methods for both churning butter and making cheese in *Little House in the Big Woods*—not surprising in Wisconsin, a state that eventually becomes famous for its dairy products.[5] Yet cured cheeses fall by the wayside out on the prairie: the Ingallses frequently make simple, uncured cottage cheese to eat fresh in South Dakota (*LTP* 28, 106;

THGY 123), but Wilder makes no mention at all in her later books of the intensive cheese-making process she described at such length in Little House in the Big Woods (186–92). Butter is mentioned even more than cheese: the family eats butter on bread with many meals over the course of the series, whenever it is available. Butter sandwiches are a staple lunch Laura takes from home to school or work (OBPC 152; LTP 66; THGY 17). In all cases, the fat calories the butter provided, as well as its rich mouthfeel, would have been much prized. As with wheat, the Ingallses' focus on dairy (milk, cheese, butter) connects them to a longstanding culinary tradition in Western culture. Fernández-Armesto attributes the enduring presence of bread/wheat and dairy in Western civilization to their "magical" qualities: "Churning milk is a process of almost alchemical magic: a liquid becomes solid, white becomes gold (4). . . . Perhaps that is the key to bread's success: it is one of those 'magical' foods, in which human mastery effects an unrecognizable change on the ingredients of the recipe" (97).[6] Even in subsistence, the quotidian routines of their lives connect the Ingallses ineluctably to a Western history of food.

The final structuring foods—garden-grown vegetables—are another culinary constant in the lives of the Ingalls family, who generally put in a garden as soon as they can when they settle in a new area. Gardens are mentioned in all of the books except By the Shores of Silver Lake and are only missing there because the family has not yet bought their own claim to farm. Garden vegetables provide most of the diversity in the family's diet. Gardens are one of the earliest sites of cultivation, and as Malcolm Thick puts it in The Oxford Companion to Food, to gardening "we owe not only the bulk, but also the variety of produce that we store in our larders" (330). The vegetables that the Ingalls family grows divide into two major types: those they preserve for the winter, and those they eat fresh when the vegetables ripen—although of course there is some crossover between those categories. Garden produce stored for winter's use is mentioned early in Wilder's first novel. The list provides a good sense of the variety of vegetables the family raises each summer:

> The garden behind the little house had been growing all summer. . . . Now the potatoes and carrots, the beets and turnips and cabbages were gathered and stored in the cellar, for freezing nights had come. Onions were made into long ropes, braided together by their tops, and then were hung in the attic beside wreaths of red peppers strung on threads. The pumpkins and the squashes were piled in orange and yellow and green heaps in the attic's corners. (LHBW 12)

Most of these stored vegetables are root vegetables, and most of them recur in later gardens in other places. Potatoes are the most frequent constant, mentioned in every book; potatoes and turnips are about the only crop the family has to harvest after the grasshopper plague in Minnesota because they are root vegetables, growing below ground and thus hidden from the voracious pests (*OBPC* 277); they are also a staple during the hard winter until the supply finally gives out (*LW* 252). Of course, the family eats many of the garden vegetables fresh at harvest time: Wilder mentions stewing the pumpkins and baking Hubbard squashes in the fall in *Little House in the Big Woods* (216–18), although the family still stores the bulk of them against the winter's need. Other vegetables are more elaborately preserved: Ma makes use of all the preservation techniques available in the late nineteenth century: pickling, drying, and canning. The family eats pickled cucumbers (*LTP* 88, *THGY* 43), green tomatoes (*LTP* 138), and beets (*LTP* 229); Ma makes preserves of tomatoes, ground-cherries, and husk tomatoes (*LTP* 137–38). To save corn from the blackbirds attacking it, Ma has the girls harvest what is mature enough, then boils it, cuts the kernels from the cob, and dries them, so that they can be stewed the next winter (*LTP* 102–4); dried corn was also the foundation for hulled corn (or hominy) (*LHBW* 218–21). Dried beans—boiled, baked, or made into soup—also form a major part of the winter diet in Wisconsin and South Dakota (*LHBW* 62, 226; *LW* 40, 44, 126, 129; *LTP* 227; *THGY* 43); baked beans in particular form part of celebration dinners such as Christmas and Thanksgiving. Not all garden vegetables are hoarded against the winter: the Ingalls family members enjoy eating them fresh when ripe, too. Corn is roasted on the cob (*LTP* 88); carrots thinned from the garden are boiled (*LTP* 106); tomatoes are served sliced with cream and sugar (*LTP* 88). Other vegetables are grown that can only be eaten fresh: lettuce and radishes (*LTP* 15, *THGY* 123). The Ingalls family's gardens are small, intensive places of food production, "weeded, dug, hoed, and harvested by hand" (Davidson 331) that add vibrancy, savor and plenty to their lives. Canning, drying, and pickling preserve that vibrancy, savor, and plenty through the entire year. Flandrin and Montanari speak of "the routines of daily life" where "even the most insignificant events have a necessary place and a precise significance" (2). The wheat and corn the Ingalls raise may place them within larger economic and historical contexts, yet the labor, craft and know-how the family exercise to feed themselves day in and day out—as well as throughout the year—are not "insignificant" at all.

* * *

Wilder is most frequently critiqued for overt racism in *Little House on the Prairie*, particularly remarks made about Indians by Ma and their neighbor Mrs. Scott, although the entire series rests on the mostly unquestioned removal of Native peoples from the lands that the Ingalls family moves to settle in. A particularly egregious example lies in the opening paragraph of that novel: "In the West the land was level, and there were no trees. The grass grew thick and high. There the wild animals wandered and fed as though they were in a pasture that stretched much farther than a man could see, and there were no settlers. Only Indians lived there" (*LHP* 2). As Caroline Fraser notes, the penultimate line of the first edition originally said that "no people" lived there, "only Indians." Once a reader complained to Wilder's publisher, her editor Ursula Nordstrom suggested changing the end of the sentence to "no settlers" for the 1953 edition. Wilder agreed to the change, apparently disturbed at the implication of her original text: "It was a stupid blunder of mine. Of course Indians are people and I did not mean to imply they were not" (Fraser 476–77). The revised version has appeared in all subsequent editions. But the "only" still marginalizes the importance of the original inhabitants of the Great Plains, and the series as a whole nonetheless retains the underlying structure of granting subjectivity to the European settlers but not to the indigenous population. In the *Paris Review* interview cited as this chapter's epigraph, Louise Erdrich comments on this issue specifically, stating that she finds "appalling" Laura Ingalls Wilder's racism, which dehumanizes Native populations by disappearing them, effectively allowing her to portray the plains as essentially unoccupied and thus free to be settled, as in that opening paragraph to *Little House on the Prairie*. Yet, despite her antipathy, Erdrich likes Wilder's details about "making sausages" (161), and in another interview, with *Teachingbooks*, she returns to her admiration of Wilder's sausages and her specificity: "When I began *The Birchbark House*, I wanted to have this level of detail, too" ("Louise Erdrich"). This section of the essay will explore the dynamic tension between ideological critique and aesthetic admiration voiced by Erdrich, a tension that gave rise to the Birchbark series and helps explains Erdrich's narrative choices, particularly in her use of Ojibwe food and foodways. To more precisely shape this analysis, we will follow Michelle Pagni Stewart's work on the Birchbark series. In her article "'Counting Coup' on Children's Literature about American Indians: Louise Erdrich's Historical Fiction," Stewart initially lays out some of the intertextual ties between Erdrich and Wilder (female protagonists, resistance to gender roles, details of daily life, loving family, hard times), and then she takes up Catherine Rainwater's use of the concept of "counting coup" from her book *Dreams of Fiery Stars: The Transformation of Native American Fiction* to apply it to the Birchbark series. Stewart defines "Counting coup" as a means by which a warrior earned "honor for his bravery and cunning"—not by killing, but simply by finding a way to touch the enemy or appropriate his possessions (216). She cites Rainwater's argument "that contemporary American Indian fiction 'counts coup' upon other postmodern texts by 'not only appropriating the semiotic "property" of the Other, but also reinventing it by making it serve "Indian" ends within the mainstream culture' (34)" (216). Stewart then applies Rainwater's concept of literarily "counting coup" to Louise Erdrich's Birchbark series, arguing that Erdrich is "counting coup" in this way specifically on Laura Ingalls Wilder's Little House books, constructing her own series so that "instead of simply reworking or countering the original texts, [she is] in fact triumphing over negative images and mindsets while celebrating more culturally sensitive depictions" (216). We would argue that Stewart's model of interpreting Erdrich's "counting coup" explains how Erdrich depicts specific foods and foodways that overlap the two series: maple sugaring, berrying, gardening, and hunting.

Maple sugaring is a spring process. Indeed, all the foods that structure this Ojibwe family's daily routines are seasonally based, following the natural cycles of the environment in which they live. The sugaring season begins in late winter and continues through March, April, and May. Whole families moved from their winter quarters to camps near sugar maple stands for four to six weeks of labor-intensive work (Berzok 87). Like Wilder, Erdrich deliberately demonstrates in detail for modern readers the old, now almost lost, ways of making food. In showing the seasonal migrations of the family, based on the foods they harvest, Erdrich "counts coup" on one of the most problematically and overtly racist moments in Wilder's novels, in *Little House on the Prairie* when Mrs. Scott claims that the Indians would "never do anything with this country themselves. All they do is roam around over it like wild animals. Treaties or no treaties, the land belongs to folks that'll farm it. That's only common sense and justice" (211). Mrs. Scott clearly privileges an agricultural vision of the land, which blinds her to the work and organization inherent in gathering and hunting societies. Erdrich demonstrates that the Ojibwe are not aimlessly "roaming"; they move to the suitable place where they engage productively with the land at the proper season, in this case, gathering and processing its bounty in collecting the maple sap from a particular stand of trees and boiling it down into syrup and sugar. Erdrich provides detailed portrayals of the procedure in three of the novels (*The*

Birchbark House, *The Porcupine Year*, and *Chickadee*), from tapping the trees to collecting the sap, boiling it down into syrup and sugar, and then packing it into birch bark cones. To combat the common prejudice that gathering takes little work as a strategy for food production, Erdrich makes clear that the process involves a considerable amount of difficult labor and skill: the many trips hauling sap from the trees, the length of time that boiling it takes, the difficulty of stirring the syrup so constantly over the fire for all that time so that it will crystalize (*BH* 197–99; *PY* 168; *C* 22–24, 35–36).

The maple sugar harvest is so deeply ingrained within Ojibwe culture, such a centrally structuring cultural event, that it is the basis of a major origin myth of the tribal nation. In "Killing the Weendigo with Maple Syrup: Anishinaabe Pedagogy and Post-Secondary Research," Lana Ray and Paul Nicolas Cormier use Michael J. Capudo and Joseph Bruchac's retelling of the myth of maple sugaring[7] to speak to the reasons the Ojibwe have to work so hard to gather and process maple sugar. In the story, the trickster god, Nanaboozhoo, realizes that the Ojibwe are benefiting from the syrup too easily, literally just "letting the syrup drip into their mouths" (165). To motivate the Ojibwe to leave this idyllic, passive existence, Nanaboozhoo dilutes the sap, necessitating that the Ojibwe collect buckets full of sap and boil them down to make syrup. In other words, the creation myth requires that the Ojibwe work and "must engage with the sap in order to reap its benefits" (Ray and Cormier 165). Although Erdrich does not reference this myth directly in her novels, she too emphasizes the details and difficulty of the work, and she demonstrates the link between that work and the comfort and joy the characters take throughout the year in the sugar they make (*BH* 24, 45–46; *GS* 18, 51). In the portrayals of sugaring and the consistent presence of maple sugar throughout the series, Erdrich demonstrates the structural power that maple sugar has in the family's life. Even in *Makoons*, when they have moved west onto the plains and out of the range of the sugar maples, the memory of the sugar and the seasonal labor that produced it remains a touchstone for the family, linking them to their past and their lost home (76–77).

In contrast, Wilder presents sugaring only once, in *Little House in the Big Woods*. That scene is lengthy and detailed, functioning to exemplify the skills required to make maple syrup as well as the communal celebration of dancing and feasting that commemorates the seasonal activity, but once the Ingallses move from Wisconsin in the subsequent books, out onto the Great Plains, maple syrup is no longer part of their food repertoire (as wheat flour and bread are), no longer a centerpiece to the family foodways. Thus, here is another way that Erdrich is counting coup, demonstrating not only the hard work that maple sugaring requires but its central importance to the family, shaping their thinking and behavior *over time*.

The way that Erdrich's descriptions of manufacturing the syrup parallel Wilder's suggests that she is counting coup in another way as well: the process that the extended Ingalls family uses to make its maple syrup is in fact derived from Native foodways, although Wilder seems either unaware of that or simply does not care about the custom's origin. In the classic text, *The Maple Sugar Book*, Scott and Helen Nearing make a lengthy and well-substantiated case, through Anglo and French testimonials of the colonial period, that maple sugar was a New World food deeply embedded in the cultures of northern tribal nations. Europeans learned of it from Native peoples and adapted the processes of harvest and cooking to make it for themselves (22–39). The French priest who visits Omakayas's family to watch them make the syrup in *Chickadee* illustrates the cultural dispersal of the technique (36–37). While maple sugar overlaps both the Ojibwe and Euro American foodways, in making it a centerpiece of food culture within the Birchbark novels, set well before Wilder's Little House books, Erdrich strategically claims it as an inherently Native food, a historical component of Native identity that long predates its colonization by the European American settlers who displaced them.

Just as sugaring requires the spring move to a camp in a stand of maple trees, Erdrich uses berries and berrying to shape Omakayas's family's summer living pattern in terms of both gathering and preserving the berries. They are either dried or made into pemmican, to create their winter food stores. In *American Indian Food*, Linda Berzok discusses broadly the "abundance and variety" (xii) of foods American Indians gathered across the continent. She claims that, in terms of wild fruit, "there may have been 250 species of berries and fruit eaten by the Indians" (74). Of that diversity, in the Birchbark series Omakayas's family gathers blackberries, chokecherries, and heart berries. Just as they move from their winter quarters to the spring sugaring camp, the family's summer home is close to berry patches. Omakayas's thoughts turn to whether the berries are ripe and worries over whether the birds are eating them almost as soon as they arrive at their summer house (*BH* 14–15). The particular seasonal food and the foodways inherent to berries and berrying are organized with the entire year in mind: that is, to make sure that enough food is saved to get the family through the winter and into the next spring. Thus, like maple syrup and sugaring, berries and berrying motivate a temporal arc that shapes the Birchbark series's narrative, particularly in *The Birchbark*

House and *The Porcupine Year*. Unlike with maple sugar, when Omakayas's family migrates west into the plains, they do not move out of range of the berries, although the kinds of berries they gather change.

Erdrich most fully develops the importance of berrying in an episode in *The Birchbark House*, when Mama finds and picks an especially luscious bush of ripe chokecherries, then assigns her young son Pinch to guard them as they dry, so that they can be eaten in winter. Pinch, tempted by the deliciousness of the ripe fruit, gradually nibbles away at the berries, depleting the supply until little remains. Erdrich uses this story as a lesson about the needs of the family versus the desire of an individual family member. When Yellow Kettle (Mama) finds a bush of "late blooming chokecherries" (*BH* 82), she is clearly pleased because this fortunate find will augment the family's winter supply. She spreads the berries out carefully on bark sheaves in the sun so that they will dry and be preserved for the winter. But she has other chores she needs to do (checking fishnets), so she assigns the duty of guarding them to her young son: "'You watch them carefully now, Big Pinch. Keep the birds away. Listen, my son.' Mama narrowed her eyes at Pinch so that he would know he was trusted with an important task. 'This is our winter seasoning and food. You'll be glad of them when we are hungry in little spirit moon'" (*BH* 83). This task is a challenge for Pinch, who is both notoriously disobedient and always hungry. His mother sets forth the importance of the job that she gives him, his responsibility for the family's needs, and his own future pleasure come winter. She asks him to exert the self-control he has lacked in the past for the sake of future need. At this important moment he should demonstrate that he can act for the long-term, collective good of the family, rather than give in to individual desire. But he fails the test: rather than doing the job his mother entrusted to him, he gives in to his usual gluttonous, disobedient hunger. Erdrich shifts point of view at this moment in the book to give Pinch's inner rationalizations: "It was hard being Big Pinch, harder than his sisters would ever know. They didn't understand how good it felt to fill a stomach that so rarely got full. They didn't realize how good it felt to shove handfuls of berries into his greedy mouth" (*BH* 83). Erdrich's narration here suggests that Pinch has the strong appetite of a growing boy who lives in a culture in which feasting to fullness is a rare occurrence, yet she also undercuts sympathy for him by suggesting that his appetite is outsized, inappropriate, "greedy." Yet Pinch's ultimate ethical failure derives from being tempted by pleasurable taste, rather than attempting to fill an empty belly. He does not maliciously gorge himself; he simply cannot resist the lure of the ripe fruit:

If only, thought Pinch sadly, those berries didn't look *so delicious*! Mama had found a patch of chokecherries that were much more luscious than most. These were the biggest, fattest berries Pinch had ever seen! It didn't seem as though it would hurt to eat a few. . . . The berries tasted as good as they looked, better. Richer, blacker, without the mouth-puckering chokecherry taste. He might just have another handful. (*BH* 83–84)

Worse, when questioned by his mother about the missing berries, he blames their disappearance on his sister's pet crow, causing his mother to attack the bird in her frustration over the lost berries. But when Pinch feels the first pangs of the inevitable stomachache from eating too many berries, his mother realizes he has lied to her. She does not punish him, either for the lie or for giving into the immediate pleasure of the palate rather than preserving the family's winter berry supply. Instead, she voices her disappointment in him: "You lied. . . . As for your stomachache, there is no medicine but enduring the consequences of your greed. You'll have to suffer, Pinch. Maybe this will teach you" (*BH* 88). His mother thus gives Pinch no sympathy, recognizing that his own body will punish him for his lack of self-control.

In "From Berries to Orchards," Chantal Norrgard makes the point that "Ojibwe have relied on berries as a form of sustenance throughout their history. . . . Berry picking also held (and holds) social and cultural meanings, linking families and communities as individuals continue to recall berry-picking stories or the significance of their time together in the berry camps" (33). In the lengthy story about Pinch and the chokecherries, Erdrich offers an affirmation through her fiction of the nutritional and sociocultural truths Norrgard observes. Like Nanaboozhoo in the maple sugar story, Yellow Kettle engages Pinch in family food customs, teaching him to see beyond immediate personal pleasure and understand the berries and their preservation as central to the family's long-term survival. At the end of *Makoons*, after the too-successful buffalo hunt, overwhelming swarms of flies plague the carcasses, the hunters, and their families, finally symbolizing the tragic end of buffalo hunting on the plains. Following the hunt, Omakayas's family and the others encounter berries on their return home to Pembina. The fruit signals the happy return of a family foodway, one that has survived the move west:

> The day cooled and the air was crisp in the morning. A tremendous relief lifted people's spirits. The buffalo berries, Juneberries, and chokecherries were ripe. Makoons and Chickadee picked as many

> berries as they could whenever they stopped to camp. . . . As they rode along, there was always a skin covered with berries drying in the cart behind them. They would add the dried berries to the pemmican. They added dried berries to everything. Although Yellow Kettle always scolded the twins when they ate the berries while they picked, she wasn't there, so they disobeyed. Omakayas didn't stop them. (122–23)

While Yellow Kettle tries to repeat the lesson she taught their uncle Pinch, Omakayas is more generous, perhaps because the family is on the move, rather than settled with more limited berry resources, or perhaps because the boys do not feast in the same gluttonous way that Pinch did as a boy. The family adds to their stock of dried berries with each campsite; the berries in season offer enough bounty for the boys to enjoy their succulent ripeness. The emotional peace that berrying offers the group derives in part from its contrast with the bloody deaths and butchering of the buffalo, and partly from a return to familiar foraging foodways despite the alien plains that have become their new home.

In the Little House books, berries are picked and dried, saved for winter stews and pies, but, like maple sugar, berries and berrying do not have the consistent structural presence that they do in the Birchbark series. Berries, fresh or dried, are flavorful adjuncts to the Ingallses' diet, particularly important for luxurious treats like pies, which are made with the family's key food signifier, wheat flour, connecting them back, once again to the European American food traditions that they are extending into the plains. For Omakayas's family, berries and berrying allow them to maintain Ojibwe culinary history as they are forced west onto the plains. Eating fresh berries is a joy and luxury for Pinch, Makoons, and Chickadee, but Erdrich portrays the berries as far more nutritionally significant than Wilder does, because they are necessary for the family's subsistence and survival during the winter. They are not turned into pies but mixed with meat (moose, bear, buffalo) to make pemmican. The vitamins of the berries and the calories and fat (fatty acid) content of the meat combine to provide optimal nutrition for winter survival (Berzok 175–79). Again, Erdrich is "counting coup" on Wilder, demonstrating the longstanding presence of berries and the custom of berrying in Ojibwe culture as well as the deep need the Ojibwe have for the berries' nutritional content, year in and year out.

Like berrying, gardening carries Omakayas's family through their westward journey. Just as garden produce adds variety and savor to the Ingallses' life at its many stopping points, so too does the produce of Nokomis's gardens add to what the family gathers and hunts in the five Birchbark novels. The family has a garden planted with corn and pumpkins in *The Birchbark House*, which Omakayas and her older sister Angeline protect from ravenous blackbirds in a scene that parallels the Ingalls girls trying to protect their corn from the same pests. (Both families wind up eating the birds—yet another place where Erdrich counts coup on Wilder.) In *The Game of Silence*, Nokomis carefully preserves the seeds from her garden to take with her when the family is forced from their ancestral home. Over the course of the journey west, she preserves some seeds but loses many. But she is also able to trade with other women at times, and gradually she rebuilds her seed bank. She rejoices when she once again gets the chance to plant a garden when the family settles in Pembina, a town just south of the Canadian border in the territory that eventually will become North Dakota (*Chickadee* 145–46). Unlike the Ingalls family, whose gardens are a sign of their ability to adapt to the changing circumstances of their westward movement, Nokomis's gardens are a sign of place, belonging, and settlement. The Pembina garden connects the family materially to its past, their home on Lake Superior, while also conveying the sense that they are once again settling, now in Dakota territory. Moreover, at the end of *Makoons*, Erdrich portrays the garden as a place of abundance (corn, beans, squash, potatoes) but, at Nokomis's death, a spiritual portal as well:

> Nokomis walked into her garden. Nokomis greeted the sun, her palms out, smiling. Then she lay herself carefully down between the rows of gentle plants. . . . As Nokomis lay on the earth, she felt a lightness in her body. Suddenly, to her surprise, she felt herself rise out of her old body . . . She said good-bye to her sleeping family. Good-bye to this world. Peacefully, she turned to the west. A path opened before her. She saw someone familiar and laughed. Her old friend Tallow! Nokomis stepped onto the path . . . and began walking lightly away. (125)

By creating Nokomis's final garden as a multidimensional *locus amoenus*, Erdrich is counting coup once again, using magic realism to demonstrate how food signifies across the Ojibwes' material, geographical, cultural, and spiritual terrains.

In the mythic American west, hunting occupies a large place in how mainstream culture has imagined both Indians and pioneers. As noted above, in the Little House books, hunting is important as long as the Ingalls family is on the edge of the frontier, before the area becomes too populated with other pioneers and the local wild game stock is decimated. Although gathering and hunting are important for the Ingallses throughout the books, as the series progresses the agricultural impulse (cultivated crops, domestic livestock) to control the land marginalizes the need to live off and from it. In the years covered in the first five books of the Birchbark series, the Ojibwe have not yet been forced to adopt Western patterns of agriculture: thus, gathering and hunting remain at the center of Omakayas's family's food life. In *American Indian Food*, Linda Berzok uses the term "gatherer-hunter," rather than the more common "hunter-gatherer," because "it was the gathering of wild plants, shellfish, seeds, berries, and related food stuffs—a female activity— that secured most of the calories for the diet" (xv), while hunting—a male activity—supplied fewer calories but was crucial for "providing fat, which was the real goal" (179). Erdrich follows this historical precedent in having most of the family's food come from what the women gather, but she breaks the gendered division of hunting labor by having Deydey, Old Tallow and Two-Strike hunt, although all of them share their kill with the community, as was customary (Berzok 128–29). Erdrich gives hunting a consistent and persistent place in the five novels, punctuating the more dominant gathering activities; she uses hunting (like gathering) to structure and shape the books' narratives, particularly the annual cycle and the journey west. Although Deydey, Old Tallow and Two-Strike fish and hunt smaller game (rabbits, birds) as nutritional stopgaps, they focus their efforts on rarer but calorie- and fat-rich large game (beaver, bear, deer, moose, and, once out on the plains, buffalo)—animals that are riskier to hunt so that kills are less reliable. In doing so, their behavior fits "the optimal hunting strategy" of Native Americans, which "was to slaughter the largest animals possible to obtain the maximum amount of edible calories for the amount of energy expended" (Berzok 179–80).

What Erdrich focuses on repeatedly in her depictions of hunting is the danger it poses to the hunters and its necessity for family survival. At the beginning of *The Porcupine Year*, Pinch and Omakayas are pursuing a deer at night (torch hunting) from their canoe, but after Pinch's shot fails, they are caught in the river's rapids and nearly die (2–9). This failed hunt is complemented by Old Tallow's successful but self-sacrificial hunt when she dies killing the bear, whose meat saves the family from starving in the winter (114–20). Two-Strike Girl's life is changed in *The Game of Silence* when she successfully kills a moose, on her own with just one arrow: "This sort of thing just didn't happen—a girl making a grown warrior's shot" (82). Her successful hunt enables her thereafter to cross gendered work lines, styling herself as a hunter and no longer doing the women's work of gathering. In *Chickadee,* Two Strike has become an adult woman who "loved to hunt" (13). One dramatic example that shows how dangerous a hunt can be is when Animikiins, Omakayas's husband, hunts for a moose in *Chickadee*: he successfully stalks and shoots it on a frozen marsh, but the injured moose charges and Animikiins nearly dies when he breaks through the ice. After saving himself, he finds the moose carcass: the tongue and liver sustain him through a blizzard, and then he is able to return to his wife:

> Now Omakayas rejoiced. They had real food. A moose would last them the rest of the winter. Piece by piece, the family hauled back the moose using the toboggan. Everyone also carried chunks of frozen meat with carrying straps. By the time they cached the meat near their camp, hoisting some into a tree, burying some in snow, they were warm and excited. Omakayas brought in the tenderest piece of meat and began to make a feast. The rest of the family had been hunting in the next bay. Now they gathered. (19–20).

In this example, the family demonstrates the foodways mentioned by Berzok: the large moose brings in plentiful rich calories, and the immediate family shares their bounty with more extended relatives. By *Makoons,* Omakayas's family has shifted to hunting buffalo since they are living on the plains. No longer able to gather some of their previous staple foods nor to hunt the woodland animals they once did (moose, deer, bear), they must rely on the buffalo herds that still roam the plains for much of their diet. Although the hunts are successful because the buffalo are still plentiful, Erdrich uses the final hunt, with the plague of the flies on the butchered animals, to foreshadow the near extinction of the buffalo and the tragic end of Ojibwe food independence.

Just as wheat is the central staple of European American agricultural society, so is wild rice the staple of the Ojibwe. As Erma Vizenor, tribal chairwoman of the White Earth Nation, makes clear, wild rice is not just an edible cereal grain but comes with a divine provenance that shapes Ojibwe identity, belief, and behavior: "For generations [the Ojibwe] understood their connection to the *anishinaabe akiing* (the land of the people) in terms of the presence of this plant as a gift from the Creator. . . . Wild rice is part of our prophecy, our process of being human, our process of being Anishinaabe. . . . We are here because of the wild rice. We are living a prophecy fulfilled" (Raster and Hill 279).[8] Thomas Vennum agrees with this view in *Wild Rice* and the Ojibwe People*: "Traditional Ojibwe life elevates rice above being simply food for consumption or barter. Stories and legends, reinforced by the ceremonial use of *manoomin* (wild rice) and taboos and proscriptions against eating it at certain times, show the centrality of wild rice in Ojibwe culture. These factors together suggest that wild rice, at least in the past, approached the status of a sacred food" (58). Just as Wanabozhoo is the primary agent of cultural change and adaptation in the origin myth of maple sap and sugaring, he also, with the help of his grandmother (Nokomis), introduces wild rice, its spread, cultivation and preparation to the Ojibwe in numerous stories (Vennum 61–68). In the 2006 article "Oral Narrative and Ojibwa Story Cycles in Louise Erdrich's *The Birchbark House* and *The Game of Silence*," Elizabeth Gargano notes that

> Erdrich describes a rich and enduring tradition that achieves a dynamic balance between continuity and innovation. The storytelling tradition can open at any point to include new elements. Hospitable to contemporary experiences, it maintains a profound cultural relevance and significance; . . . In her two novels for children, *The Birchbark House* (1999) and *The Game of Silence* (2005), Erdrich creates histories that are also cultural texts in this specific revitalizing sense. (27)

As she does with so many of the other gathered and hunted foods in the Birchbark series, Erdrich spends significant narrative space on wild rice, reviving knowledge of the myth, camps, social life, harvesting, processing (parching and hulling), storage and preparation within an active culture of storytelling.

Erdrich regards ricing culture as so central that she makes the harvest time a significant scene in each of the first two books. *The Birchbark House* provides a careful description of how the family processes the rice but also begins to develop Omakayas's relationship with Two Strike and the latter girl's resistance to following gender guidelines as she dances the rice, a job usually undertaken by boys. Thus, the ricing experience is integrated within the larger family saga that Erdrich is beginning to develop. The rice harvest in *The Game of Silence* develops generational and intragenerational conflicts: Omakayas gets in trouble with her parents for harvesting the rice early in a bid for adult attention, all because she was trying to compete with Two Strike's choice to hunt rather than harvest or process rice. Yellow Kettle has promised her daughter that she is "old enough and strong enough to help" harvest the rice in the canoe with her (*GS* 74); Omakayas is excited because she sees knocking rice as the job of a "grown woman" (*GS* 76). Angered by Two Strike's disdain for the work assigned to girls and jealous of how successfully her cousin transgresses gender roles without being sanctioned by adults, Omakayas persuades her more conventional cousin, Twilight, that the two of them can earn attention by getting started early on the rice harvest. Despite Twilight's objections that no one can start until the rice boss gives permission, Omakayas rationalizes the decision: "'If we were just coming back with a jeemaan [canoe] full of manoomin [rice], do you think they'd really scold us? They'd praise us because we proved how hard we can work!' Omakayas was carried away with the romance of her idea. In her mind's eye, she saw only triumph, a return in which she was the center of attention" (*GS* 77). When the two girls return in the wake of Two Strike's incredible moose kill, however, they find only adult disapproval of their act: Mama announces she will not allow her daughter to rice with her, and Deydey makes clear why what Omakayas has done is so wrong:

> "You struck the manoomin too green into your boat," he said abruptly, "ruining the plants. My daughter, there is a way we do things. We do it to take care of the rice. We listen to the old people—they who check the rice and watch for the exact right moment for us to humbly accept the gift. You went against the way things are supposed to go. You didn't listen to your old ones, your grandmother among them." (*GS* 81)

In her thoughtless bid to display her maturity, Omakayas has instead acted childishly by disregarding tradition and disrespecting the knowledge of the tribal elders. Deydey's rebuke makes clear the values that underlie their cultural traditions: caring for the rice itself as a resource the people venerate and living harmoniously with the rice's natural cycles. Omakayas feels shame and guilt but also feels conflicted in the face of all the attention given to Two Strike's moose kill. She inwardly justifies her action by evaluating the state of the rice she harvested: "She wouldn't cry and she wouldn't say she was wrong. The rice had fallen easily from the stalks, the lake was generous" (*GS* 81). Erdrich uses food to signal Omakayas's movement into adolescence, showing the girl's faith in her own judgment, while still suggesting that she needs to learn to exercise it within her cultural traditions.

* * *

Both Wilder and Erdrich chronicle life in the northern woods and plains of Wisconsin, Minnesota, and the Dakotas in the nineteenth century, albeit from opposing cultural viewpoints, and food lies at the heart of each of their portraits. Both spend considerable effort in representing the foodways of each culture in great detail, and they tie the production, processing, and cooking of food to the action and character development in both series. Wilder portrayed the foodways of her youth, which were already disappearing in her old age when she wrote her novels, so vividly that she inspired generations of readers young and old to recreate the foods of her youth—some no doubt helped by *The Little House Cookbook* that Barbara Walker created in 1979. While Wilder wrote with a conscious political slant, intending to demonstrate the virtues of pioneer self-reliance as an antidote to the New Deal for her original Great Depression–era audience, the less overt food ideology that underlies her text suggests cultural blind spots and a disregard for the people that her family and pioneers like them displaced. The European American pioneers remade the landscape in ways necessary for imposing Western agricultural practices: deforestation, the broad destruction of native animals through hunting and obliteration of habitats, the "breaking" and "busting" of deep prairie sod required for planting crops (especially wheat) in fields. By doing so, they destroyed the foodways of the Native peoples dependent on that landscape.

Erdrich's Birchbark series depicts the foodways of the nineteenth-century Ojibwe in detail equal to Wilder's, by her conscious design. As a turn-of-the-millennium writer, Erdrich, unlike Wilder, is not drawing on personal recollection of foodways used by her characters, given that she sets her story 150 years or more in the past. But many of the foodways she depicts have indeed survived into modern times: they remain central to Ojibwe cultural self-definition. The Ojibwe have fought through treaty and law to ensure that the fundamental staples of their people (berrying, maple sugaring, and ricing, as described above) remain viable within their control: access to the natural resources are still central to their identity as a people. For the Ojibwe—and a number of other Native nations as well—food sovereignty is a fundamental part of tribal sovereignty. Amanda Raster and Christina Gish Hill define food sovereignty as "the right of a cultural group to define its own food system" (268). In "The Dispute over Wild Rice: An Investigation of Treaty Agreements and Ojibwe Food Sovereignty," Raster and Hill discuss the link between ricing and Ojibwe identity within the history of treaties and legal negotiations that the Ojibwe continue to pursue to preserve that link against encroachments and threats from US agriculture. To that end, they speak to the underlying assumptions of Ojibwe food sovereignty:

Understanding the complexity of the interactions between the people, animals, and plants that share the land, Ojibwe people have fostered their relationship with wild rice in a way that emphasizes respectful management of the landscape that supports its productivity. By acknowledging Ojibwe rights to hunt, gather, fish, and harvest rice using traditional techniques in their acknowledged territory, the treaties that Euro-Americans signed with Ojibwe bands actually recognized that this management relationship developed in relation to an entire landscape, not just the Ojibwe's right to access specific resources, such as wild rice. (268)

The activism charted in Raster and Hill's article shows how native cultures, particularly since the rise of the American Indian Movement (AIM) in the late 1960s, have reasserted their active and continuing existence through literary, aesthetic, political, economic, legal, culinary, and other sociocultural forms. The Ojibwe insistence on maintaining treaty guarantees to ricing as Raster and Hill document, and to berrying as Chantal Norrgard attests, shows a focus on food sovereignty in their activism that suggests the fundamental nature of these foodways to continuing cultural identity—a primacy that Erdrich supports through her portrayal of how the nineteenth-century Ojibwe practiced them.

As a member of the Native American Renaissance, Erdrich uses postcolonial/postmodern narrative play to disseminate and vivify her Native Ojibwe culture. Her success in the Birchbark series comes, in part, from her use of Ojibwe foodways within the conventions of children's books that she adapts to Ojibwe storytelling, as Elizabeth Gargano points out (27). Because she traces her characters over a series of books, Erdrich shows the complexities of such foodways over the course of many years. Mainstream American culture has been slow to recognize that Native foods and foodways constitute cuisine at all—many different cuisines, in fact. Only one book has been published that explores the multifaceted cuisines of the indigenous nations of North America: Linda Berzok's *American Indian Food* (2005). In its preface, Berzok offers a general description of indigenous cuisine:

Native American food holds a unique position in the culinary lexicon as the oldest gastronomy in North America. It is characterized by abundance and variety. Wild plants, fish, meat and cultivated crops were freshly caught, gathered or harvested, and prepared simply. Much was eaten raw, although some was dried or smoked and preserved for the lean winters. Except for trading, American Indians ate only those foods grown, fished or gathered within a relatively small radius of their homes. (xii)

She then notes how remarkable it is that these distinct cuisines still exist, given that "foodways were one of the first layers of culture attacked by the invaders" (xii–xiv). Yet, despite the systematic governmental policy decisions to produce food genocide and thus induce the genocide of both Native peoples and their cultures, native foodways—and the cultures that practice them—have survived and persisted (xiv). While the Birchbark series is not *about* food sovereignty, Erdrich's focus on food fits a larger cultural trend right now to restore an active knowledge of native foods and foodways. Indigenous chefs like Sean Sherman (Oglala Lakota) and Karlos Baca (Diné/Tewa/Nuche) work to create contemporary precolonial Native cuisines, using local ingredients, foraging, hunting, and preparation that reflect their tribal traditions.[9] In an interview with *Indian Country Today*, Baca says, "There's a symbiosis that people have lost—not just tribally but worldwide for the most part—of eating with the seasons and the earth providing what your body needs at that point in time" (Butler). In the *Toasted Sister* podcast, Andi Murphy (Navajo) talks "to Native chefs and foodies about what Indigenous cuisine is, where it comes from, where it's headed and how it's used to connect them and their people to their origins and traditions." Tribal colleges in Minnesota, Montana, and North Dakota have classes (Phillips 14–20) and sponsor summits (Sorenson 32–34) meant to teach and actively bring back historical foodways.

The survival and perpetuation of these Native foodways, particularly in the face of the long-term and ongoing cultural erasure of Native peoples by mainstream American culture, is a cause for celebration; they need nurturing at many levels, and literature for young readers provides an important one. Erdrich's novels affirm the richness and complexity of her Ojibwe characters in their original cultural setting, illustrating the pleasures of foods taken directly from the land that provides them with only minimal cultivation, even as she chronicles the loss of their homeland and consequent evolution of their lifestyle. Wilder's novels have been a part of the erasure of Native history for child readers, particularly in their characterization of so many of the lands her family moved into as empty until "settlers" came—or even worse in acknowledging the Osage presence in Kansas with Pa's calm expectations that the American government has always "let settlers keep the land. They'll make the Indians move on again" (*LHP* 273). Once the land is under white control, it will be remade: agriculture is the only form of land use that the Ingalls family and their neighbors the Scotts recognize and value, despite treaties in which Native peoples sought to preserve their lands and the foodways dependent on them. Although treaties were designed to allow for different visions of the land and its purposes, the American government violated treaty after treaty, moving Native peoples onto lands that would not support their traditional foodways and forcing them to become dependent on foods the government gave them instead, while pioneers like Wilder came to see the changes that they wrought in the land as inevitable. Thus, in the Little House books, Wilder invokes a nostalgia for pioneer life which reinforces Frederick Jackson Turner's vision of manifest destiny and the European Americans, citizens or immigrants, who made western expansion possible; to counter this vision, in the Birchbark series Louise Erdrich invokes Ojibwe life in a way that shows it has a history, a present, and a future.

Chapter 6

"A PROFOUND LOVE FOR LUSCIOUS THINGS"

Food as Symbolism and History in Maurice Sendak's *In the Night Kitchen*

Maurice Sendak has freely admitted in multiple interviews (Cott 68, Haviland 25) that food appears to be one of his obsessions: the children and child stand-ins in his stories and drawings often eat freely and with delight; some of them also threaten to eat those they are angry with—or creatures very much larger than they are threaten to consume them. Kenny, both Max and the Wild Things, Jennie the dog, the Nutshell Library characters (Pierre, Johnny, the boy in *Chicken Soup with Rice*, and the alligator family of *Alligators All Around*), the sea monster of *Hector Protector and As I Went over the Water*, the children of Sendak's fantasy sketches—all take their turns eating and evading being eaten (or even occasionally being consumed and regurgitated). *In the Night Kitchen*, however, stands out in Sendak's oeuvre in its overt representations of and homage to the beloved Jewish foods and kitchen utensils of Sendak's childhood; Mickey, its protagonist, becomes a hero by navigating the challenges of the Night Kitchen to become essential to producing the delights of breakfast.

All of Sendak's books mine his childhood, transforming the particulars of his individual experience into stories of universal experience. Sendak recognized that *In the Night Kitchen*, however, was an especially personalized story, produced, he claimed in an oft-quoted phrase, "from the direct middle of me, and it hurt like hell extracting it" (qtd. in Cech 177). In another interview, he describe it thus: "So the book became a huge, I hope beautiful, garbage pail for memories past and present, and for me a picture book that had enormous significance and far and away at that time in my life was my favorite" ("Getting to Know Maurice Sendak"). He has commented in interviews on the book's various inspirations from his life experience; critics such as John Cech and Jonathan Cott have explored the food imagery within the story, albeit briefly. Sendak expressed his own awareness of his stories' biographical origins, particularly those of the "trilogy" (as he termed it) of *Where the Wild Things Are*, *In the Night Kitchen*, and *Outside Over There*. In order to understand Sendak's second picture book more fully, then, we must explore the cultural and historical context of the food Sendak encountered in childhood and then transformed as the material background of the Night Kitchen itself.

In our 1999 article, "Power, Food, and Eating in Maurice Sendak and Henrik Drescher: *Where the Wild Things Are*, *In the Night Kitchen*, and *The Boy Who Ate Around*," we used theorists like Mary Douglas, Stephen Mennell, and Julia Kristeva to explore Sendak and Drescher's deployment of food as social code and how their characters resist and capitulate to their encoding into the social fabric. Our approach reflected Jean Perrot's 1990 article, "Maurice Sendak's Ritual Cooking of the Child in Three Tableaux: The Moon, Mother, and Music." Perrot used Claude Lévi-Strauss's theory of "cooking" from *The Naked Man*—which recognizes the signifying power of food and its preparation as socializing agent—to explore Sendak's similar use of food in *Where the Wild Things Are* and *In the Night Kitchen*. What neither we nor Perrot did, however, is study the particular food codes that Sendak brings to the creative process: that is, how he is encoded and, thus, encodes in turn. Given the wealth of biographical information on Sendak, the next logical step beyond the theoretical focus of our earlier essay on the cultural and narrative structures of Sendak's work is analyzing the particular food codes and history in which Sendak and his characters are enmeshed.

Sendak was born in Brooklyn in 1928 to parents who had immigrated to the United States from Poland shortly before World War I as part of the huge wave of Eastern European Jews that began in the 1880s. Initially, the majority of these immigrants settled in the Lower East Side of Manhattan, but as their population increased, other enclaves developed in Brooklyn and the Bronx. Food was of central importance as a signifier of their past and present as well as their future prosperity in the United States. Food played a large role in Sendak's childhood—as it does for all children—in defining home and pleasure; as a Jewish child in 1930s Brooklyn, his experience of food reflected the larger patterns of food within the immigrant Jewish community there, both in terms of foods cooked at home (reproduced from the old country and/or adapted in the new) and commercially produced foods bought for the household, which were readily available because of the growing technological production of food in America in response to a rising population. Occasional treats of more mainstream American foods, available on rare trips to Manhattan, were memorable as well (Cech 199–200), but the daily mainstays of Sendak's cultural milieu in the Jewish enclaves of Brooklyn underpin the images of In the Night Kitchen. Although food is a central concern of Where the Wild Things Are, Sendak codes his Jewish background within the Wild Things that threaten to eat Max rather than in the food Max desires to consume. In his portrayal of the eponymous Night Kitchen, however, Sendak pays a conscious and overt homage to that immigrant past, fusing the intimate foodways of home and the industrial foodways of American society as the setting for his hero's search for agency. In the Night Kitchen thus uses the city of food to portray ethnic Jewish experience set within mainstream American culture.

To understand how Sendak processes these personal, familial, and immigrant experiences, it is important to place Sendak within the wider context of Jewish American writers and their interrogation and conceptualization of the immigrant experience, of the tensions between assimilation and integration, forgetting and remembering, inclusion and alienation that shaped Jewish cultural identity for generations.[1] In "Of Crucibles and Grandfathers: The East European Immigrants," Priscilla Wald notes,

> The sense of alienation that arises from the pressure (internal or external) to forget bears witness to more than the contemporary terms of identity in the U.S. It attests to the childhood memories of family and place from which we derive our sense of being human and of being in and to the world. We can move away from that, of course, but we cannot forget. The literature of Yiddish New York tells the story of the memories and movements of people for whom family and place, however uncertain, nevertheless formed the basis of the identities that they were asked to build anew. (67)

Assimilation, in Wald's essay, is about immigrants melting into the new culture, a kind of forgetting of the ways of the past, of the home country. She focuses on the early generation of Jewish writers in New York from the late nineteenth century to the 1920s. She sees their literary work as reacting to the pressure to forget and assimilate; thus, in its resistance to that cultural coercion, it comes to preserve and define a cultural identity that is both undeniably American and distinctly immigrant Jewish—to use cultural memory as the basis of identity.

The immigrant Jewish authors Wald discusses captured the experience of the generation to which Sendak's parents belonged. Sendak himself belongs to the next generation beyond Wald's focus, yet his work shows the same resurgence of cultural memory that Wald finds in the writers who are his cultural forebears. Sendak achieved mainstream success with *Where the Wild Things Are*, a book that lacks overt markers from Sendak's past. Although Sendak admitted to sourcing the Wild Things in his memories of his aunts' and uncles' visits during his childhood ("Getting to Know Maurice Sendak," Haviland 25, Lane 88), their form as Wild Things hides their original Jewish identity. Max as the hero is a universal "everychild" whose dream journey affords him the freedom to act out a fantastic version of his desires and then practice reining them in; he then ends his adventure back "in his very own room with his supper waiting for him" (*Where the Wild Things Are*). In contrast, seven years later in his next major picture book, *In the Night Kitchen*, Sendak shifts from the assimilationist approach of the earlier picture book to one that more freely acknowledges his Jewish roots, producing a book that is marked with "childhood memories of family and place" and thus follows the pattern Wald discerned (67). In *Exiles on Main Street: Jewish American Writers and American Literary Culture*, Julian Levinson claims that Jewish American authors "elaborate some set of images, tropes, or metaphors through which the past manages to speak once again—and in the American present" (193). A close examination of *In the Night Kitchen* reveals how Sendak uses the food of his childhood to that end.

JEWISH IMMIGRATION AND FOOD

In his 1917 memoir, *An American in the Making: The Life Story of an Immigrant*, Marcus Ravage writes extensively about the poverty, degradation, and economic disparities he witnessed on the Lower East Side of New York as a new Jewish immigrant from Eastern Europe in the early twentieth century. When he visits his successful countryman Couza in his tenement sweatshop after having just arrived in the city, Ravage despairs over the misery he sees yet marvels at a breakfast served with "German-silver coffee-urn and pressed-glass bowl, and silver-plated spoons and white linen" (63). Nor is he only impressed with the tableware: he is amazed at the richness of food available: "Cake for breakfast! If I had been offered swan's eggs or steak or broiled pigeons . . . I should have kept my self-possession. But the very idea of serving cake for breakfast struck me as an extravagant fancy of which only millionaires were capable" (63). As much as the book serves to condemn the inequities suffered by turn-of-the-century immigrants in New York, Ravage regularly turns to wonder at and appreciate the food he encounters and the abundance it represents, despite all the other wretchedness he experiences. As much as food reflects the problems he sees, it also refracts as a signifier of hope. This vision of food is reinforced in Sanford Sternlicht's much later autobiographically based literary analysis, *The Tenement Saga: The Lower East Side and Early American Writers* (2004): "However, food was very important since it reminded these strangers in the New World just who they were and where they had come from. When the new immigrants were poor and hungry, they realized that food was amazingly abundant in America, and that hard work, daily prayer, and a little mazel (luck) could allow them to eat as well and as much as they wanted" (55). Similarly, in *Hungering for America: Italian, Irish, and Jewish Foodways in the Age of Migration*, historian Hasia Diner notes that after suffering hunger and deprivation back home in Europe, Jewish immigrants "strove vigorously to have good food regularly, and to feast as they wanted upon luxuries once associated with the sacred times. They saw the meals on their tables as America's gift and the fruit of their own aggressive efforts to get what they wanted" (178).

In *We Are What We Eat: Ethnic Food and the Making of Americans*, historian Donna Gabaccia speaks to all the entrepreneurial food businesses which thrived to serve the enclave community and then to move beyond it to serve a mainstream audience:

> In 1899 the . . . Jewish Lower East Side in New York City boasted 140 groceries, 131 kosher butchers, 36 bakeries, 9 bread stands, 14 butter and egg stores, 24 candy stores, 7 coffee shops, 10 delicatessens, 9 fish stores, 7 fruit stands, 2 meat markets, 10 sausage stores, 20 soda water stands, 5 tea shops, 11 vegetable stores, 13 wine shops, 15 grape wine shops, and 10 confectioners. . . . The unpredictability in enclave markets repeatedly encouraged small businesses to look farther afield, beyond the boundaries of ethnic communities, for a wider market of more diverse consumers. (64–65)

For the Jewish immigrant community in New York in the late nineteenth and early twentieth centuries, food was not only an aspirational ideal but also a pragmatic economic engine both to realize the promising plenty of America for themselves and to gain a foothold in the American mainstream.

SENDAK: FROM INSIDE OUT, HOME TO COMMERCIAL KITCHEN

An important category of this immigrant cuisine is sweets. In Donna Gabaccia's list of Jewish businesses, it is worth noting how many specialize in sweets of one kind or another. In all the general abundance of food, sweets seem to rate a special, often sentimental, mention, especially sweet breads. Marcus Ravage's first notable impression of food in New York is of cake, as noted above. In his autobiographical *Walker in the City*, Alfred Kazin talks about coming home from school on Friday afternoons "to the warm odor of coffee cake baking in the oven." He goes on to speak of the many dishes for the Sabbath dinner, culminating with the sweet: "compote of prunes and quince, apricots and orange rind; applesauce; a great brown nut cake filled with almonds" (Diner 195). In Sanford Sternlicht's rehearsal of his own experiences of food in New York, he dedicates a paragraph to sweets, noting his grandmother's skill in making the thin dough of strudel, which his mother was unable to reproduce. No baker, his mother turned to "store-bought schnecken (sticky buns), ruggelach (square-shaped pastries wrapped in dough and filled with raisins and nuts), and various kuchen (cakes) and hamantashen (a poppyseed pastry, usually filled with prunes or apricot jam, in the shape of a tricorn hat) at Purim" (53). Besides homemade and store-bought pastries, there was also a burgeoning restaurant culture that privileged sweets. Diner observes that "The New York world of Jewish food allowed individuals to eat away from family as well. Cafés and restaurants, 'coffee and cake parlors' [Roskolenko 191] dotted the neighborhood" (199). Beyond New York, the growing reach of early twentieth-century immigrant Jewish cuisine in the United States may be best noted in the success of the *Settlement Cookbook*, which was first published by "Milwaukee's Jewish-oriented settlements" (Gabaccia 137) in 1901 and went through twenty-nine editions by midcentury. As the first nationally famous cookbook to feature Jewish cuisine, it includes a full chapter on kuchen (identified in later editions as coffee cakes[2]), as well as parts of earlier chapters with recipes for kuchen fillings (Kander 354–62).[3] All of this sweet cookery grew of out of the baking expertise of German and German Jewish immigrants, who used that expertise to gain an economic foothold in New York and in cities across the country (Gabaccia 112). In *In the Night Kitchen*, Mickey's heroic journey provides the collective "we" of the final sentence with "cake every morning," an accomplishment that resonates not only with the nation's sweet tooth but with the history of Jewish immigrant food as it moves from enclave to mainstream.

Like Saul Bellow and Philip Roth, Sendak was the native-born son of immigrant Jewish parents, and he grew up at a time when the food milieu described above was well established. As a child, food was significant for Sendak. In his many interviews, food is a regular topic, brought up by both the interviewers and Sendak as a way to understand the artist and his work. In the 1971 interview with Virginia Haviland, Sendak says, "The business of eating is such an immensely important part of life for a child" (25). We can see the truth of this general sentiment more precisely in other interviews and scholarly commentary. According to John Braun in his 1970 interview with Sendak, "Because of his illness, Maurice was home a lot. He spent a great deal of time in the kitchen with his mother" (222). In Sendak's rare trips to Manhattan as a child, with his older sister, the first order of business was eating at a restaurant, but Sendak recalled alluring bakery smells on the trip into the city, welcoming him to the fantastic and worldly foodland that was Manhattan:

> Those trips were ravishing. It was going to a 1001 Nights, it was going to a seraglio, it was going to the most devilish place in the world. It was crossing the Manhattan Bridge, and as you crossed the Manhattan Bridge, right along the river there was a bakery. The aroma of fresh bread poured into the subway trains, and it was like an aphrodisiac. It made me wild, so that the connection of wonderful bread or foods and New York City was fixed in my mind. New York was a place where you went to eat. . . . (Cech 199–200)

Herein lies the experiential inception of the urban visuals of *In the Night Kitchen*, a food world, a table land, where all the ingredients for cake manifest themselves through a cityscape. Sendak's personal journey from home kitchen to Manhattan (and, thus, to the larger world) corresponds to the Jewish immigrant experience from inside the enclave to out into the mainstream. As much as food provided a path outward for Jewish immigrants, so, too, does Sendak tap into a similar path. Regarding *In the Night Kitchen*, John Cech notes, "This nocturnal fantasy transformation of the kitchen is based, of course, on Sendak's composite memories of the family's kitchens where Sadie Sendak made her own version of a 'morning cake.' Sendak filed a copy of her recipe among his notes and drafts for *In the Night Kitchen* . . ." (196–97). Cech goes on to say that "the kitchen was the real center of most American households for Sendak's generation . . . charged with a family's literal and psychic history" (Cech 197). While the family kitchen was a center of Sendak's life as a child, the intense experiences of his sojourns to Manhattan moved him beyond that kitchen.

Turning to cake, if Sendak's mother's "morning cakes" were a nascent autobiographical detail that fueled *In the Night Kitchen,* so too was his visit to the 1939 World's Fair and his experience of the Sunshine Bakery demonstration kitchen:

> . . . this aroma came out of this white building—it was the smell of biscuits and cake and flour and milk, and it was better than sex, better than anything in the whole world, and I just stood there sniffing. And then these little fat bakers with mustaches came out and stood on the balcony and they waved, and I stood downstairs and waved back to them—I don't know how long we waved at each other. . . . [T]hat scene at the bakery was emblematic and it became the emblem for *Night Kitchen*—the bakers, the lusciousness of cooking, of kneading with your hands, of undressing and floating in this sensuosity of milk . . . I really love that book much more than *Wild Things,* because it's really a gut book with a profound love for luscious things." (Cott 52–53)

Sendak focuses on the wonder of that childhood moment in this particular memory: the enormous sensory pleasure created by the scent of baking sweet breads in the middle of this huge public fair, and the mutual recognition between the baker/actors and himself (as he perceived it at the time). In designating it "emblematic" he enlarges its significance from the individual experience of a single child to stand as a profound experience of American childhood. But in other interviews, Sendak's memory of the Sunshine Bakery, through its advertisements, is much more ambiguous:

> When I was a child there was an advertisement which I remember very clearly. It was for the Sunshine Bakers. And the advertisement read, "We Bake While You Sleep." It seemed to me the most sadistic thing in the world, because all I wanted to do was to stay up and watch. It seemed so absurdly cruel and arbitrary for them to do it while I slept. And also for them to think I would think that was terrific stuff on their part, and would eat their product on top of that. It bothered me a good deal, and I remember I used to save the coupons showing the three fat little Sunshine bakers going off to this magic place, wherever it was, at night to have their fun, while I had to go to bed. This book was a sort of vendetta book to get back at them and to say that I am now old enough

to stay up at night and know what is happening in the Night Kitchen. (Haviland 26)

In this oft-quoted discussion of the genesis of the picture book, Sendak emphasizes his lack of power and choice as a child, and his anger at that lack of agency, reflecting the common childhood frustration of being sent to bed and missing out on the events of the mysterious night, reserved for adults. The slogan Sendak recalls, "We Bake While You Sleep," was clearly intended to suggest a commercial luxury to adult consumers who might well remember the tedious process of having to make bread by hand early enough to be eaten for breakfast. This expected attraction for adult customers contrasts powerfully with the interpretation of Sendak-the-child upon reading the text, and with his anger which sparked his imagination both as child consumer and as adult artist. Sendak's experiences with Sunshine Bakery have both a public and a private dimension: the home consumption of their breads and of the advertising for them, and the public viewing of the production site at the World's Fair. From home kitchen to a city bakery to the Sunshine Bakery,[4] Sendak as child experienced the passage from home food to industrial food, from enclave to nation. It is this food journey that Sendak captures in *In the Night Kitchen*.

DREAMING THE KITCHEN

For all of its obsessive narrative and visual focus on everything food and food related, the most notable absence in *In the Night Kitchen* is any mention, verbally or visually, of the family kitchen. (The same is true for *Where the Wild Things Are*.) As quoted above, John Cech claims the centrality of "the kitchen ... for Sendak's generation ..." as a receptacle for "a family's literal and psychic history" (197), yet Sendak has left out a simple portrayal of Mickey's family's kitchen in this food idyll. As Nancy Carlisle and Melinda Talbot Nasardinov note in *American Kitchens*, in the period from 1890–1945 urban kitchens "were used for visiting, bathing, sleeping, and working, leaving little room for preparing food or storing cookware" (133).[5] Sendak spent a lot of time in the kitchen while he was growing up, and given that his relationship with his mother was sometimes difficult and contentious (Cech 222, Cott 24–25), the kitchen may not have been a locus of sentimental nostalgia; moreover, Sendak said in an interview with Bill Moyers, "I often went to bed without supper cause I hated my mother's cooking. So, to go to bed without supper was not a torture to me" ("Author"). It is as if Sendak wants to make a clean break with that "literal and psychic history," and, rather than a realistic portrayal of a small family kitchen, he sublimates it into an expansive space that is open to the city skyline and the night sky. Although one item in the dreamscape, Mama's Cream of Tartar, functions as a maternal metonymy—allowing Sendak's mother a veiled, refracted presence—the world of In the Night Kitchen is an essentially male space, where Mickey is free to follow his desires and become the hero of his own narrative. Sendak's portrayal echoes Michael Symons's claim in The History of Cooks and Cooking that throughout history, when cooking moves from private kitchen to public space, female work is "downgraded" (402) as domestic; thus, the female cook is supplanted by the male chef. As a result, the female cook is erased from history while the male chef becomes a visible public figure: "the more tasks moved outward, the more 'male' they became" (301–2). So the three male Oliver Hardy bakers reign over the enormous, industrial-sized kitchen Mickey dreams of, rather than a giant maternal figure as cook, and it is their dilemma that Mickey solves.[6]

By illustrating only the dream kitchen, Sendak allows Mickey to enter the hero narrative unfettered by the realities of his quotidian life as a small boy. So, when an unknown noise awakens Mickey from his bed, he is annoyed, rather than scared—angry enough (paradoxically) to shout for quiet rather than call for his parents. The noise is undefined, merely represented in the images as words: thump, dump, clump, lump, bump. Mickey does not know what has caused the noise, nor does he seem to want to go back to sleep: his mind is too active and leads him into a long, slow fall (à la Alice down the rabbit hole to Wonderland). He tumbles through a dream version of his home, landing in the urbanized space of the Night Kitchen. Sendak models the look of the Night Kitchen on memories of his 1930s childhood: he enlarges objects from home kitchens, such as food containers and cooking implements, to the magnitude of a vast city, turning a domestic cooking space into one built on a metropolitan, industrial, and cosmic scale. Sendak derives his fantastic architectural kitchen from both his remembered frustration and the wonder he felt for the Sunshine Bakery and its bakers at different points in his childhood, using it as the setting that his hero Mickey explores in his quest.

Like the young Sendak, Mickey is curious about what happens at night when he is supposed to be asleep; he wants to understand and explore the enticing and unknown world he finds. Sendak bestows on Mickey the gift of the bakerly dream as a conceptual focus for the undefined night noises;

it is a way that Mickey gives shape to the noise, his frustrations, and his desire to be a hero. Mickey is drawn as a very young child, with the stubby limbs common in children not long past the toddling stage. Given his age, it is unlikely that Mickey has experienced an industrial bakery like that of the Sunshine Bakers or knows anything about baking. But Mickey knows at least one of the products that can come from an industrial bakery: cake. Like many Americans who eat the foods produced by the industrial food chain, Mickey knows the food but not where it come from or how it is made. Like Charlie Bucket in *Charlie and the Chocolate Factory*, Mickey too desires to know where his favorite sweet food comes from and tours an imagined, magical, *industrial* source. For Mickey, that experience comes as a dream of a giant, open-air kitchen, where bakers cook while he sleeps—most nights, but not this special night. Lacking any experience with industrial kitchens, Mickey draws on the kitchen items he does know, such as a homestyle kitchen range (labeled the "Mickey Oven") in which the cake will be baked. John Cech speaks eloquently of the material memories that Sendak used in creating this imaginary urban landscape:

> Sendak . . . stayed close to his own roots, constructing the Night Kitchen out of bottles, packages, jars and cooking implements that were familiar sights in any 1930s kitchen. Sendak built this fantasy world out of familiar things, the sorts of detritus of everyday life that fascinates us as young children: the egg beaters, whisks, funnels, and other utensils that, if turned upside down, could well become a tower of a building; the packages of baking soda and jars of jam and pickles that, if lined up on a shelf or counter and viewed from the diminutive perspective of a four-year-old in a dimly lit kitchen, could well resemble the skyline of a city. (196)

In essence, Sendak pursues a Freudian dream logic, taking elements of the day residue a small child's waking experience and reworking it through Mickey's unleashed but well-directed id to produce a wondrous, gargantuan foodland.

Besides appearing like a psychoanalytic mindscape, Sendak's cityscape also seems like a crowded reflection of programmatic architecture, which populated the American landscape beginning in the 1920s as a form of commercial advertising. John Cech briefly notes the influence on Sendak of artists associated with ironic pop art, such as Warhol, Steinberg, and Oldenburg, as well as "the fanciful nature of some vernacular American roadside architecture" (197). Landscape historian Charles Liebs, in *Main Street to Miracle Mile: American Roadside Architecture*, describes how businesses erected outsized buildings in the shape of objects like "giant milk bottles, watermelons, dogs, and root-beer barrels . . . [to] physically [illustrate] the name or nature of the business or the merchandise sold inside" and attract customers (48). Programmatic architecture (also called novelty or mimetic architecture) was popular in buildings that were associated with food, and restaurants were often shaped like the products they sold: "Some operators adopted the Coney Island approach to roadside marketing by casting their stands into bizarre shapes that often mimed the name or function of the restaurant. Thus, ice-cream stands took the form of giant ice-cream freezers and milk cans" (Liebs 205). Although programmatic architecture was tailored to roadside car culture, its nineteenth-century precursor was urban; according to Liebs, city "merchants freely exploited a variety of easily recognizable images of everyday objects, from clocks to teapots, for their commercial value. Giant watches hung above jewelers' shops, mortars and pestles graced druggists' doorways, and oversize boots announced to passersby that a cobbler was close at hand" (49). The cityscapes of *In the Night Kitchen* tap into an American tradition that—like amusement parks or "movie palaces" (Liebs 48)—normalizes the surreal and fantastic. In other words, Mickey is not just having a weird dream, because mainstream Americana provides both its structure and content.

Sendak projects his personal history into the giant buildings that form the Night Kitchen, choosing not to use actual brands of specific items of the time. Instead, using advertising-style graphics, he brands many items with labels drawn from personal connections and experiences that he then draws onto the public space that the Night Kitchen represents. Although many of the buildings have labels on them to show what kind of foods they contain or represent (beans, cream, jam, salt, canned tomatoes, yeast, coffee, rolled white oats, bread, and cake), all apparent brand labels refer to people in Sendak's life—the ingredients of which he is composed, perhaps.[7] Some labels are loving family homages: two buildings in separate panels but on the same page, both representing canned tomatoes, bear the names of Sendak's parents: "Philip's Best" and "Sadie's Best." Two other buildings carry differing versions of Eugene Glynn, who was Sendak's life partner: a building labeled with the possessive "Eugene's" and a gabled dairy container with "E. Glynn" inside the gable—and a circular label that says "Pure" on the side. Both seem to offer a tender vision of their relationship, simultaneously offering a tribute to their partnership while being opaque enough to hide it, for Sendak feared how being identified as homosexual would affect his career as a children's author and illustrator at the time. He did not publicly reveal that he was gay until 2008, a year after Glynn's death (Cohen E1). When Sendak becomes self-referential in the illustrations, he slides in a sly note of self-mockery and light comedy about his own babyhood: the building that bears his own birthdate ("Patented June 10th 1928") is a container of "Cocoanut."

One other label of particular note, which occurs on one of the bakers' cooking ingredients rather than on one of the food container buildings, is the canister of Woody's Salt. The salt container appears prominently, held up by one of the bakers, in the first panel that shows the Night Kitchen. Lane identifies the faux brand name as referring to Sendak's friend Woody Gelman (182). Sendak depicts a large Star of David in between "Woody's" and "Salt," a symbol that indicates the Jewish background of his friend, and perhaps also provides a joking reference to the popularity of kosher salt in American cooking. This is the most overt reference that Sendak includes in the book to the Brooklyn Jewish cultural milieu in which he grew up. Aware of his mainstream audience, Sendak does not reference specific traditionally Jewish foods such as matzo or bagels or blintzes in his cityscape, and yet he does put the Star of David in a highly conspicuous spot at the very beginning of the Night Kitchen images, an open visual tribute to the ethnic background he shares with the friend honored in the label. Here, through the label on a common product container, Sendak subtly fits a Jewish food—and thus metonymically Jewish culture—inside a popular American art form. As discussed earlier in the essay, for twentieth-century Jewish American artists, assimilation is not a means of erasure and forgetting but a trigger for cultural memory (Wald 67). Or, to apply Julian Levinson, Sendak uses the image of Woody's Salt as an object "through which the past manages to speak once again—and in the American present" (193).

We can see the same kind of bridging happening on the last page of the book. Through the narrative and graphic arcs of *In the Night Kitchen*, Sendak fuses the public/industrial and private/home, deconstructing the family kitchen to remake it into fantasy commercial space, which, in turn, reflects the growing dependence Americans had (and have) on industrially produced food. In this modern milieu, Mickey gains agency and becomes hero. Sendak fills the surreal dream scenes with the ingredients and implements for making cake, but the three bakers are oblivious to the mistake they are making by identifying Mickey as the milk needed for their cake batter. In their segment of the production line, the bakers are tasked with mixing the dough after the milk is poured in. Getting and pouring the milk is not their job. So when Mickey rather than milk pours into the cake, the bakers do what the routine of their job requires of them: they mix, like cogs in an industrial machine. And it takes Mickey, who comes from outside the production line, to recognize the problem and fix it, like an industrial engineer, providing the milk that allows the cake production to flow smoothly again. Mickey is a hero for the modern age. The last image of Mickey, standing in his dough suit against the radiant sun as a sign of providence and plenty, signals his emblematic recognition as hero. Ironically, Mickey does not eat in the book—nor is he eaten—but he fulfills his destiny to provide "food . . . for the community" (Bodmer 276), so "*we* have cake every morning" (*INK*, emphasis ours). Plus, it is not just ordinary food that the hero Mickey provides: not mundane bread, but *cake*, the rich, luscious dessert-like treat that children dream of for breakfast and sometimes get in the form of morning coffee cakes, long a tradition of German-Jewish baking and so much desired by Marcus Ravage. In "Max-Mickey-Ida: Sendak's Underground Journey," George Bodmer describes Mickey in the terms of a conventional mythic hero who,

> like many heroes, is in danger himself of becoming a sacrificial meal in the 'Mickey oven.' Instead he is able to use his wits to secure the means for others to be nourished. By sacrificing his personal interests, he achieves the status of sun-god at the end of his task. James G. Frazer in *The Golden Bough* describes many European and Indian cultures who in fact fashion a doll of dough of their harvest god and eat it as a way of insuring fertility for the crops. Mickey is incarnated as a Mickey-cookie with a head bitten off, and his own head reassuringly shining through. (276)[8]

The last image and Bodmer's take on it are fascinating. In the final image of Mickey stalwartly standing while cradling the milk bottle in front of the radiant sun, he appears very much the mythic, god-like hero that Bodmer interprets him to be. But the image also looks very much like a commercial label or logo.[9] *In the Night Kitchen* transforms a mundane, commercial process into magic, and Mickey ends up the hero *of a commercial venture*, solving the milk problem, which allows the Sunshine Bakery to provide cakes in the morning for the burgeoning population of modern America. Mickey may be a hero, but he is also a potential CEO, for he occupies the liminal space of both the product and the company's savior.

A DIFFERENT WAY BACK

For the "inside-outside" trajectory that this essay has explored, it is interesting to contrast *Where the Wild Things Are* and *In the Night Kitchen*. The former is all "inside": inside the house, inside his room, inside Max's imagination. Max acts out, rebels against his mother's authority, and is sent to his room; in the reverie/fantasy, Max processes his id energy and allows ego controls to reassert themselves; on his return to his room and waking up, the space is marked by the food his mother has left for him. She metonymically reasserts control, and Max is taken back, just as Peter Rabbit is taken back in by his mother at the end of *The Tale of Peter Rabbit*. Some readings of the end of *Where the Wild Things Are* explore the possibility that Max does not fully capitulate (the presence of the wolf suit, the moon from the reverie which remains in the window[10]), but the mother-food signifier nonetheless anchors Max back home on the last two pages as he pulls off his wolf suit to transform from Wild Thing to little boy. In *In the Night Kitchen*, besides the one exclamation of "Mama! Papa!" as Mickey passes through the floor on the fourth page, Mickey is outwardly directed. Although he is younger than Max, he is the more mature character. While it seems easy to read the tall bottle of milk as a mother signifier (since mothers seem like large containers of milk to their infants), it is unmarked, unconnected in Sendak's private labeling system to his mother, who is referenced instead by name on the tomato building and by implication in the "Mama's Best Cream of Tartar," on the table after the bakers pull the cake out of the oven. And when Mickey returns home to his bed, he does so without a mother-food signifier to lull him back to sleep and rein in his accomplishments. Mickey's dream is not about exorcising id energy for ego control but about problem solving. He is responsible, and others can depend upon him. Mickey has moved independently between home and world and has done so through food. He bridges the "inside" and the "outside," and his return to home and bed defines a much more empowered relationship between the two realms than Max manages.

While Sendak incorporates food and eating in so many of his works—e.g., *Pierre, Hector Protector and As I Went Over the Water, Higglety Pigglety Pop!* and, of course, *Where the Wild Things Are*—he uses food in *In the Night Kitchen* in a far more complex and sophisticated manner. In *Where the Wild Things Are*, which Sendak viewed as his first full picture book, food is integral to the plot but in generic symbolic ways that lack any specific cultural encoding. Max operates in the family home and the land of the Wild

Things, threatening to eat others and being threatened with being eaten, but specific foods never get mentioned beyond the visually presented bowl and cake (or sandwich—reader interpretations differ) given by his forgiving mother at the end of the story. *In the Night Kitchen*, on the other hand, offers a much more richly coded food story. Mickey's journey to the Night Kitchen empowers him far more than the adventure with the Wild Things does for Max: Mickey saves not just himself from potential annihilation by escaping the cake dough but also solves the bakers' problem of providing cake for everyone. Mickey's night kitchen is a bountiful, culturally grounded table land built from a complex variety of legible social codes. Food embeds such codes, as Mary Douglas argues, and its "messages . . . will be found in the pattern of social relations being expressed. The message is about different degrees of hierarchy, inclusion and exclusion, boundaries and transactions across the borders" (61). Maurice Sendak, growing up as a native-born child of immigrants in a Brooklyn that he perceived (as an adult) as essentially a "shtetl" (Braun 220), experienced that simultaneous sense of membership and marginalization within the Jewish community and the wider American community, which like other Jewish American artists he expressed in a pattern of aesthetic coding of cultural memory. These feelings create the universalizing resonance for which the stories he wrote for children are so venerated. His experiences in a marginalized subculture mirror those of children, the primary audience of his work. As a marginalized group, children are deeply aware of social hierarchies and their place within them: they understand their lack of power, and they hunger for it. Mickey fulfills children's dreams for power within a context they can understand: the food they consume in their daily lives. By visiting the Night Kitchen, saving the day by providing the milk that the inept bakers need, Mickey demonstrates desirable confidence, skill, and competence, fulfilling a hero's quest to become a valued member of the community. Furthermore, he creates not just a mundane meal, but a fantastically appealing one: *cake* for breakfast. And in that luscious breakfast, which everyone can share thanks to Mickey, Sendak encodes both the personal experience of the Sendak household's "morning cake" that his mother made and the wider American experience of commercially made, convenient coffee cakes, the sweet treat so many children (and adults) enjoy waking up to.

DANGEROUS ANGELS: THE WEETZIE BAT BOOKS

Food, Place, and Sparkly Glam Slinkster Cool Vegetarianism in Los Angeles

As with all the works covered so far, Francesca Lia Block's Weetzie Bat books are marked by the volume of food signifiers throughout the series. The world of these novels consistently hinges on food: its preparation, consumption, location (i.e., restaurants or home), and its effects on characters' moods and well-being. As Block emphasizes in the opening paragraph of the first novel, Weetzie is deeply enamored of the food culture that surrounds her, that is very particular to Los Angeles: "the wildest, cheapest cheese and bean and hot dog and pastrami burritos at Oki Dogs," the skate-wearing waitresses "at the Jetson-style Tiny Naylor's," and "all-night potato knishes at Canter's" (*Bat* 3). Throughout the series, Block celebrates her Weetzian vision of Los Angeles by commemorating its funky and idiosyncratic restaurants. The food served in them reflects historical Los Angeles culture, both the home-grown glamor of iconic hotspots from Hollywood's early and mid-twentieth-century heyday and the emerging ethnic and transnational foods of contemporary, multicultural Los Angeles. As a city obsessed with style and brimming with newcomers from all around the world, it is no surprise that Los Angeles has long been a place that values both restaurant chic and food innovation, often (but not always) in the same venues. As food critic Jonathan Gold puts it, "Los Angeles is a city where a great meal is as likely to come from Koreatown or the three million strong Mexican community as it is from Beverly Hills, a city where inspiration is often as close as the cold case of the local Vietnamese deli" (vi). When the novel opens, the adolescent Weetzie appreciates all sides of LA food culture when dining out; as she matures and feeds her family and friends, she develops an unstated but coherent food philosophy that emphasizes healthy, vegetarian food made at home. This cuisine is based on love—of self, of family, and of community—and becomes an ethical resolution to care for the health of humans, animals, and the earth itself in a place where anyone, as the architect Jan Rowan describes Angelenos, is "able to choose what you want to be and how you want to live without worrying about social censure" (quoted in Banham, xxxiv).

Although Block sets her novels in the immensely large and complex metropolis of LA, she nonetheless creates a social landscape that functions as an open, neighborly, intimate, and transformative community, much like the vision of Laurel Canyon in The Mamas and the Papas' song "Twelve Thirty." Block uses food to map out a safe and familiar territory for her characters in a way instantly recognizable to fellow Angelenos, such as Patricia J. Campbell, who finds that the setting of the novels in Laurel Canyon, as well as contiguous environs north and south, reflects her own experiences growing up in the neighborhoods of Los Angeles:

> Driving north on Fairfax in my old VW van, I pass the Farmer's Market, where I sold melons and figs when I was in college, and where Weetzie Bat bought plastic palm tree wallets and tomahawks. Up the street is the silent movie house, with pictures of Charlie Chaplin looking like My Secret Agent Lover Man, and Canter's, where I adore the hot pastrami but Weetzie prefers the potato knishes. A little farther on, the street is lined with Jewish bakeries, falafel restaurants, and dark shops like the place where Witch Baby found the globe lamp. (57)

This vision of Los Angeles as large, multifarious, and intimate is reflected by the Pulitzer Prize–winning food writer, Jonathan Gold, a native Angeleno, who penned his restaurant review column, "Counter Intelligence," for the *LA Weekly* and *Los Angeles Times*, from 1986 to his untimely death in 2018.[1] Gold wrote about restaurants from all over the Los Angeles region because LA food culture is so rich and diverse. He notes in the introduction to his collection *Counter-Intelligence: Where to Eat in the Real Los Angeles* that "Metropolitan Los Angeles can be an overwhelming place, endless and illogical" (vi), yet over the course of his career, via his reviews, he organized his understanding of the region through the specifics of cities, neighborhoods, enclaves, cuisines, and then restaurants. Gold's reviews were never simply about a restaurant and its food but always took into account the complex of cultural forces that allow a restaurant and its food to exist and thrive within local, regional, and international contexts. Gold uses a Carrollian rabbit hole to describe what he does as a food journalist and frame his tripartite approach of food, wonder, and place:

> What I'm trying to say, I think, is that the most authentic Los Angeles experiences tend to involve a mild sense of dislocation, of tripping into a rabbit hole and popping up in some wholly unexpected location. The greatest Los Angeles cooking, real Los Angeles cooking, has first a sense of wonder about it, and only then a sense of place, because the place it has sense of is likely to be somewhere else entirely. (vi–vii)

His perspective seems particularly applicable to the Weetzie Bat series. Like Jonathan Gold, who popped us up in small, various, and intimate places throughout Los Angeles exploring particular foods as cultural ciphers, so too does Francesca Lia Block use food in the Weetzie Bat series as a lens into a particular, circumscribed place, a trail that runs from the foothills north to Hollywood and south to downtown, a circuit where Block's characters live, work, and play.

In a map of Los Angeles and Hollywood,[2] one can clearly see the limited space in which Block's characters live most of their lives: bordered by the Hollywood and Ventura Freeways on two sides, bisected by Santa Monica Boulevard, with Studio City to the north and the Farmer's Market to the south, and Universal Studios, Hollywood, the Hollywood Bowl, and Mann's Chinese Theater and the Walk of Fame nearby. This specificity is reinforced by *The Ultimate L.A. Food Guide* (1983), which identifies its reviews of markets, bakeries, groceries, and other food outlets by neighborhood and offers up local history as part of its descriptions. For example, in their sketch of the Farmer's Market at the intersection of Beverly and Fairfax, authors Jean Brady and Merle Miller note that "this famous Los Angeles landmark . . . began during the Depression, when eighteen hard-pressed farmers set up stalls in a large vacant field on the outskirts of Los Angeles in order to sell their produce and eke out a living," but it has transformed into a foodie heaven, with stalls selling "mouth-watering selections of fresh fruits and vegetables . . . the finest prime beef, lamb, pork, fish, and poultry; a cheese shop and international delicatessen; a grocery stocked with thousands of imported and domestic gourmet items; and bakers and candy-makers working behind glass for all to see" (176). It is no wonder that Weetzie adores the date shakes she buys there (*CBGG* 163). It is very easy for outsiders to regard Los Angeles as a huge, abstract, urban wash, snaked by freeways that never allow one into the city, and as a huge, unknowable, and undifferentiated urban expanse; however, Block and her characters, like other Angelenos, obviously see LA as contiguous circuits of neighborhoods whose highlights and pleasures they know and in which they indulge.

Jan Susina's 2002 article, "The Rebirth of the Postmodern Flaneur: Notes on the Postmodern Landscape of Francesca Lia Block's *Weetzie Bat*," is a superb study of the geographies—literary, cultural, and physical—of the first book in the series. It can also function as a useful platform for analysis of food throughout the series. Susina initially turns to Mike Davis's groundbreaking book, *Cities of Quartz: Excavating the Future in L.A.*, focusing on Davis's epigraph, a quotation from Walter Benjamin's essay, "The Return of the Flaneur": "The superficial inducement, the exotic, the picturesque has an effect only on the foreigner. To portray a city, a native must have other, deeper motives—motives of one who must travel into the past instead of into the distance. A native's book about his city will always be related to memories; the writer has not spent his childhood there in vain" (qtd. in Susina 189). Susina uses Benjamin to distinguish between Davis's hard-edged, critical, prophetic vision of "Fortress L.A." and Block's "magical Los Angeles framed as a fairy-tale Hollywood" (189). Davis is a native southern Californian, who writes out of disappointment at the loss of a neighborhood Los Angeles and its replacement by a corporatized LA that has concentrated power in fewer and fewer hands, disempowered everyone else, and organized the city to maximize the flows of capital (e.g., the greater LA freeway system). For Davis, this organization creates deep-seated and powerful resentments that will inevitably explode (e.g., the Rodney King riots). Conversely, Alex Raksin offers a popular culture counterargument to Davis's dark urban vision in his *Los Angeles Times* review of *City of Quartz*, contending that "the ideals and aspirations of this community have been defined in countless novels, films and songs" that offer an aesthetic response rather than one grounded in socioeconomic analysis. In the song "Twelve Thirty," their paean to Laurel Canyon, the Mamas and the Papas also offer this view of Los Angeles culture, where the narrator opens up emotionally to respond to fellow Angelenos, experiencing a genuine sense of community for the first time.

Like Raksin, Block in the Weetzie Bat books offers a contemporary and living history of neighborhood Los Angeles, one that reflects the way Angelenos generally think of their city, as seen in the Gold and Campbell quotations above, as a complex mix of Shangri-LA and Hell-A. Susina meticulously documents the specificity of place, present and past, in *Weetzie Bat* as a signifier of the novel's postmodern landscape:

> *Weetzie Bat* conveys vivid descriptions of a sense of place which often makes it read more like a travelogue of Los Angeles than a novel.... In the novel's opening paragraph, Block recounts that for Weetzie, Los Angeles means Marilyn Monroe's handprints outside of Grauman's Theater, the canyon where Jim Morrison and Houdini lived, the roller-skating waitresses at the Jetson-style Tiny Naylor, and the plastic palm tree wallets for sale at Farmer's Market [sic]. (191)

Following Reyner Banham and Mike Davis, Susina also focuses on freeways as markers of Block's postmodern landscape: "It is the very process of driving the freeways which is the defining motivation of the characters. Their constant driving reveals the essential placelessness that defines their sense of place" (190). As much as freeways do define and facilitate life in Los Angeles, freeways function less as metonymies of movement in the Weetzie Bat novels than as simple borders, framing and foregrounding the significant places and the significance of place throughout the books.[3] The foods in the books are much more indicative of the static nature of Los Angeles culture and the memories that remain rooted there despite the transitory nature of the roads, a rootedness that allows a therapeutic ethos to develop and shape the culinary arc of the series.

To continue with poetics, Block does not treat Laurel Canyon as synecdochic for all of Los Angeles. Laurel Canyon is just Laurel Canyon. In fact, all the places in the novels (including places to which the characters venture outside Los Angeles, such as the Castro District in San Francisco and the Meat District in New York) exist in their specificity, not as synecdochic representatives of some greater whole. That specificity is articulated by a vast variety of details (social, architectural, personal, and interpersonal), but of all the details those that seem to dominate—that are most striking and most telling—concern food and the places to enjoy eating it. The restaurants she references function as signs of historical continuity and remembrance. Invoking Hollywood mythology, Block has Weetzie go to Schwab's for strawberry sundaes and Canter's for bagels. Weetzie also goes with Dirk to the original and locally infamous Oki Dog for the "cheese and bean and hot dog and pastrami burritos" (*Bat* 3). Jonathan Gold also speaks lovingly of Oki Dog:

> For a while in my late teens, long before I could have told you the difference between a quesadilla and quenelle, I ate at Oki Dog more often than I did at home.... About two in the morning, after an evening

of slamming to the Germs or the Dead Kennedys at the old Starwood, I'd end up with everyone else at the Oki Dog in West Hollywood, which was the closest thing there was to a punk-rock after-hours club. If your hair resembled a chemotherapy side-effect, Oki Dog seemed a logical place to go. (224)

Gold's memory is of the same period in Oki Dog's history as and coincides well with Block's romanticization of it as a place for "punk princess" Weetzie to hang out in after clubbing with her friend Dirk (*Bat* 5; "Punk Pixies" 1). Yet, as Gold points out in his review of the new Oki Dog on Pico Boulevard, the original was "a magnet for punks and hustlers, groupies and teenage runaways" whose success became so "colorful" that it was shut down in 1990 after "a decade of neighbors' complaints" (224). Thus, by the time *Witch Baby* was published in 1991, the original Oki Dog was already a memory, an example of what, in *The History of Forgetting*, Norman Klein calls the "phantom limbs" of the Los Angeles cityscape (2–3).

Another restaurant landmark that Weetzie loves is the Tick Tock Tea Room, where her father Charlie Bat takes her for the restaurant's famous turkey platter when he comes to town to visit her. It is a nostalgic invocation of old Hollywood that, unfortunately, only makes Charlie feel his age rather than the young, ambitious screenwriter and family man poised for success that he remembers having been when he first arrived in Hollywood in the 1950s. Set in the middle of old Hollywood on Cahuenga Boulevard, a block off Hollywood Boulevard, the Tick Tock Tea Room was a product of the Great Depression, serving inexpensive sit-down meals to families of modest means in a homey setting. At the height of its success, the Tick Tock served two thousand meals a day. It closed in 1988, a year before the publication of *Weetzie Bat*, because, according to George Geary in the coffee table book *L.A.'s Legendary Restaurants: Celebrating the Places Hollywood Ate, Drank, and Played*, "Hollywood was on the decline, new competition had emerged, and the heart and soul of the tea room had died out" (98). The Tick Tock in its faded glory serves as the perfect backdrop for Weetzie's meal with her father: both a reminder of Hollywood's heyday that Weetzie's parents sought to be part of and, in its ersatz home cooking, a substitute for the home that Charlie Bat can no longer offer his daughter in Los Angeles. And, like the original Oki Dog, the Tick Tock Tea Room is a "phantom limb," another absent presence that populates the novels. Thus, as Block lovingly recreates the Los Angeles of her adolescence for her protagonist to enjoy, she makes young Weetzie an aficionado of the local restaurants of the day. Block then uses those restaurants to structure a happy, glittering nostalgia, a longing made up of evanescent experiences, presences fading into ghostly absences marked by a sense of wonder that makes it all, given Jonathan Gold's understanding of food and restaurants, "real."

As Weetzie matures, the narrative remains food focused, but the emphasis shifts to the food Weetzie makes for the family she collects around her. A strong pattern of food philosophy emerges: Weetzie gradually embraces a cuisine that is largely vegetarian (and occasionally pescatarian) and that reflects Los Angelenos' preoccupation with healthy foods. Weetzie uses such food as a means of comfort and healing, helping her friends and family when they are in distress. When My Secret Agent Lover Man is sick after his experience with Vixanne Wigg, Weetzie makes "him drink grapefruit juice and herb tea" (*Bat* 45). When Dirk goes hunting his missing lover Duck, Weetzie packs "bags and picnic baskets and thermoses and Spiderman lunch pails full of bagels, string cheese, chocolate chip cookies, milk, apples, and carrot sticks" to nourish him on his trip (*Bat* 64). The vegetarian philosophy is confirmed even more explicitly in the second novel, *Witch Baby*. Weetzie makes vegetarian lasagna for her family (*Baby* 91) and avocado sandwiches for another road trip that Dirk and Duck take (*Baby* 100–101). At a party at the beginning of *Witch Baby*, the family and friends celebrate with "Weetzie's Vegetable Love Rice, My Secret Agent Lover Man's guacamole, Dirk's homemade pizza, Duck's fig and berry salad, and Surfer Surprise Protein Punch, Brandy-Lynn's pink macaroni, Coyote's cornmeal cakes, Ping's mushu plum crepes and Valentine's Jamaican plantain pie" (*Baby* 75). Such healthy homemade vegetarian food is always served as a sign of love and community bonds. Nor do conventional gender roles govern who cooks: although serving good food to her family manifests Weetzie's maternal nature, the men (both gay and straight) also cook and follow Weetzie's lead in making vegetarian dishes.

The home that Weetzie Bat and Dirk inherit from his grandmother, Fifi, in the hills above Los Angeles, serves as the setting where the members of this large, alternative and extended family eat plentiful amounts of delicious, creatively prepared food, the place where they gather to revel in good food, music, and companionship in a repeated expression of gourmandism. In *The Physiology of Taste* (1825), Brillat-Savarin defines gourmandism as "an impassioned, considered and habitual preference for whatever pleases the taste. . . . Morally, it is an implicit obedience to the rules of the Creator, who, having ordered us to eat in order to live, invites us to do so with appetite, encourages us with flavor, and rewards us with pleasure" (148). To partake of a Weetzie feast is a guarantee of good feeling, fitting in, security, and satisfaction with both self and the world at large. Gourmandism is one of the key elements of the series' inclusive, comedic impulse. This capacity for food to create a social community is reflected in Brillat-Savarin's meditation on the "Effects of Gourmandism on Sociability" from *Physiology*: "Gourmandism is one of the most important influences in our social life; it gradually spreads the spirit of conviviality which brings together from day to day differing kinds of people, melts them into a whole, animates their conversation, and softens the sharp corners of the conventional inequalities of position and breeding" (153). In *Weetzie Bat*, Weetzie uses food as an inclusive means by which to create a healing, healthy, and whole community. Throughout the novel, food serves constantly as resolution, as source of comfort, as pleasure, as a sign of belonging. When Dirk and Duck return home at the end of the novel, the entire family, "all six of them, held onto one another in a football huddle," then "they all ate linguini and clam sauce that My Secret Agent Lover Man made, and they drank wine and lit the candles" (*Bat* 69). For Weetzie, food inevitably provides a comic resolution: "I don't know about happily ever after . . . but I know about happily, Weetzie Bat thought" (*Bat* 70). By the end of the first novel Weetzie has everything that she desires; as Witch Baby observes in *Missing Angel Juan*, "Weetzie thinks life's so slinkster cool as she would say because all her wishes came true" (263).

In Weetzie's home in Los Angeles, Meadows and Mallard's apartment in New York in *Missing Angel Juan,* and even in Duck's mother's house in Santa Cruz, Block foregrounds home food as safe, inviting, and primarily vegetarian. As the novels progress, this therapeutic food comes to dominate. It can best be labeled what Warren Belasco would call "countercuisine" (4). In *Appetite for Change: How the Counterculture Took on the Food Industry,* Belasco writes about the food revolutions that came out of the 1960s, focusing on the rise of vegetarianism as a way of rethinking "whole systems" (15), providing holistic healing, and challenging the food industry and the unhealthful, overprocessed, chemically preserved foods that it sold the American public. Besides the heavy sociopolitical impulse, Belasco also notes a lighter touch to the counterculture that used food to create a "hip pastorale . . . a way to have fun and live conscientiously" (66). Although the Weetzie novels are set one to two decades after the height of the counterculture, Block seems to adopt a similar ethos to the food she uses in the novel, as a healthful and therapeutic medium to protect her main characters from the dangers of the world in enclaves open to and inclusive of their creative sensibilities. Her characters seem to reflect a microcosm of Reyner Banham's description of the people drawn to Hollywood, "an unprecedented and unrepeatable population of genius, neurosis, skill, charlatanry, beauty, vice, talent, and plain old eccentricity" (16). To take the therapeutic vegetarian ethos back further, Tristram Stuart's history of vegetarianism, *The Bloodless Revolution*, points out that vegetarianism has been a way to redefine humans' relation with the world to focus on kindness, benevolence, nonviolence, and sympathy (xvii–xxiii). Correlative to Stuart's history, Anand Saxena in *The Vegetarian Imperative* offers a twofold, pragmatic redefinition of humanity's place in the world: avoiding the deprivation of future children through unsustainable practices (like meat eating) and consuming nutrition directly from plants rather than secondarily through animals (which feed on plants). Both of these elements result in greater health (223–30). Weetzie's daughter Witch Baby challenges Weetzie's holistic ethos after the conclusion of the first novel but comes to agree with her mother's food philosophy by the end of the series.

The sense of good feeling and belonging through vegetarian cuisine resolves Weetzie's character. In the sequels Block shifts the narrative focus primarily to Witch Baby, Weetzie's "almost daughter" (the biological daughter of My Secret Agent Lover Man and his former lover Vixanne Wigg). Witch Baby has a much harder time finding well-being and belonging, as signified by how food, vegetarian and otherwise, consistently cannot comfort her. Food usually fails to provide good feeling, pleasure, and a sense of belonging for her. Weetzie can eat a bagel and feel better, whereas food does not provide Witch Baby a remedy for her alienation. As the family celebrates the completion of their film *Dangerous Angels* with the vegetarian feast referenced above, Weetzie successfully distracts My Secret Agent Lover Man from his depression over finishing the film by offering him a "paper plate sagging with food," thereby reintegrating him into the family (*Baby* 75). Witch Baby, however, takes no part in the celebration, remains separate, and rejects Weetzie's offer of familial inclusion in the form of the Vegetable Love-Rice (*Baby* 78). Witch Baby recognizes the implicit fellowship that the feast represents and chooses emotional isolation and a growling empty stomach instead (*Baby* 75).

Each of the three *Weetzie Bat* sequels begins with Witch Baby's isolation and refusal to partake in the communal family feasts, and throughout the sequels she consistently refuses food in social settings. She only eats solitarily, on the sly, as when she steals Duck's Fig Newtons. Only when she is with Angel Juan does food tempt her; her willingness to eat peanut butter and banana sandwiches with him (*Baby* 120) serves as a sign that their relationship is healthy. When she finds her mother, Vixanne Wigg, the leader of a Jayne Mansfield cult, she is unable to establish a good relationship with her; in contrast to Weetzie, Vixanne has no good food to offer her daughter, only sugar in the form of candy and Cokes, which "aren't allowed at [Weetzie's] cottage" (*Baby* 145). Still for all of its illicit attraction, the food at her mother's house leaves Witch Baby feeling "sick and bloated from all the sugar" (*Baby* 145). The drinks fail to quench her thirst: "her throat, no matter how many sodas she is given, is parched" (*Baby* 147). Her biological mother cannot nourish her either physically or emotionally. By contrast, Witch Baby's return home is marked by special parental attention from Weetzie and My Secret Agent Lover Man, accompanied by a feast of substantial healthy foods: "homemade Weetzie pizza with sun-dried tomatoes, fresh basil, red onions, artichoke hearts, and a spinach crust" (*Baby* 150). Witch Baby is finally willing to partake of the food and fellowship her family offers and momentarily feels a part of the house and family. The resolution that Witch Baby feels at the end of this novel is characterized by a sense of melancholy, of which "her own sadness was only a small piece of the puzzle of pain that made up the globe" (*Baby* 154). Her blues, however, are tempered with a sense of emotional connection: "But she was a part of the globe—she had her place. And there was a lot of happiness as well, a lot of love" (*Baby* 154). Witch Baby has moved away from the emotional isolation of the novel's beginning, and at the conclusion her emotional state parallels Weetzie's mood at the end of *Weetzie Bat*: both are aware of pain but choose in the moment to focus on the love and happiness of the world.

This sense of connection for Witch Baby proves to be fleeting, however. In the next two sequels, *Cherokee Bat and the Goat Guys* and *Missing Angel Juan*, Witch Baby once again feels estranged from the family and refuses to eat. In *Cherokee Bat and the Goat Guys,* she refuses to participate in her birthday party, even though Cherokee and Raphael "made three kinds of salsa and a special dish of crumbled corn bread, green chiles, artichoke hearts, cheese and red peppers," until Angel Juan shows up, at which point the "half-starved young girl" joins the party for the ice-cream birthday cake (*CBGG* 170–71). The adults are absent in this novel, off making a movie, and the youngsters are on their own. During this period of independence, they discover their sexuality: Cherokee with Raphael and Witch Baby with Angel Juan. Their band becomes successful, aided by magic real animal gifts: feathered wings and goat haunch jeans, goat hoof boots, and goat horns. The first two, Coyote reminds Cherokee, "were gifts the animals gave you without death, untainted" (192). The latter two, however, have disturbing elements of animal corpses: "The hooves . . . bristled with tiny hairs" (*CBGG* 229). As the teens' band, The Goat Guys, becomes more successful, they sink further into the drug-induced haze of the club scene, and joyful sexuality shifts to disturbing carnality, love becomes lust as the tainted animality of the animal talismans creates destructive effects. Raphael smokes, first tobacco then marijuana; they drink whiskey and tequila while performing; they go to parties where cocaine is common; Angel Juan begins cutting himself onstage so that he is covered in blood. Cherokee, like Witch Baby, becomes anorexic: "[Cherokee] took the armload of fur and bone into the bathroom, pulled off her clothes, and stared at her reflection—a weak, pale girl, the shadows of her ribs showing bluish through her skin like an X-ray" (234). After Coyote rescues Cherokee from a suicide attempt when she wears all the animal gifts at once, she wakes from her drug- and depression-induced stupor to the love of her friends: Raphael is with her, promising to stop taking drugs and smoking, and then "Coyote, Witch Baby, and Angel Juan came in with strawberries, cornmeal pancakes, maple syrup and bunches of real roses and irises that looked like the windows come to life" (244). The healthy vegetarian food, removed from the fleshly carnality/sexuality of the club scene, heals Cherokee and restores all four of the teens to a healthy, loving relationship once again. The novel ends with yet another Weetzie feast of luscious vegetarian cuisine:

> At the end of the summer, The Goat Guys set up their instruments on the redwood stage their families had helped them build behind the canyon house. . . . A picnic of salsa, home-baked bread still steaming in its own crust, hibiscus lemonade and cake decorated with fresh flowers was spread on the lawn. Summer had ripened to its fullest—a fruit ready to drop, leaving the autumn tree glowing faint amber with its memory as the band played on the stage for their family and friends. (251)

Here at the conclusion of the novel, place, time, and cuisine converge as Block figures the season itself as food. The harvest party celebrates the reunion of the family and the harmony of the young musicians who play their music outdoors in the fresh air for the pleasure of their family and themselves, not for the fame and idolatry they had sought in the smoke and drug-riddled club scene.

This food-fueled resolution once again proves to be short lived when the next book starts. In *Missing Angel Juan*, the inevitably isolated Witch Baby takes the biggest risk in the series: in order to find the boy she loves, she leaves behind the safe cottage in Laurel Canyon for the wilds of New York City, which, coherent with Weetzie's vegetarian ethos, turns out to be a haven of vegetarian food—when Witch Baby is willing to open herself to it and the love it represents. All too frequently, however, Witch Baby reverts to her anorexic patterns, emotionally isolating herself as she refuses to eat. The two gay almost-uncles, Meadows and Mallard, who look after the apartment that belonged to Weetzie's father Charlie, insist on feeding Witch Baby when she arrives, starting with the groceries they have stocked for her to take up to the apartment: "As he closes the door, I feel loneliness tunnel through my body. I look inside the bag of food and there's granola, milk, strawberries, bananas, peanut butter, bagels, mineral water and peppermint tea. I sit on the old trunk and eat a banana-and-peanut-butter bagel sandwich to try to fill up the tunnel the loneliness made" (*MAJ* 285). The two old men insist on taking Witch Baby out for macrobiotic cuisine at a restaurant the next night, and Witch Baby feels in her body the comforting effects of their companionship and care in the food they provide for her: "Miso-oniony, golden-pumpkiny, sweety-lotusy, sesame-seaweedy. The food makes me stop shaking" (*MAJ* 289). But Witch Baby knows she will lose this temporary emotional high, that "tonight with its macro-heaven dinner and goddess music will fade, leaving me just as empty as before" when her almost-uncles leave on a trip (*MAJ* 291). She recovers the sense of well-being and emotional connection, however, when she meets her ghostly almost-grandfather and Virgil-like guide Charlie Bat, who takes her the next morning for breakfast to Sylvia's soul food restaurant in Harlem, a place that "smells like somebody's kitchen" where Charlie used to bring Weetzie so that she could experience a kind of home cooking when she visited him (*MAJ* 300–301). Although she initially orders only coffee, the scent of food and Charlie's gentle urging persuade her to eat "the best breakfast [she's] ever had" of "eggs, grits, and sweet-potato pie" (*MAJ* 300–301). The next night, again at the prompting of Charlie, Witch Baby goes to an Indian restaurant, where she eats "saffron-yellow vegetable curry with candy-glossy chutney, rice and lentil-bread" (*MAJ* 316). She gives in to the pleasure of the spicy food, feeling "sort of high" from it (*MAJ* 317). Throughout these early adventures in New York City, Witch Baby has her protectors in this faraway land, who feed her food that Meadows defines as "apotropaic," that is, food that protects her by warding off evil (*MAJ* 284).

Charlie, the ghost, cannot eat: he misses the pleasures of the flesh and wants Witch Baby to eat not just because it is good for her but so that he can vicariously enjoy her meals. Although her emotional distress over the missing Angel Juan makes her less inclined to eat, he pushes her to pay attention to food in ways for him that she would be unlikely to notice for herself. When they go to a market, "Charlie is flickering from the rainbow pastas to the stuffed grape leaves, from the egg rolls to the greens, between the beans, seeds, nuts, cheese, dried figs and dates and pineapple, muffins, corn bread, carrot cake, pastel puddings, fruit, cookies." Despite Charlie urging her to sample widely, Witch Baby will only buy "a pink sushi roll and a fortune cookie" (*MAJ* 305–6). Once home, Charlie wants to know how it tastes. Witch Baby replies with a list of ingredients for the vegetarian roll—"Seaweed, sesame, spinach, carrot, radish sprouts"—that Charlie finds unhelpful:

> "Witch Baby, remember that I'll never get to eat another thing."
>
> "Okay, okay." I close my eyes to get the tastes better. "The avocado's silky and the rice is sweetish—that might be pink sugar or something. The ginger's got like a tang. The horseradish burns right through my nostrils to my brain."
>
> "Thank you," he says. He sighs like he's just eaten a big meal. (*MAJ* 307)

As a spirit, Charlie literally cannot experience the pleasures of the flesh; he can only enjoy food in a language-mediated form, which describes texture and flavor but is a poor substitute for the embodied experience of taste and eating. Yet in articulating her own experience to meet his need, Witch Baby can enjoy her own food on multiple levels.

Yet despite Charlie's desires, Witch Baby gradually moves further away from the meals her guardians want her to consume. Her primary food becomes rice cakes. When Charlie chides her for how little she's eating, she tries to please him: "'Couldn't you put something on that thing? . . . It tastes—I mean it looks like you are eating cardboard. . . . You're getting so skinny.' Because I want him to enjoy my meal a little, I go and get some peanut butter" (*MAJ* 328–29). Her refusal to eat makes Witch Baby easy prey when she encounters the villain of the novel, the unhealthily named Cake who owns a diner, Cake's Shakin' Palace, in the meat-packing district: "I make great hamburgers. . . . Or milk shakes if you are a grass-eating vegetarian" (*MAJ* 347). Cake's disdain for the vegetarian ethos Witch Baby has grown up with in Weetzie's home marks him as unethical and dangerous. Witch Baby, weakened by her self-starvation, succumbs to his carnivorous seduction:

"I'm okay," I say. I don't want to eat but all of a sudden my stomach starts making noises like I haven't had food in it for weeks. Then I remember I really haven't eaten anything except some rice cakes in a while.

. . . [H]e starts scooping and mixing and whirring until he has made this amazing thick frosty snowy whipped-cream-topped vanilla milkshake. He puts it in a tall parfait glass, plops on one of those poison red candied cherries Weetzie won't let us eat, sinks in a straw and sets it on the counter. Then he presses raw meat into a patty and slaps that onto the sizzling grill. I haven't eaten a hamburger in a long time because no one at my house is into meat anymore but that meat smells pounceable. I feel dizzy. I skulk over to the milkshake on the counter and take a sip. . . . But the sweet milkiness is like warm kisses so I just keep inhaling on that straw even with my head and chest frozen and hurting.

The man finishes the hamburger, slides it onto a fat sourdough bun, adds lettuce and onions and a juicy slab of tomato, stabs the whole thing with a toothpick and then sets it in front of me on a plate. I almost fall on top of it. I can taste the meat before my teeth plunge in. (*MAJ* 348–49)

The "poison" Maraschino cherry signifies the general unhealthiness of Cake's meal: artificially bleached and recolored, preserved in heavy sugar syrup (Davidson 165), the adulterated cherries certainly do not fit Weetzie's beliefs in healthy eating, with which Witch Baby contrasts Cake's cooking. Yet Witch Baby finds the milkshake alluring, comparing its sugar with kisses despite the fact that drinking it hurts: the milkshake is thus a food that creates a disturbing linkage between eroticism and pain. The hamburger is described wholly in succulent, even sexualized terms here ("pounceable" is a term that Witch Baby and her family usually use to describe sexual attraction), but Witch Baby soon feels its ill effects on her body as she realizes that she feels "drugged by [her] meaty hamburger" (*MAJ* 349). She wakes up in a bed hung with silk, afraid to think about who put her there (*MAJ* 353): a moment that links the carnivorous with dangerous carnality.

Cake's plan to drug Witch Baby and freeze her into a white plastic mannequin bears marked parallels to the witch in Hansel and Gretel, who also get ensnared with tempting food and nearly baked before escaping. While Gretel turns on the Witch, shoving her into the oven and baking her to rescue her brother Hansel, Witch Baby turns Cake into a mannequin in a moment of magic realism, thus avoiding becoming a mannequin and freeing herself and Angel Juan. When the two return to Charlie Bat's apartment, they find that Mallard and Meadows have returned and left more healthy groceries for them, which they consume before sleeping. Buoyed up by this vegetarian rush, Witch Baby ends the novel with a lengthy self-reflection that returns her to a centered, psychological wholeness, allowing her to return to her family in Los Angeles while also contentedly accepting Angel Juan's choice to make his way in New York. She is secure enough to both receive the love of her family and not "clutch" Angel Juan, the love of her life.

Throughout the series, Block recognizes the value of food as a useful delimiting agent that signifies the nurturing of life or its absence, the exploitation of life. *Missing Angel Juan*, like the other Weetzie Bat books, concludes with a feast, but Witch Baby's epiphany differs significantly from Weetzie's: Witch Baby comes to realize that community depends on letting people go and return in their own time, and that she must let go of Angel Juan rather than force him into a relationship he is not yet ready for. As such, the end of *Missing Angel Juan* represents a great step forward and extension of the cottage community in Laurel Canyon. Vegetarian gourmandism and the community implicit in it serve as a grounding principle for both emotional and physical well-being.

* * *

In *Space and Place: The Perspective of Experience*, the geographer Yi-fu Tuan explores how humans manage two fundamental categories of the ways we experience the world around us, space and place, and he describes the relationship between the two as follows: "What begins as undifferentiated space becomes place as we get to know it better and endow it with value" (6). Tuan spends the rest of the book investigating the multitudinous ways that we make space into place as knowledge creates value. One avenue Tuan pursues is the senses, in particular taste (as well as smell and touch, important adjuncts to taste): "the French verb 'savoir' (to know) is closely related to the English 'savour.' Taste, smell, and touch are capable of exquisite refinement. They discriminate among the wealth of sensations and articulate gustatory, olfactory, and textural worlds" (6). Jonathan Gold made sense of metropolitan Los Angeles through his restaurant reviews, taking a region "overwhelming" (vi) in its size and complexity and transforming it into known and edible places for himself and his readers, valued for the extraordinary quality and quantity of available cuisines. For the geography of the *Weetzie Bat* series, Block does something similar, linking knowledge, taste, and place as central to the narrative arc of the series. Initially, taste and place are marked by nostalgia, a desire for foods and restaurants of the Los Angeles past, but as the novels progress, the culinary signifier that dominates the value of place is vegetarianism. And the signal effect of that culinary shift is also a shift in place from restaurants to home, where the heterogeneous community of the novels can more easily gather and where vegetarian food can more easily be prepared and provide physical, emotional, ethical, and intellectual support, thus reinforcing and shaping the nature of home. For all the wild eclecticism of Block's world, it is a comfortable home with a well-stocked kitchen full of healthy vegetarian ingredients—where knowledgeable cooks happily work together making meals—that makes such eclecticism possible and sustainable. This open, wide-ranging, inclusive vision of food, people, and place allows the unifying comic impulse of the novels to finally settle and rest.

RATATOUILLE AND RESTAURANTS

A Portrait of the Artist as a Young Rat

> Animals fill themselves; men eat; but only wise men alone know the art of eating. (15)
>
> —JEAN ANTHELME BRILLAT-SAVARIN, THE PHYSIOLOGY OF TASTE (1825)

Rat tales are food tales. While mice are sometimes granted nonfood interests, such as Leo Lionni's Frederick, rat stories nearly always revolve around the rats' obsession with food. Templeton, from E. B. White's *Charlotte's Web*, is typical in his gluttonous preoccupation with the leftovers from Wilbur's trough and the "veritable treasure of popcorn fragments, frozen custard dribblings, candied apples abandoned by tired children, sugar fluff crystals, salted almonds, popsicles, partially gnawed ice cream cones, and the wooden sticks of lollypops" (123) at the fair. Before they are captured, the rats in Robert C. O'Brien's *Mrs. Frisby and the Rats of NIMH* forage after hours in a farmers' market that is a rat's paradise, feeding on "peas and beans that fell from the trucks, tomatoes and squashes, pieces of meat and fish trimmed as waste—they lay on the sidewalks and in the gutters; they filled great cans that were supposed to be covered but seldom were. There was always ten times more than we could eat, and so there was never any need for fighting over it" (100).

This quick sketch of a couple of famous rat tales suggests that authors who use rats as characters are well aware of the species's real-life behaviors and adapt them for their own narrative purposes. Rats live off what humans throw away; they are associated with gluttony and uncleanness. Robert Sullivan, in *Rats: Observations on the History and Habitat of the City's Most Unwanted Inhabitants*, notes that human and rat lives are indissolubly intertwined:

"Rats live in man's parallel universe, surviving on the effluvia of human society; they eat our garbage" (2). Humans categorize both rats and mice as vermin, as rodent threats to human safety, health, and cleanliness: they infest human dwellings, eat human food, and leave excrement and insect hazards in human habitats. Nonetheless, mice have long occupied a homey niche in stories for children: while no one wants a mouse in the house, readers apparently enjoy stories of tiny, underdog mice.[1] In her foundational work, *Animal Land: The Creatures of Children's Fiction*, Margaret Blount claims that stories about mice "outnumber those about any other kind of animal" (152). Oddly, in a book devoted to animal characters, she mentions only two rat characters: Templeton from *Charlotte's Web* and Rat from *The Wind in the Willows* (perhaps not realizing his true species as a water vole). In neither case, however, does she discuss the general function of rat characters in fiction, as she does for so many other kinds of animals (both real and imaginary) within her study. Catherine Elick, in *Talking Animals in Children's Fiction: A Critical Study*, initially folds rats into her discussion of mice in animal fantasy rather than exploring the species's distinguishing attributes (19), although she does later devote a chapter to discussing O'Brien's *Mrs. Frisby and the Rats of NIMH*. Most people, though, would choose to deal with a mouse infestation rather than a rat infestation; humans see rats as by far the more alarming rodent because they are larger, more aggressive, and thus carry a much stronger vermin taint. It is not surprising, therefore, that rats are much rarer fictional characters in children's stories; distinguishing rats from mice as separate categories of animal characters is essential in discussing rat tales. Even in a fictional setting, authors have more difficulty in erasing the vermin taint from rat characters as opposed to mice.[2]

Disney•Pixar's *Ratatouille* takes on the challenge of the vermin signifier, focusing on a rat who wants to be a chef, to make his career in the kitchen, in essence triggering humans' fears of dirt and disease in proximity to food. An inherent oxymoron—the vermin who can produce the best food—thus lies at the heart of the story. The film tackles this contradiction head on in the opening scene, which first features Remy's expulsion from a kitchen (carrying the cookbook that is his bible) and then his declaration as narrator about his freeze-framed self: "This is me. What's my problem? First of all, I'm a rat, which means life is hard." The visual artists emphasize Remy's ratness, and his status as Other, by shifting the visual scene to a menacing rat darting out from behind a barrel, silhouetted by sunset; the rat then scuttles on all fours across the ground and joins a large group of rats which scurry through the grass to a compost heap. This scene brilliantly captures the physical movement of rats, a realism the Pixar artists were able to create because a "tank of rats sat in the animation hallway for more than a year for research on how the little creatures moved their feet and paws, what happens with their tail as they run and how their noses and ears work" ("Ratatouille Edit Bay Visit!"). This detailed, intensive study of rats, designed to recreate them on screen realistically, is the exact opposite of how humans usually treat rats, according to Sullivan: "rats are ignored, destroyed but rarely studied, disparaged but never described" (2). Instead, this film celebrates and describes attentively rats' abilities and intelligence. Most importantly, in the end, *Ratatouille* does not destroy its rat characters or suggest that they should be exterminated: it presents a vision of human/rat coexistence, albeit on a limited scale. The film makes us aware of the parallel between rats and humans. Sullivan notes that rats are "our mirror species," and *Ratatouille* forces us to look in that mirror and acknowledge the connection.

Thus at its heart, *Ratatouille* runs counter to the most common pattern of animal story that Kathleen Johnson traces, in which a human becomes attached to an animal but must then sever the emotional ties between them, most frequently through the death or abandonment of the animal, in order to achieve maturity (81). Remy's story, however, features a growing attachment between human and animal, and although those bonds of affection get strained at times, the film ultimately affirms them through the mutual success of Remy and his human friends Linguini, Colette, and Ego. Rather than objectifying the animal, the film grants him subjectivity. Using Bakhtin, Elick sees animal stories as moral spaces where readers "enter into a dialogic relationship with animals that stimulates ethical interactions with them" (9). Although *Ratatouille* is a film, not a novel, it serves the same function, creating a reflective process that invites viewers to value the subjectivity of characters that could be defined as Other. Elick protests the common assumption in animal fiction for children that "abandoning or killing an animal should be requisite to maturity" (6). Conversely, then, true maturity should be reached through emotional engagement with animals, recognizing that they possess at least a kind of subjectivity. Throughout the film, Remy and his family are constantly threatened with extermination. In fact, Remy's relationship with Linguini begins when the garbage boy is assigned to kill the rat found in the kitchen but cannot bring himself to do it. He thus starts their relationship with empathy and compassion, which grow into friendship, developing a strong emotional bond rather than severing it. The film's movement beyond that common story pattern suggests a better ethical arc, one that that acknowledges the value of the continuing existence of an Other's, in this case a rat's, subjectivity.

Ratatouille pursues this ethical arc through food. If rat tales are food tales, *Ratatouille* is the foodiest of them all, and thus where better to set the story of a would-be rat chef than Paris, the acknowledged world capital of haute cuisine? To the strains of "La Marseillaise," the opening voiceover equates Frenchness and fine food: "We French know the truth: the best food in the world is made in France, the best food in France is made in Paris, and the best food in Paris, some say, is made by Chef Auguste Gusteau." Gusteau will be the mentor for Remy's *Künstlerroman*, which will chart the rat's blossoming as chef and creative artist, from the realization of his extraordinary palate, to the exercise of his keen sense of flavor and ingredient combinations, to his training in Gusteau's kitchen, to becoming executive chef, when he exhibits the full flowering of both his culinary and organizational genius. Remy is first a student and then a practitioner of the complex kitchen culture represented by Gusteau's restaurant, where the cooking is based on a set of practices that developed in France after the French Revolution and that produced French haute cuisine. Lying at the core of French national identity, this Parisian food culture raised food preparation to a high art, chefs to artists, and restaurants to "culinary temples of art," as Katherina Balazs claims (135). Priscilla Ferguson reinforces the same idea in *Accounting for Taste: The Triumph of French Cuisine*: "it is the tour de force of French cuisine to be defined as at once national and cosmopolitan" (4). Remy's development as a French chef thus required Pixar to depict the many nuances of the discipline of haute cuisine—canonized as a "codified cuisine" (Trubek 11, 13–25)—that were developed in the nineteenth and twentieth centuries through leading chefs and that are still used in high-end restaurants around the world. Thus, an understanding of the specifics of how French haute cuisine developed yields a fuller understanding of Remy's *Künstlerroman* arc.

Remy's story strongly reflects the development of French cuisine over the last two centuries, after the demise of the Ancien Régime and the highly privileged culinary culture it funded. In the wake of the Revolution, cooks had to carve a niche in the new public sphere. Restaurants proliferated, and a broader swath of French society could afford fine food. A new generation of chefs, particularly Marie-Antoine Carême (1784–1833), simplified the food (ingredients and presentation) for a bourgeois budget and created a standardized set of preparation techniques and recipes, pioneering "the effort to systematize the principles of the modern cuisine that emerged after the French Revolution" (Rao et al. 799). Later in the nineteenth and into the twentieth centuries, Auguste Escoffier (1846–1935) "simplified professional kitchen organization further" (800) and wrote cookbooks (for example, *Le Guide Culinaire* [1903], which standardized and disseminated haute cuisine for restaurants and home kitchens alike). Gusteau's kitchen follows the same model that Carême and Escoffier created, as Remy confirms when Gusteau's spirit catechizes him on kitchen organization as they watch the cooks in action from the skylight window: chef, sous-chef, saucier, chef de partie, commis, plongeur, etc.

Carême, who was abandoned as a child on the streets of Paris by his father (Ferguson, *Accounting for Taste* 55), successfully pulled himself up from the bottom of the social ladder through a passionate dedication to food. Whether Pixar deliberately intended such an allusion or not, Remy does the same. Like Carême, who intensively read French culinary literature to adapt historical knowledge to a post-Revolutionary social context, Remy reads Gusteau's *Anyone Can Cook* as a transformative text whose knowledge puts him on the path to culinary artistry and propels him from ratdom to a hybrid rat-human existence. Remy's interest and studies should qualify him to begin work in the world of French restaurants, but of course his status as a rat sets him up as a perpetual outsider. French culinary culture, though, has historically been structured to be receptive to innovation: as Jean François Revel said in *A Feast of Words*, "Great cuisine is by definition open cuisine" (quoted in Beaugé 7). The restaurant kitchen ethos thus enables Remy as a rat, in this animal fantasy, to insert himself in a place to which his Otherness would seem on the surface to deny him entrance; paradoxically, it gives him the hard-won freedom to inhabit the top of the social scale as culinary artist, although such triumph does not occur without setbacks and complications. For Rao et al., in "Institutional Change in Toque Ville," the organizational history of French cuisine has developed with a logic that emphasizes "individual autonomy" (795) as the primary engine of change. Changes in haute cuisine come not only through ingredients, techniques, technologies, and recipes but, most importantly, through actors: creative individuals who can transform the past into the future. Through its portrayal of Remy and his struggle to explore his inherent food-oriented talent to become a chef, the film shows how even within the hierarchical and privileged world of haute cuisine an outsider like Remy with a creative vision can move to the inside. In their film review "Sociology at the Stove," Priscilla Ferguson and Gary Alan Fine interpret Remy as casting off his identity as vermin to come above ground and take his place as a productive, recognized member of society: "Remy offers a startling case of social mobility, from the dank underground and its rank refuse to the glossy restaurant and its silky creations" (59). Thus, haute cuisine serves as a surprisingly optimal cultural ground for an animal character in a work of fiction, like Remy in *Ratatouille*, to explore the ethics—the possibilities, really—between center and margin, the hegemonic and subaltern: to blur the divisions between what viewers are happy to digest and what makes us feel abject.

This blurring can be seen as bootstrap empowerment. Remy's arc is embodied in Gusteau's cookbook title, *Anyone Can Cook,* which is liberally restated at key moments of plot and character development throughout the film because it is, as Eric Herhuth argues, one of the three central themes in *Ratatouille*: "anyone can cook," "the new needs friends," and "change is nature" (469). Yet, despite the story structure of progress and hope, the vermin signifier persists to the end, where it is at best obscured only slightly. In spite of having learned to prepare and eat fine cuisine, at the end of the movie the rats remain segregated—dining apart from the privileged (mostly white, French) humans they serve in Gusteau's as well as seated in a separate (but equal?) space from the human customers in Remy's eponymous bistro, Ratatouille. While the rats might seem to represent a radical/carnivalesque restructuring of haute cuisine, paralleling the way Elick develops a Bakhtinian interpretation of animal fantasy, they actually end up in the untenable position of reinforcing its traditional hierarchy through their cooption into the strict order of the *haute* kitchen and restaurant. Thus, countering the film's empowering thread, Remy and his fellow rats represent what Amy Trubek characterizes as the paradoxical linkage of the egalitarian and the elite in post-Revolutionary haute cuisine: with democratization, "haute cuisine became part of a much broader and deeper configuration of elite culture" (145). In *Ratatouille*, even rats can uphold *hauteness* while they are also oppressed by it.

* * *

The film starts in a country house of an old woman who does not know about the rat colony that lives in her attic. The old woman clearly cares about good food and is the film's first proof of Gusteau's egalitarian philosophy, articulated in the title of his cookbook, *Anyone Can Cook*. The kitchen is well stocked: Remy runs past pears, carrots, apples, red grapes, strawberries, and cheese on the counter and later investigates her spice rack while searching for saffron. Although we do not see the woman in her kitchen, her supplies indicate that she is a good cook. A perfect audience for Carême and Escoffier, who disseminated recipes and technical skills down the social scale and from the city to the country, the old woman lives in the French countryside, "is a food lover" (by Remy's own estimation), and owns the cookbook of a Parisian chef. Unbeknownst to her, she shares these skills and interests with an ambitious rat who lives in her house, uses her kitchen, and is becoming a food connoisseur.

The old woman's country kitchen is the preparation station, the mise en place, for the *Künstlerroman* plot. An irony underlies its role, for within her house, right above her apparently clean kitchen, lurks a large rat colony. Reflecting Robert Sullivan's point about rats forming a "parallel universe" to humans (2), the two species' living spaces are separate in the beginning of *Ratatouille*: the rats' maintenance of their colony depends on human ignorance of its existence. The only rat to cross the social boundary—always in secret—is Remy, who has been using the well-stocked human kitchen to teach himself about French foodways and cooking, both through reading the old woman's copy of Gusteau's cookbook and during occasional chances to watch Gusteau's cooking show on her television, when she is dozing. Priscilla Ferguson, who focuses her interpretation of the film on Remy's growth as an artist, notes Remy's social ambition as well as his individuality: "Like other chefs who find themselves at odds with their milieu, this would-be chef is distinctly different from his fellow rats. . . . This unusual rat wants to cook because he wants to create" (Ferguson, *Word of Mouth* 198). Given that chefs are artists whose medium is food,[3] Remy demonstrates Elick's defining characteristics of animal fantasy: "Animal protagonists in many classic fantasies are artists of various types. . . . Some animal fantasies . . . even make artistic creation their central subject and become veritable *Künstlerromane*," because "artistic creation suggests animals' affinity with humanity while it concomitantly underscores animal agency and empowerment" (19–20). The film thus plays with the paradox that food is an ideal medium for a cartoon fantasy rat seeking an artistic outlet while simultaneously invoking the standard human response of disgust to rats as a vector for filth and disease, particularly in relation to the food that feral rats seek in human habitations.

Ratatouille establishes Remy at the beginning of the film as a talented naïf who has begun to explore his untutored but highly sensitive palate. He has already developed the ability to parse out flavors and ingredients, as he shows when analyzing a discarded piece of cake: "Flour, eggs, sugar, vanilla bean. Oh! Small twist of lemon!" The lemon offers a note of surprise for Remy, a suggestion that he is on the lookout for subtle novelty. Remy's father Django, impressed with his son's outstanding scent and taste abilities, appoints him as the poison checker for the colony.[4] But Remy finds merely checking food for poison a monotonous task; his boredom sends him into the human kitchen, the site of invention and creativity, where a panoply of tastes can be more temptingly realized and experienced. His trips to the kitchen become his "secret life," shared only with his good-natured, gluttonous brother Emile, who accepts but does not understand Remy's increasingly refined tastes. Emile, in true rat fashion, prefers quantity to quality and is quite happy eating garbage in greater safety outside, rather than risking exposure in the human kitchen.

Beginning to discover his aptitude as he learns to combine foods and cook, and thus becoming more like the humans who fascinate him, Remy breaks the status quo, the barrier between human and rat worlds. As he asserts his humanity, however, the vermin signifier asserts itself just as forcefully. While he was learning both reading and cooking skills in the old woman's kitchen, Remy was able to remain invisible. But when he creates cuisine outside out of items he has foraged, scavenged, and cooked (the smoked mushroom cheese puff seasoned with rosemary and accidentally flash-grilled with lightning), he feels the need to enter the house in search of the finishing touch—the saffron in the spice rack—that will give his culinary creation the perfect combination of flavors. Once he does so, Remy violates the rat-human barrier irretrievably. When the old woman wakes up and discovers Remy and his brother Emile in her kitchen, she cannot perceive Remy as a fellow cook, nor does she see the grilled mushroom cheese puff. The vermin signifier acts as the only lens through which she can see Remy, a perspective the film reinforces by switching out of Remy's narration to her point of view: while Remy (following the conventions of animal fantasy) uses language to alert Emile of their danger in his account of the story, at this crucial moment the film deliberately breaks his dominant viewpoint, switching from fantasy into realism. The film alternates back and forth from Remy's dialogue with Emile to focalizing the old woman's view of two rats on her floor and countertop that are squeaking, not speaking. Driven by revulsion and the overzealous need to protect her house and kitchen, she uses a shotgun to try to exterminate them. Instead, she brings the whole rat colony down upon her, destroying the status quo, ridding herself of vermin, and wrecking the house with finality, a neat symbol for the mutually destructive nature of humans' long war of extermination against rats. The forcible expulsion of the rats from the house is an abjectifying act. Within the arc of the film's thesis on rat subjectivity, Remy's humanity comes to outweigh his status as vermin in his growth as artist and individual, but within the human world the vermin signifier is much slower to change. The tension between these two modes of being and perception functions to drive the plot, while the film searches for a more productive and symbiotic resolution to the relationship. Elick's Bakhtinian take on *Stuart Little* best parallels the construction and development of Remy's identity and its impact on the viewers of the film: like E. B. White's classic novel, *Ratatouille*

> disturbs the clear demarcations humans have drawn between themselves and other living beings in order to maintain ascendancy in a human-devised species hierarchy. White's insistence on Stuart's indeterminacy and unfinalizability—he simply *is* both a mouselike animal and a human and must remain so—gives readers the posthumanist license to acknowledge that all humans *are* animals and to look for ways to level those systems of value and behavior that allow humans to exploit nonhuman species. (Elick 169)

Although Remy's rat identity is more fixed than Stuart's mousehood, his status and capabilities as an artist shift him further along the spectrum from animal toward human, moving both the film and the viewers away from easy acceptance of vermin extermination. Remy's subjectivity becomes accepted by more characters within the film, leading to the end scene at the Ratatouille bistro where the vermin and human signifiers are in close proximity and the human/rat relationship is tantalizingly indeterminate and open.

The key to understanding Remy's arc as an artist is his improvisation of the mushroom cheese puff. His first culinary creation does not result from simple replication of one of Gusteau's cookbook recipes but through inspiration as he extemporizes a dish from what he and Emile have found while foraging and scavenging: "You found cheese? And not just any cheese. *Tomme de chèvre de pays!* That would go beautifully with my mushroom. And . . . and . . . and . . . this rosemary! This rosemary with maybe, maybe a few drops from this sweet grass! . . . There are possibilities unexplored here." Remy is not inventing in a vacuum. His comments to Emile reveal that he is an autodidact: even before the opening scene of the film he has learned to read and has extensively studied Gusteau's cookbook and television show. Empowered by literacy, which Elick contends "is crucial to the animal characters' success in dealing with humans" (19–20), this metaknowledge inspires him to create something new, beyond the static recipes he has read. Moreover, what impels him is not simply the desire to be a cook in a kitchen but the ambition to be a heroic, creative chef, an artist who is true to his own vision and medium. Daring the dangers of the kitchen to find the saffron, which will perfect the puff, Remy's ambitions for bold culinary adventures are reinforced by Gusteau himself, who declaims on television that "Great cooking is not for the faint of heart. You must be imaginative, strong hearted. You must try things that may not work. And you must not let anyone define your limits because of where you come from. Your only limit is your soul. What I say is true: anyone can cook, but only the fearless can be great." This statement is essentially Remy's raison d'être as artist and chef, and it frames what becomes the plot driver of the *Künstlerroman*. Remy's daring, his first act of culinary creation, almost gets him killed, first by lightning and second by the old woman and her shotgun. Remy must abandon the unfinished puff, because the attempt to complete its cooking accidentally severs both Remy and the rat colony from their home in the attic of the country house, sending them all to Paris, the food capital of France, which will become the scene of Remy's triumph as hero-chef. In Paris, Remy's three acts of creative daring at Gusteau's restaurant (soup, sweetbreads, ratatouille) organize and impel the plot.

While the early scenes in the movie display Remy's already considerable abilities as a cook, once he is in Paris, about to enter Gusteau's kitchen, Remy shows how much he knows about the professional organization of the kitchen when Gusteau's spirit quizzes him about the hierarchy. Out of the seething commotion of a restaurant kitchen in full swing for the dinner shift, Remy correctly identifies who the chef is as well as his subordinates, their individual responsibilities, and how they work together in an orderly manner despite the apparent chaos. His administrative knowledge of the kitchen hierarchy is one important requirement to become a fully fledged chef. He must, however, find his own place within the kitchen. When Remy sees with alarm that the newly hired *plongeur*/garbage boy, Linguini, has ruined the simmering soup on the stove by adding random ingredients to make up for what he spilled, the rat leans too far and falls through the skylight window into the kitchen.

The film cleverly parallels Remy's earlier expulsion from the old woman's kitchen through its window, particularly in Remy's abjectification in both incidents. Just as he was ejected as a rat from the home kitchen, Remy operates as an undesirable vermin in his first minutes in Gusteau's kitchen, getting a hellish tour and nearly being killed several times as he seeks to hide himself: almost drowned in dishwater, stepped on, burned by the stove's fire, even nearly cooked in a casserole dish. The vermin signifier is very strong: Remy runs on all fours, scuttles from shelter to shelter, scales shelves, all in his attempts to escape. Yet as he nears success, racing toward the open window by the stove, he is arrested by the soup's stinking aroma, which makes him gag—an equally alarming moment of abjection for him and one that shifts him out of his vermin persona back to his preferred identity as culinary artist. He simply cannot resist tossing some herb leaves (perhaps basil or oregano) down to the soup. Although escape beckons and he starts to leave, he goes back once again to add another spice, then checks the results by drawing steam into his nose with his paws. For a third time he starts to leave, but once again he goes back and adds another spice, white cubes that are likely garlic. Once again staring toward the open window, Remy pauses, eyes shifting to his right as he looks over his right shoulder back to the simmering soup pot, when Gusteau's spirit pops in, startling him. Gusteau urges him to act like a chef: "You know how to fix it. This is your chance!"

Following his conscience—his ethical duty to the soup and its potential consumers—Remy resolves to stay and rehabilitate the soup. He turns the fire down so that it will simmer slowly rather than boil too fast, hygienically washes his front paws, adds stock and "crème liquide" for body, and sniffs around to choose ingredients (red and white onions, shallots, parsley and other herbs, uncut garlic, a little mustard). After once again using his front paws to check the aroma, he begins to throw other ingredients in enthusiastically: celery, garlic, salt, cheese, a spoonful of parsley. Frequently Remy pauses, falling into cooking reveries in which he loses track of the world around him, lost in the delicious smells and tastes of his creation. This proves to be his downfall when Linguini spots him in such a reverie, snapping him out of his identity as chef and back into rat mode. Whereas back in the old woman's kitchen Remy was unable to finish the puff, this time, fortunately, he completes the soup just before he is transformed back into vermin in another one of the identity reversals Remy suffers throughout the film. His prowess as a chef, however, is confirmed when the soup is taken out to a customer before Linguini can prevent it. The diner, however, is pleased—and turns out to be no ordinary patron but an important critic, Solene LeClair, who writes in her review that "the soup was a revelation, a spicy yet subtle taste experience," adding that it has made her reevaluate the restaurant: "Against all odds, Gusteau's has recaptured our attention. Only time will tell if they deserve it." Unknown to anyone, Remy has become necessary to the restaurant's success: he has proved himself as a creative chef to a discriminating restaurant critic and found a place—of sorts—for himself in the restaurant.

For the article "Some Like it Haute," Katharina Balazs conducted interviews with three-star Michelin chefs in France to help determine the reasons for their success as culinary artists and businessmen running a restaurant. From those interviews, she delineates a set of seven lessons that explain their success within a culture that has long privileged the culinary. A distillation of her seven lessons reveals three underlying axioms: (1) history: creativity is grounded in knowledge and an openness to the new (bridging the past and future); (2) reproducibility: the restaurant must be properly organized to reproduce the chef's creations; (3) audience: the chef must possess a keen awareness of what customers want and expect. In Paris, first at Gusteau's and then in his own restaurant, Remy grapples with each of these axioms on his way to mastery. His first culinary responsibility requires him to salvage the nearly ruined soup; to do so, Remy draws on his knowledge of Gusteau's techniques, but he is also open to the potential of all the ingredients that surround him, creating a soup that is new and that thus pleases the critic, Solene LeClair. Remy here reflects Balazs's claim that the successful chef links history with creativity: "Turn life into a learning process. Learn the basics thoroughly but don't get stuck in them; try to surpass them. . . . They [Michelin chefs] possess the 'art of reframing,' of looking at things with fresh eyes and seeing possibilities where others see routine" (138). The linkage between history and creativity is even more starkly illustrated with Gusteau's old sweetbread recipe, which the chef Skinner pulls from the old recipe box. It has not been a part of the restaurant's recent repertoire because it had been a failure, and Skinner fully intends for Linguini, who is getting the credit for Remy's creations, to fail—to get "stuck" in making it. Remy reimagines the dish, "surpassing" Gusteau's written recipe, in response to customer requests for something new, and it becomes a tremendous success. Remy's improvised and improved sweetbreads create an immediate demand, which the kitchen is prepared to fulfill. Their ability to do so illustrates the connection Balazs sees between creativity and reproducibility: "Consistent quality is not necessarily the anathema of creativity. . . . Gastronomic restaurants are examples of organizations characterized by the presence of both a high level of creativity and the strong formalization of work and production processes" (139–40). The job of the complex set of kitchen brigades, derived from Escoffier, is to reproduce the chef's dishes in quantity with no failings in quality. Creativity belongs to the chef, as the head of the restaurant's organization, not with the cooks—as Colette makes clear when training Linguini. She asserts that Gusteau has "something unexpected" in each dish, but when Linguini writes a note to remind himself to do just that she immediately contradicts him: "No! Follow the recipe.... It was *his* job to be unexpected. It is *our* job to follow the recipe" (emphasis added). When cooking the soup, Remy essentially produced it by himself off in a corner of the kitchen. The sweetbreads represent a new artistic milestone, one in which he innovates as a chef by borrowing ingredients from many preparation stations but also integrates with the kitchen by creating a dish that they replicate as orders pour in for it from patrons whose curiosity and appetites have been piqued by this special addition to the restaurant's menu.

This integration is possible only because of the relationship Remy develops with Linguini. Although the young man is Gusteau's son, he does not find that out about himself until later in the plot; at this point, as the *plongeur*, he is the youngest, least skilled, and least knowledgeable of the kitchen staff. Both he and Remy (as a rat) thus occupy places of social abjection. Remy, in fact, dismisses Linguini when Gusteau's spirit is quizzing him on the kitchen staff ("Oh, him? He's nobody."), only to be chastised by Gusteau for doing so: "Not nobody. He is part of the kitchen." When Remy scoffs that "he's a *plongeur*, he washes dishes, takes out the garbage. He doesn't cook," Gusteau rejoins, "But he could." Remy's rejection of Linguini's potential is ironic for two reasons. First, many chefs historically have started as *plongeurs*, learning the kitchen from this lowest rung on the hierarchy upwards as they get promoted, so that they understand all the cogs of the kitchen machine (Leschziner 19–21). Second, Remy's own path toward being a chef, the most visible rank in the kitchen hierarchy, is contradicted by his vermin status as a rat, which necessitates his invisibility. Remy does in fact become more visible, gradually: the film plays with how much he is seen and by whom.

First, Remy's presence in the kitchen is exposed to Linguini, who traps him with a colander, then to all the kitchen staff, who pick up the closest kitchen implements with which to kill the unwelcome vermin. Linguini as *plongeur* is ordered to dispose of Remy. At this moment, paralleling the old woman in the country house, the interspecies interaction is guided by the traditional extermination pattern between humans and rats. But faced with actually killing the rat, Linguini wavers, a hesitation that can best be explained by Peter Singer's discussion of the moral status of nonhuman animals in *Practical Ethics*. Working from Jeremy Bentham's discussion of animal rights,[5] Singer asserts that nonhuman animals' capacity for suffering and their interest in avoiding suffering gives them claim to be treated morally: "A stone does not have interests because it cannot suffer. Nothing that we can do to it could possibly make any difference to its welfare. A mouse, on the other hand, does have an interest in not being tormented, because mice will suffer if they are treated in this way" (50). The others in Gusteau's kitchen do not feel this moral claim about a rat invading their cooking space, but alone with Remy on the banks of the Seine, Linguini experiences this dilemma. Experiencing a moral quandary and bemoaning his own situation, Linguini begins a monologue: a set of rhetorical questions that set up an interspecies dialogue as the young man gradually realizes that the rat he is speaking *at* can respond to him. Per Singer, at the beginning of the conversation, Linguini gives Remy a kind of personhood: he is deeply ethically disturbed by having to kill the rat, particularly as he recognizes Remy's terror. This is the first step to granting the other being's subject status. The film flits between the positions of Remy as trapped, abject vermin, cowering on all fours and caught in a jar, and as chef with subjectivity. The film gradually reinforces the latter in several ways. Linguini's angry order "Don't look at me like that!" recognizes that the gaze of the rat represents a perspective. Linguini compares himself with the imprisoned rat, further drawing attention to their parallel statuses: "You aren't the only one who's trapped. They expect me to cook it again! I'm not ambitious, I wasn't trying to cook. . . . You're the one who was getting fancy with the spices! What did you throw in there? Oregano? No? Rosemary?" His monologue here acknowledges Remy's abilities and agency in saving the soup, contrasted with his own incompetence. Remy's tiny nods and headshakes, responding to Linguini's questions, gradually reinforce his personhood, especially once he sits up on two legs rather than cowering on all fours. Although half of the "conversation" is conducted in gestural language, it nonetheless opens up a true interspecies dialogue. Elick argues the profound significance of such an act: "To ascribe language to animals . . . is to grant them subject status at the start. When authors include animal utterances competing with human ones, a novel's world becomes more equalitarian, its sense of truth more dialogic" (Elick 19). The dialogue between Linguini and Remy is predicated on Linguini's recognition of Remy's abilities as a chef: cooking precedes even language in giving Remy subjectivity in human eyes. Linguini's name for Remy, "Little Chef," serves to recognize formally Remy's subjective status, which is founded on Remy's food-based skills.

Remy and Linguini prove the possibility of moving beyond the traditional rat/human, parasite/extermination relationship. Their rat-human communication gives rise to the dual being of Remy/Linguini—mind and body, if you will—functioning cooperatively, if awkwardly, through a shared and practiced body language that takes the form of puppetry, with Remy hiding in Linguini's toque and yanking his hair to control his limbs. Linguini sees the benefits to them both: "You know how to cook, and I know how to appear human. We just need to work out a system so that I do what you want in a way that doesn't look like I'm being controlled by a tiny rat chef." This hybridity gives Remy what he needs to develop as a cook. As hero-chef in training, he can no longer cook alone: he needs help, thus demonstrating the theme Herhuth identified, "the new needs friends" (269). He must integrate into the kitchen. As the new Remy/Linguini being, they learn essential restaurant cooking technique from Colette as well as all the ins and outs of the kitchen (layout, organization, contents); eventually they can work together successfully as an integral part of the team that produces the dinner service. The culminating accomplishment of this dual being—as Remy moves from cook to chef—is making the aforementioned sweetbreads recipe with all of its improvisations on Gusteau's original failed recipe. As Remy takes Linguini on a tour of the kitchen to grab ingredients from many different preparation stations, this scene visually demonstrates Remy's mastery of the space *within* the kitchen, as opposed to his earlier understandings of it from above (with Gusteau's spirit) or underfoot (as a rat). The Remy/Linguini hybrid being serves as a kind of cloak or mask, under which Remy is hiding his rodent identity. This frustrating hybrid is ultimately unstable, however, and finally implodes when Linguini admits to the kitchen staff that he is not the talent behind the innovative dishes that they have been serving, unveiling Remy in an attempt to give credit where it is due. At this moment, with Linguini's help, Remy casts off their shared secret identity to assert himself as an individual agent once again, now able to manage the kitchen and the dinner service himself.

When critic Anton Ego dares Linguini as the new owner and supposed new chef of Gusteau's to try to impress him, Remy has the challenge he needs to prove himself in the three main responsibilities of a head chef: as a culinary artist and kitchen manager with keen audience awareness. His ability to manage the second, without which he cannot achieve the first or third, is compromised when the entire restaurant staff quits en masse after Linguini exposes Remy as the truly gifted cook. They share no language that would help them see Remy as an equal—much less as their superior in the kitchen hierarchy: all they can see is a disgusting rat that pollutes the kitchen. Faced with disaster, with a restaurant full of patrons, no staff, and Ego poised to destroy them, Remy accepts his father's offer of the rat colony as a labor force to "man" the kitchen. The kitchen finally becomes the truly rat-infested space that former chef Skinner has been trying to persuade the health inspector to investigate—although Remy hygienically steam cleans the whole clan in the dishwasher. Remy trains and organizes the clean rats into militaristic brigades à la Auguste Escoffier and the classic haute cuisine kitchen. Then adapting components of classic French technique (knife technique, mother sauce [tomato], cooking method) (Trubek 13–25), Remy extemporizes a dish, transforming a country ratatouille into a haute cuisine *confit byaldi*[6] for the food critic Anton Ego. In this act, Remy realizes the third key focus of an executive chef, the audience:

> The chefs are great believers in personal relationships with their clients. . . . Their ambition is not only to serve a perfect dish, but, as far as possible, to serve the perfect dish for the person who is going to eat it. . . . The secret of gastronomic restaurants stems from the ability to take the most basic human need of eating and turn it into a unique event, a fulfillment of their customers' dreams. (Balazs 142)

Remy's haute cuisine version of ratatouille bridges both geographical and chronological barriers for Ego, transporting him into a Proustian reverie of his boyhood in the French countryside when his mother served him ratatouille as a sign of her love. Remy thus gives Ego what he didn't know he was looking for in the cuisine of a starred Parisian restaurant: his mother's comfort.

Although Ego's reclamation occupies only a small portion of the film, his epiphany serves as the film's climax. It is the moment in which Remy successfully passes the test Ego set for him—he cooks in a way that satisfies a difficult and discerning critic: "I don't *like* food, I *love* it. If I don't love it, I don't *swallow*," Ego proclaims (emphasis added). He also sets himself up as a self-described "opponent" of Gusteau's primary chef (whom he believes to be Linguini at that point), warning him, "I will return tomorrow night with high expectations. Pray you don't disappoint me." Ego is consistently portrayed as distant and emotionally rigid, living and dining in solitary splendor, visually associated with death imagery such as his coffin-shaped study and skull-like typewriter on which he composes reviews that become obituaries of the restaurants that fail to please him. In his clinical analysis and refusal to swallow any food that does not please him, Ego denies the life-giving and social properties of the food that he has made his life's focus. When Remy chooses ratatouille as the dish to impress him, Colette is doubtful: "Ratatouille? It's a peasant dish. Are you sure you want to serve this to Ego?" Remy follows up his nod by demonstrating to her a new way of preparing the ingredients—the haute cuisine *confit byaldi*.

When the dish is served to the emotionally repressed Ego, his first suspicious bite awakens his memory of childhood. Ego completely surrenders to the experience, symbolically dropping his pen (his analytical tool) as his eyes widen and he smiles. He looks down at the dish in wonder, then eagerly forks up another bite, while rolling his eyes and uttering an enthusiastic "Mmmm!" At this culminating moment the film moves Ego back in memory from the city of the present to the country of the past. Ego, as sophisticated urban critic, is reclaimed by his childhood memories of authentic French country cooking—a connection Remy, also raised in the country before coming to Paris, instinctively understands will appeal to the critic. Proust too saw a close connection between rural and urban life, locating the heart of "Frenchness" in the dialogue between them, as Priscilla Ferguson argues: "The Recherche produces a national culinary landscape that reconciles province and capital, periphery and center, a landscape in which the French recognize an idea of country" (*Accounting for Taste* 112). Remy's version of ratatouille thus represents an authentic French dish, uniting both the country traditions and urban nouvelle cuisine innovations in a way best described by a chef interviewed by Balazs:

> We have a legacy of knowledge that has been left to us like a gift, sound, solid foundations on which we can build, and which we have to pass on to future generations. Only if one knows one's traditions and is able to make the classics impeccably, then it is possible to modify them, to invent new dishes. . . . We are able to project ourselves into the future, while forgetting nothing of our culture, of our past. (137)

This uniting of past and present lies at the heart of the film's great Proustian moment, when food reawakens a key childhood experience. The Pixar team clearly references the most famous moment in Proust's *À la Recherche du Temps Perdu* in setting up the scene of Ego's memory: in both cases a country boy arrives home, emotionally upset, and his mother offers him food which produces an immediate emotional reaction. Proust's experience provides a permanent emotional touchstone of "all-powerful joy" (48), one that the narrator can never recapture because for Proust (like his fellow Modernists) that past is irrecoverably lost, destroyed by the ravages of the Great War, and he is haunted by an aching sense of nostalgia and loss as a result. The filmmakers change one significant Proustian detail: rather than arriving home on a cold and rainy day, the young Anton Ego enters the house framed in a doorway with sun-drenched fields outside. The background symbolizes the filmmakers' equally sunny view of childhood and the possibility of tapping into memory and finding uncompromised joy. *Ratatouille*'s makers, with an audience of children (and their gatekeeping adult caretakers), work in an ideological context that is fundamentally Romantic. They assume that childhood offers the means of emotional salvation: recovering the pleasures of childhood, in Ego's case the love represented by the food that his mother made for her upset son, holds the key to adult emotional health.

By creating the *confit byaldi* version of ratatouille that pleases Ego so much, Remy demonstrates his mastery of French cooking: he has transformed country cooking into not only haute cuisine but also nouvelle cuisine, a style that has dominated French and global cooking since the 1960s. But Remy's technical expertise is ultimately less important than the authentic emotional effects his work produces on those who consume it—and even on those who help him produce it. For Colette, the process is difficult. She returns to the kitchen to help Linguini because she loves him, not because she believes in Remy as a chef; in fact, when she reenters the space and sees the kitchen overrun with the rats, who are following Remy's shouted orders, she gasps and then gags and turns for the door. She growls out her assent to Linguini: "Don't say a word. If I think about it, I might change my mind. Just tell me what the rat wants to cook." Remy's choice of ratatouille puzzles her but wins her over when she sees his innovations as they cook together. Ego is converted by the food itself, which opens his mind enough to accept the fantastic story of Remy as chef when Linguini and Colette reveal it to him. He is so won over that he writes his review praising Remy as "nothing less than the finest chef in France," albeit in couched language, never revealing Remy as rat. Nonetheless, he deliberately chooses to risk his reputation in "the discovery and defense of the new"—in this case, Remy's talent—and thus shows himself in agreement with Gusteau's advice early in the film that Remy took to heart: "You must try things that may not work. And you must not let anyone define your limits because of where you come from. Your only limit is your soul. What I say is true: anyone can cook, but only the fearless can be great."

Remy's performance of the new is indeed great, and it convinces Colette and Ego to give up their prejudices as Linguini has done and recognize that Remy is a sentient and civilized being. In other words, given that French society deems food the symbol of its national identity, as a chef Remy embodies what Norbert Elias terms the "special character" (4) of its particular civilization. Correlatively, Eric Herhuth makes the point that that, just as Remy is becoming human through cooking, Linguini, Colette, and Ego tap into their becoming animal, in this case, rat (477–78), by accepting Remy as civilized. The rat-human connections that they form neutralize the vermin signifier—at least to some extent. Thus, the new relationship represents a progress unthinkable at the beginning of the film—even if it still suffers from some limitations. Echoing Elias, Ferguson notes that *Ratatouille* takes its place in a long line of works that proclaim the civilizing effects of cooking (*Word of Mouth* 202), and, echoing Trubek, she offers a useful overview of the rat-human connection within a culinary culture that is both exclusive and inclusive: "*Ratatouille* reconciles the irreconcilable, joins the everyday in the exceptional, and preaches the democracy of opportunity and the elitism of achievement" (200). If this were simply a *Künstlerroman*, Remy's arc would be over in his moment of triumph. But, of course, as Remy himself puts it, "The food didn't matter. Once it got out there were rats in the kitchen, oh man, the restaurant was closed. . . ." Although he is an artist, Remy remains a rat. The vermin signifier reasserts itself one more time.

* * *

The lengthy dénouement of the movie, which ends with the main characters happily cooking and eating in the eponymously named bistro Ratatouille, is predicated (though not obviously) on the horrific scene in which Django takes Remy to see the fate of fellow rats in the window of an exterminator's shop, where seventeen dead rats hang by their necks from traps.[7] If Robert Sullivan is right, and rats and humans live in intertwined but parallel social universes, Django takes a precautionary approach by arguing for segregation. Although shocked by what he sees in the window, Remy does not take his father's bait and instead argues for the need to change rat-human interactions:

> REMY: No. Dad, I don't believe it. You're telling me that the future is—can only be—more of this?
> DJANGO: "This" is the way things are. You can't change nature.
> REMY: Change is nature, Dad. The part that we can influence. And it starts when we decide.
> DJANGO: Where you going?
> REMY: With luck, forward.

Walking away upright instead of on all fours as he arrived from the sewer, Remy has decided to be an agent of change; however, the "forward" that the film manages is not a fantasy world where rats and humans live fully integrated, egalitarian lives together. At the end of the film, Remy's own new restaurant is a highly delimited and demarcated space that allows humans and rats to coexist but not comingle, except within one demarcated private space. Rather than a large restaurant with a fully staffed kitchen, where it would be difficult to manage or suppress the vermin signifier, this is a bistro with a very small human staff (Colette as sous-chef, Linguini as waiter, with Ego as investor) that is rat-friendly. The bistro has two dining areas: one for humans on the main floor, the conventional public space, and another in the rafters for the rats, hidden decorously by green plants—a structure that curiously mimics the social organization of the country house at the beginning of the film. Although Colette, Linguini, and Ego clearly know about the rats above, the film gives no indication that the rest of the patrons do.

Earlier in the film, Remy told his father, "All we do is take, Dad. I'm tired of taking. I want to make things. I want to add something to this world." Remy has now achieved that ambition and has become the artistic, productive member of society he wanted to be. As for the rats, they are no longer eating garbage in the alleys as backstreet thieves and scavengers; instead, they converse while dining on prepared cuisine at tables in a restaurant, and thus have become "civilized." Critics like Ferguson are impressed with the film's ending: she notes the transformation of the rat colony into "a different community, one created by commensality and by the food talk that makes eating together a truly social occasion" (202). Clearly, in Ferguson's estimation, food forms the basis of the human-rat bond in the film. Of course, real rats depend on human food sources, as Sullivan's study makes abundantly clear, but in reality, the vermin signifier always dominates, and humans seek to exterminate wild rats as polluters of food sources and vectors of disease. Because *Ratatouille* is an animal fantasy, it can explore what Elick sees as the possibilities inherent in the genre: such texts depict animals as "capable of unbalancing human hierarchies and enjoying equitable relationships with people" (6). The final bistro organization, with Remy as chef in the kitchen and rats dining at tables in the rafters, certainly calls normal hierarchies into question. The issue of "equitable relationships," though, is more complex. Ferguson sees the final social organization positively: "Sooner the lion lie down with the lamb, you may object, than rats dine with humans. But in true Disney fashion, the impossible happens, though the two species do not actually dine together. They remain separate communities, connected by the chef artist" (202). Remy has achieved a kind of equality in the kitchen, proving Gusteau's thesis that "anyone can cook," but how far up the social ladder have the other rats truly gotten, despite the improvement in their diet? Is dining separately from the humans a statement of equality?

The rats' lives do seem to have changed for the better, but their general socio-economic status remains ambiguous. When they dine at Ratatouille, it is unclear how or even if they are paying for their meals. Do they dine off the largesse of Remy? If so, they are being financially floated by the diners below and in a sense are still living off the castoffs of human society: their essential historical role as rats remains untouched with the exception of chef Remy. The family difficulties Remy experienced with his father seem resolved—Django even seems proud of what Remy has accomplished. But Django himself, as colony leader, seems to have nepotistic tendencies: during the climactic scene at Gusteau's, he volunteers the rat colony to replace the staff that just walked out in disgust. He rationalizes their free labor as family service: "We're not cooks. But we are family. You tell us what to do, and we'll get it done." The rats seem to find happiness in the elevated subjectivity they achieve by cooking under Remy's direction, but notably they are the dark Other serving the wealthy white patrons of Gusteau's without wages, and the evening's work does not lead to long-term employment for any of them. The implications of this—and the separate dining space—are particularly disturbing if one chooses to read the rats as a metaphorical stand-in for groups of humans in a way that has traditionally been common in animal fable—in this case, the marginalized postcolonial immigrant population of France, where the film is set, or the African American population of the United States, where the film was produced.

Rather than seeing the movie as presenting a sunny path to a more egalitarian, civilized, and inclusive future, it would be more accurate to see its world as still quite fragile: where marginalized beings find social improvement and thus emotional contentment as well as discovering that some of the human beings who would have exterminated them are willing to live with them in a mutually beneficial economic and cultural symbiosis. The premises underlying the fantasy world of the film allow the rats to speak to each other but never to humans, who can only hear squeaking; interspecies communication remains extraordinarily difficult and time consuming—and it is the rats who learn humans' language rather than humans learning to understand the rats' own language. Yet inside the restaurant the extermination paradigm, which has motivated so much of the action in the rest of the film, has been suspended. Cooperation has resulted in a better life for the film's primary characters, rats and humans. The rats live safely, without fear for their lives: their food is cooked and not poisoned. Remy is free to exercise his talents to feed his family and friends, rather than spending his days ensuring their safety by sniffing the garbage they have scavenged. As for the humans, Linguini finds a job he can do successfully, Collette is now promoted to sous-chef,[8] and Ego lives the joy of commensality. Moreover, the film offers no looming threat of the vermin signifier's return: no health inspector lurks, no former Gusteau's employee seeks revenge, and no nosy customer discovers the rats' dining room. But the movie does not portray a universal revolution of "separate but equitable" social spaces. Outside the restaurant, there is no indication that the social structure which produced the oppression and violence at the beginning of the film has changed. The filmmakers recognize the difficulties of changing society's paradigm and do not pursue a utopian (or intersectional zootopian) resolution. Instead, the film's ending affirms Elick's Bakhtinian view of animal fantasy. The bistro is a space for ethical inquiry to engage in possibilities, where "dialogic relationship" persists between humans and animals, stimulating "ethical interactions" (9): it shows how groups whose interactions have been characterized by loathing, mistrust, and oppression can find a way to live in harmony. In a world supposedly grounded in equal rights and the values of life, liberty, and the pursuit of happiness, the difficult relationship between oppressor and oppressed, center and margin, still needs to be explored, owned, and worked through. In the aphorism that begins this chapter, the epicure Brillat-Savarin links food consumption to stages of becoming, from filling to the art of eating, animal to wise man. It offers a vision of culinary uplift, but one whose stages—separated decisively by the semicolons—are exclusionary. Although *Ratatouille* proposes a modest rethinking of how animal and man—or, symbolically, two categories of being that seem antithetical—could live with one another, it does so with the assumption that the stages from animality to wisdom are fluid, interconnected, and inclusive. Food and the opportunity to prepare it can effectively fuel a far more egalitarian world than Brillat-Savarin could imagine when he published *The Physiology of Taste* in 1825.

Chapter 9

"BEATING EGGS NEVER MAKES THE EVENING NEWS"

Politics and Kitchens in Rita Williams-Garcia's *One Crazy Summer* and Its Sequels

Food plays a major role in all three of Rita Williams-Garcia's novels set in from 1968 to 1969: *One Crazy Summer* (2010), *P.S. Be Eleven* (2013), and *Gone Crazy in Alabama* (2015). They each won the Coretta Scott King Award for the year they were published; *One Crazy Summer* also won a Newbery Honor Award and the Scott O'Dell Award for Historical Fiction, and was a National Book Award finalist, all in 2011. The novels focus on the three Gaither sisters, Delphine, who is eleven at the beginning of the first book, and her younger sisters Vonetta and Fern, who are nine and seven. The girls grow up in the Bedford-Stuyvesant section of Brooklyn but have extended family in Prattville, Alabama. In the opening novel, they visit their estranged mother Cecile in Oakland, California, who left the family when Fern was a newborn infant, and whom the girls have not seen since. *P.S. Be Eleven* is set immediately afterwards, when the girls return to their father and grandmother in Brooklyn, and unfolds over the course of Delphine's sixth-grade year. *Gone Crazy in Alabama* is set primarily on the girls' great-grandmother's farm the following summer. Each place is marked by distinctive foods and foodways that reflect the particular historical moments of African American culture of that time and place: the Black Power movement in Oakland in 1968, the Great Migration in Brooklyn as it adapts to post–World War II convenience culture, and the Jim Crow American South.

A passage from *P.S. Be Eleven* neatly brackets the kinds of foods and socioculinary behaviors the sisters have grown up with: the rural foodways of Alabama (either in situ or imported to Brooklyn by Big Ma) and the quick and convenient foodways that shape modern urban life:

Big Ma never made quick-fast-in-a-hurry food. She made food that needed washing before it touched a knife, pot, or pan. Or she made beans that soaked overnight and simmered with neck bones for a good part of the next day. And stewed meat in heavy enameled pots, with bay leaves and carrots and potatoes that soaked up gravy. Big Ma cooked food meant to stick to your insides and keep your belly full. She cooked food that took time.

If cooking hadn't started by two or three o'clock, we'd have to eat quick-fast-in-a-hurry, which were the meals I cooked. Franks and canned pork and beans. Fried chicken, boiled potatoes, and frozen green peas. Sometimes I made spaghetti with catsup and any kind of cut-up leftover meat from the night before. A few times when Big Ma was sick, Uncle Darnell brought in a pizza pie. Big Ma never liked that and always got well the next day so we wouldn't get used to take-out food. (223–24)

What this passage does not capture is Cecile's deconstruction and remaking of the kitchen and her relationship to it in *One Crazy Summer*. Cecile's profound rejection and revision of the "yoke" of women's service to men and family (*OCS* 110) lies at the heart of Delphine's critique of Cecile's mothering techniques, yet Cecile's kitchen-cum-art studio serves as the place where they negotiate the nature and limits of their fundamentally new relationship in the present moment of the novel, a relationship that does not fit the conventions of the mother-daughter relationship as conceived by a conservative character like Big Ma. An essential—and pragmatic—component of Cecile's rejection of the traditional kitchen lies in her relationship to the Black Panthers and the Free Breakfast for Children program, which Williams-Garcia incorporates (just slightly anachronistically[1]) into her story. The radical view of the place of the kitchen in 1968 Oakland sharply contrasts with Delphine's previous kitchen experiences, as defined in Delphine's musing in the passage cited above. As Williams-Garcia moves her next two novels forward through her young characters' lives, into 1969, she simultaneously explores backwards into the roots of the two generations preceding them, each defined by its own customs for the buying, bartering, raising, and cooking of food: the conveniences of the big-city destinations of the Great Migration and the farm-based slow cooking of the Jim Crow South. These daily food-based customs—bound by the racial/racist restrictions of the North (restrictive real estate covenants) and South (Jim Crow)[2]—form the background against which the remaking of the urban power structure of Oakland is captured in *One Crazy Summer*.

KaaVonia Hinton and Angela Branyon's article, "'Your Hair Ain't Naughty:' Representations of Women in Rita Williams-Garcia's Novels," provides a useful model for mapping food and foodways within the series. Hinton and Branyon map different constructions of the figure of the strong Black woman onto three of the mothers in the novels (Big Ma, Cecile, and Marva), exploring their strengths and weaknesses and showing how, in particular, Delphine must navigate among these forms of Black womanhood as she works toward forging her own identity. Hinton and Branyon claim that "Williams-Garcia emphasizes the connection between Black girls and multiple models of Black womanhood, as Black women in the trilogy are diverse and contradictory, yet they are presented as essential to Delphine's socialization" (328). Moreover, as a result, "Williams-Garcia places Delphine in a position to push back against myths and interlocking oppressions and gives her role models to consider as she begins to assume the fullness of who she is as an emerging young Black woman" (341). Although Hinton and Branyon seldom mention food, their analysis of how Williams-Garcia's three major mother figures reflect cultural values parallels the way each woman approaches food. We see food and foodways in the novels providing similar cultural, experiential, and developmental arcs for Delphine and her sisters to negotiate as they mature over the course of a significant year of cultural tumult in the history of African Americans and the United States.

* * *

In the third novel of the trilogy, *Gone Crazy in Alabama*, which is set in the summer of 1969, Delphine and her sisters visit their grandmother, Ophelia Gaither, commonly called Big Ma, who has returned to the family farm near Prattville, Alabama. Ophelia lives there with her mother, Naomi Trotter Charles, whom the girls address as Ma Charles. More family lives nearby: Naomi's estranged half sister Ruth Trotter and her great grandson James, commonly called JimmyTrotter, who is fifteen. Both families live on farms they own; the Charles family has a close neighbor, Mr. Lucas, who grew up with Big Ma and who largely runs the two properties, doing the chores the women can't manage. The Charles and Trotter families live together in a near-self-sufficient food arrangement that reflects food traditions from the nineteenth-century past. They grow, raise, hunt, and barter for the food they prepare and eat: produce from their gardens, eggs and chicken meat from the Charles chicken coop and run, milk from the two Trotter cows. When the Trotters have venison from shooting a deer, they share it across the creek with the Charles family.

This barter relationship exists in spite of the animosity between the two half sisters, who have hardly seen or spoken to each other for decades. Clearly, the food ties overcome personal enmity, a solidarity that has enabled the families' largely independent survival through the Jim Crow era, which has only recently ended de jure with the passage of the Civil Rights Act of 1964 and the Voting Rights Act of 1965. The families' self-sufficiency derives in large part because they own their land, a significant advantage over many southern African Americans who were forced to sharecrop for white landowners. The Charles and Trotter families fit Anne Yentsch's discussion of independent southern African American farmers remarkably well. She notes an increase in Black farmers from 1890 to 1910, who had greater self-sufficiency and autonomy and consequently greater self-esteem. As a result, they "raised a large variety of foodstuffs," which they shared "with less-fortunate kin" (78):

> Black landowners still had to deal with racist storekeepers, but because their yard space was not in white hands their vegetable gardens could be any size a family chose. They could plant fruit trees. They could raise more than chickens and add a hog, a mule, or a cow, or they could plant a flowering crepe myrtle. Some farms boasted pecan trees, fig trees, cane fields, and sweet potato patches. Gardeners grew collards, okra, tomatoes, watermelons, and irrigated tiny rice fields. Fruit and vegetables composed a larger percentage of farm products. (Yentsch 79)

The garden on the Charles property is mentioned only occasionally, but in it grow vegetables that are used fresh in season or canned, insuring the family's self-sufficiency. Pecan and peach trees also grow in the yard, providing nuts and fruits used for snacks and desserts, especially cobblers and pies.

The most striking example of food cooperation among the branches of the family is the exchange of eggs from the shared Charles and Lucas chicken coop and milk from the Trotter cows. Delphine sees the arrangement in action her first morning in Alabama, when she finds her cousin JimmyTrotter taking eggs from the chickens, having brought over a quart of milk from Sophie, the Trotter cow that is currently lactating. JimmyTrotter takes the eggs he gathers up to the house and delivers the milk, then eventually returns home to his great grandmother with their eggs from the exchange (GCA 38–41). Delphine, helping her cousin gather the eggs (albeit a little hesitantly), is immediately integrated as a part of the food production system of her country southern family. She knows from the family's visit three years ago what the realities of country eating entail and seeks to protect Fern from the experience of seeing a chicken slaughtered for the family meal—an innocence that Big Ma has no patience with when a chicken is needed (GCA 56–57). The incident confirms Fern's budding vegetarianism: already refusing to eat bacon or ham after reading *Charlotte's Web* on the bus on the way down to Alabama (GCA 43–44, 56), Fern likewise refuses to eat chicken that night, or venison when the Trotters kill a deer and barbeque it (134–35).

The younger sisters have to grapple with the differences between the factory-made foods they are used to and other home-produced food, besides meat. For example, Fern must be coaxed to eat eggs with the assurance that no chicks are developing in them (because the henhouse has no rooster). The milk that JimmyTrotter brings is another notable case in point. Vonetta is initially repulsed by milk still warm from the cow, in part because she and Fern have never considered the true source of the milk they consume in Brooklyn:

> "Where do you think milk comes from?" I asked her.
> "The store. In a red and white carton."
> "With a picture of a cow on a farm," Fern said.
> "That farm's across the creek," JimmyTrotter said. "That cow is Sophie. And in a month, that milk'll come from Butter." (GCA 44)

Rather than the idealized textual representation of a farm which milk companies use to advertise their product, the girls confront the unappetizing reality of nonprocessed farm food. Vonetta and Fern's desire for their accustomed cornflakes outweighs their initial disgust at milk fresh from a cow, although Vonetta suggests JimmyTrotter should arrive earlier so the milk can be cooled in the freezer for breakfast to conform to her city-based expectations (GCA 44). Learning to consume raw milk from a family cow draws the girls into the family's custom of eating mostly homegrown or homemade meals as opposed to industrially produced food:

> "All this talk about where milk comes from," Ma Charles said. "Milk comes from a cow. Maybe a goat. In all my eighty-two years I never drank a drop of factory milk and I won't start now. Never had an egg come out of a carton or a loaf of bread that didn't rise up in my own oven, and furthermore, it's a sin to throw a nickel on a head of cabbage or a bunch of carrots that already grows up out of my own dirt." (GCA 45)

The Trotters do sell their extra milk as a source of income: JimmyTrotter regularly delivers their "family-farmed milk" to four other families, the bakery, and the grocery store (*GCA* 122–23). But they work for customers who wish to maintain the ancient connection to locally produced food. The Trotters' cows serve people in town "who didn't trust big dairy farms. They gladly paid for what they could get from family farmers like the Trotters" (*GCA* 123). Thus, the cows and chickens represent not just self-sufficiency for the family that owns them but a local, small-business alternative for a limited number of families and local businesses.

This communal resourcefulness, evident in the novel as well as in history, can best be conceptualized by Tony Whitehead's definition of culture from his article, "In Search of Soul Food and Meaning: Culture, Food, and Health": "Culture is part of a larger ecological system, which is historically created, intergenerationally reproduced and moderated, and functions to allow humans to meet basic biological needs in ways that blunt that impact of deleterious environmental agents and exploit agents that sustain life and culture" (96). The African American community of family farms in *Gone Crazy in Alabama* have had the fortune to maintain an interdependent independence for over ninety years (*GCA* 21) in the midst of the Jim Crow South. Certainly, they regularly face the pressures and restrictions of de jure and de facto racism—which Williams-Garcia illustrates through scenes like JimmyTrotter's interaction with the town sheriff and the KKK riding on horseback by Ma Charles's house—but their food independence blunts the impact of that racism and helps buoy significant self-esteem. Thus, as Hinton and Branyon point out, the novel features generations of strong Black women (Ma Charles, Great Aunt Trotter, Big Ma), who have found ways to exercise their strength within the severe restrictions of southern racism. Using food as key to their strength and longevity, Big Ma's family reflects a creative culinary engagement that extends back further than the Jim Crow South. As Charles Joyner puts it in *Down by the Riverside: Slave Folk in a South Carolina Slave Community*,

> food played a role in slave culture beyond mere sustenance. . . . It had immense cultural and ideological significance: the choice of particular foods and particular means of preparation involved issues of crucial importance to the slaves' sense of identity. Slave cooks not only maintained cultural continuity with West African cuisine but also adapted the African tradition creatively to the necessities and opportunities of a new culinary environment. (106)

In "Soul Food as Cultural Creation," William C. Whit links the creative past to the creative present, when, concerning soul food he says, "As the cultural production of African Americans, soul food demonstrates the manner in which, in the face of unfavorable social conditions, slaves involved themselves collectively in creating a new cuisine that addressed problems of nutritional adequacy and ethnic and racial identity" (55). In the present moment of the novel, this now-traditional African American cuisine[3] has functioned successfully for a long time. Williams-Garcia grounds *Gone Crazy in Alabama*'s central conflict in a challenge to it.

The milk that binds together the local strands of the Alabama family becomes the focal point of the family conflict that underlies the story's climax; it also embodies the conflict between older rural and newer urban foodways. Vonetta, who has accepted milk from Sophie the cow because she finds it necessary to the morning cereal she demands, becomes worried as Sophie runs dry, several weeks before anticipated. Herein lies the conflict between the urban and the rural ways of managing food: Vonetta, as a city child, expects milk to be available at any time she wants, provided by the grocery store that depends on factory dairy farming, whereas her Alabama relatives adapt their meal plans when the milk gives out. JimmyTrotter and his great grandmother try to time their two cows' calf bearing to keep milk available year-round as much as they can, but Sophie's milk cycle ends early, threatening her future as one of the cows they rely on for milk to drink and sell.

This problem precipitates several conflicts. First, it sets off another round of bitterness between the two half sisters Ma Charles and Great Aunt Trotter, with Ma Charles threatening to withhold eggs if she does not get milk in exchange, despite JimmyTrotter's pleas that he has brought to them what little milk Sophie produced. Sophie going dry thus destabilizes the barter system that they have in place—although Big Ma is unwilling to see the Trotters go without eggs and undercuts her mother's authority by telling JimmyTrotter to go ahead and take eggs. Second, Vonetta pleads for milk from the store, which Ma Charles refuses to allow:

> Ma Charles stood up, her finger pointed. "No milk but cow's milk, straight from the cow! Not in this house."
>
> I [Delphine] spoke up. "But Ma Charles, store milk comes from cows. At the dairy farm."
>
> "I know what I said and why. They don't have grass at the dairy factory," Ma Charles said. "And if they do, believe me, those factory cows

don't graze on grass that springs out of dirt. I'm not ignorant. . . . I've seen 'em penned and chained worse than convicted killers. No, sir, . . . You won't pour a bowl of prison milk in this house." (GCA 177–78)

Ma Charles grounds her refusal to allow store-bought milk in an ethical argument about the treatment of animals: on small family farms, cows have the freedom to graze on wholesome grass as food (which cows evolved to eat), while factory farms imprison them and give them corn-based feed. Ma Charles's stance in demanding the ethical treatment of animals mirrors Fern's boycott of all meat on similar ethical grounds. Third, Vonetta's desire for milk worsens the split between her and her Uncle Darnell. Although she is his favorite niece, she has refused to forgive him for stealing the money the girls had saved for a Jackson 5 concert months earlier, when he was under the influence of drugs. Hurt by her refusal to speak to him despite the amends he made in the form of a Jackson 5 album, Darnell conveniently forgets to pick up milk at the grocery store because Vonetta refuses to ask him for it herself. When he arrives home without milk for a second night in a row, he offers to drive over to the McDaniels' farm, but Big Ma refuses his proposal: "The world doesn't spin and stop on a bowl of cornflakes. . . . Son, you been working and going to school. You go lie down" (GCA 185). Big Ma intends to teach Vonetta lessons in thoughtfulness and food flexibility, but Vonetta refuses to learn. Cornflakes with milk take priority over anything else in her mind: "As long as I have milk for my cornflakes . . . I don't care about anything else" (GCA 179). While Fern and Delphine have integrated into the rural food rhythms of the house, Vonetta remains urban and alienated and thus is unreceptive to Big Ma's lesson to accept the natural cycle that dictates what the family traditionally eats. All this leads Vonetta to vow to get milk for herself and not share it with her sisters, with whom she has also quarreled (184). She takes the acquisition of her milk into her own hands: she gets up early to bike to the store in town and get the milk she craves, in defiance of her grandmother and great grandmother's edicts. Unfortunately, she chooses the morning that a tornado blows through and goes missing in the storm and its aftermath.

The storm tears the family asunder by taking Vonetta, but it also heals other breaches. The girls' mother Cecile comes from Oakland; their father and his new wife drive down from Brooklyn. Great Aunt Trotter, JimmyTrotter, and their cows survive the storm, although their house does not. They move into the Charles house, and the sisters are finally reunited after a rift of decades' standing. Mr. Lucas, the neighbor who has been courting Big Ma, likewise moves in because his house too is destroyed. For the first time, they are all under one roof. When Vonetta returns from a hospital, injured but safe, the family celebrates its gratitude with a family dinner: "At the table that night, with Pa and Mrs. on one side and Cecile, Vonetta, Fern, and I on the other, our family gave thanks that Vonetta was home safe" (GCA 263). The family dinner heals the estrangement between Vonetta and Uncle Darnell, who "walked in with a gallon of cow's milk from the McDaniels' farm," prompting Vonetta to burst into tears (GCA 263). Just as lack of milk triggered the major familial rupture, the gift of milk repairs and restores broken relationships. Williams-Garcia's choice of milk as the linchpin for both the conflict and its resolution carries suitable symbolism. Milk is a fundamental foodstuff across many cultures, overtly symbolizing nurture. It represents family, motherhood, and the bonds between mothers and children; here, it becomes a symbol for family wholeness. The family raises other foods, but it is not the eggs, the chickens, or the garden produce, but the milk that drives the plot, leading to the book's emotional climax.

The final family dinner also provides a crucial resolution for Delphine's long-held desire. Williams-Garcia comments on that moment in her speech accepting the Coretta Scott King award for the novel: "All Delphine wants in this final story of the Gaither sisters is to have all of her family members at the table. So I granted Delphine's wish. I gave her the gathering, the celebration of family, but not without the storm. The feast at the celebration can only taste but so good if you haven't passed through the storm" ("CSK" 81). But this gathering is temporary, and the family scatters into its usual diaspora afterwards: Cecile returns to Oakland; the girls, Pa, and Marva return to Brooklyn; the Alabama family remain in Alabama, though gathered into one house rather than three. The dinner here functions as feasts conventionally do, as a unifier for all participants, while the particular food served functions, as Anne Bower puts it in her introduction to *African American Foodways*, to powerfully signify "something African Americans share throughout and beyond the United States" (7–8). Although, according to Adrian Miller in *Soul Food*, traditional southern country dishes became a source of nostalgic reconnection for African Americans after World War II (41) and then were rejected by the Black Power movement in the 1960s because they were seen as "slave food" (45), Williams-Garcia uses this dinner to bring representatives of the northern and western African American Great Migration diasporas back to the table of their southern heritage. The resolution of the trilogy both unifies and disseminates, reflecting the culinary and cultural tensions of the time.

Even though it was the last book of the series to be written and published, *Gone Crazy in Alabama* functions essentially as the foundational book because it reveals the bedrock of family and culture, especially food culture, on which the action of the other two books are built. Williams-Garcia did not start with a trilogy in mind, but the writing of each book led her to fill in the background she could see peeking out from behind the main action of each story:

> It wasn't until I was midway through *One Crazy Summer* and asked questions of myself about the other characters (Pa, Big Ma, Uncle Darnell) to better understand the three sisters, that I realized there was a sequel to this story. Then, early on in the writing and plotting of that sequel, *P.S. Be Eleven* (2013), I could feel the story's inevitable but somber ending. Questions came to my mind—in particular, who did Big Ma come home to when she returned to Alabama? And where exactly in Alabama was home? According to Vonetta in *One Crazy Summer*, home was just "Alabama," but according to Delphine, home was in a "one-cow town" (Williams-Garcia, 2010, p. 77) near Prattville, Alabama. I had a picture of place, story possibilities, two cows, and a title: *Gone Crazy in Alabama* (2015). A trilogy was born! ("Between Delphine and a Hard Place" 211)

Although Williams-Garcia started with the revolutionary experience that Delphine and her sisters experience in Oakland in the first story, she worked her way down through layers of African American history and culture as she progressed through the series: by portraying in the sequels first the Brooklyn culture the girls grow up in and then the Alabama culture of their grandparents and forebears, she defined what Cecile and the Black Panthers were both celebrating and protesting against. Thus, the food analysis of *Gone Crazy in Alabama* takes precedence over that of the following novels, because it depicts the food traditions that evolve and change, first in Brooklyn, the setting of *P.S. Be Eleven* and then in Oakland in *One Crazy Summer*.

* * *

In the bridging novel *P.S. Be Eleven*, food plays a much smaller role than it does in the other two. Although it appears at a few important points, it does not structure the plot in the same deep ways as it does for the first and third novels. The food that is portrayed draws in part from the country food that the older Gaither generation grew up on in Alabama and in part from the urban environment they have moved to. Big Ma still cooks "food that took time" most nights, with slight adaptations for city life because the ingredients are bought in grocery stores rather than harvested on their own farm. Delphine is accustomed to her grandmother's food that is made from whole produce and meat chunks: she cites beans that need overnight soaking as well as full-day simmering, and meat stewed with carrots and potatoes and flavored with bay leaf (*PSBE* 223).

Delphine contrasts the Alabama-style cooking of Big Ma with what she has herself learned to do as a makeshift replacement on the occasions when Big Ma is ill or too busy to prepare dinner herself. Delphine defines her own cooking as "quick-fast-in-a-hurry" meals: "Franks and canned pork and beans. Fried chicken, boiled potatoes, and frozen green peas. Sometimes I made spaghetti with catsup and any kind of cut-up leftover meat from the night before" (*PSBE* 224). These dishes are dominated by industrially prepared foods, which are canned, frozen, dried, or bottled, all easy and convenient to find in an urban grocery store and requiring far less time and cooking talent to make. (They are, of course, also available at the grocery store in Alabama in 1969, but the family there eats less expensively and more nutritiously with their own produce, as discussed above.) Some are more traditional—the fried chicken and the boiled potatoes—but those are also not difficult for a novice cook, like Delphine, to manage.

Overall, the "quick-fast-in-a-hurry" foods of urban Brooklyn suggest that convenience is the dominant value in terms of Brooklyn food choices when Big Ma is not cooking. The fast food, take-out pizza that Uncle Darnell favors—a food that had become popular in postwar America—also embodies this as a value. The premium on ease and rapidity of food preparation fits the general shift in American urban eating patterns after World War II, patterns adopted by Black families who were part of the Great Migration of African Americans out of the South and into the urban North from 1916–70.[4] In *Something from the Oven: Reinventing Dinner in 1950s America*, Laura Shapiro points out that the food industry, coming out of the technological innovations developed during World War II, produced convenience foods which were dried, powdered, boxed, and frozen; these new foods were then promoted to the mainstream American consumer to make meal preparation easier and quicker, thus freeing women from spending so much time in the kitchen. According to Shapiro, food manufacturers envisioned "a day when all contact between the cook and the raw makings of dinner would be obsolete" (xvi–xvii). Delphine's "quick-fast-in-a-hurry" cooking reflects the convenience style that came to dominate American cooking in the latter half of the twentieth century, while Big Ma's slow, country cooking stands in absolute contrast to it. The novel does not show Delphine cooking very much, but she defines the two types of food at a moment of crisis, when she must step in with her version of cooking because Big Ma is so traumatized and depressed by her son Darnell's disappearance that she cannot rouse herself to cook dinner (*PSBE* 223–24).

Marva, the "snappy and mod" young woman from the "now generation" whom Pa marries in the course of the book (*PSBE* 48, 213), also cooks "quick-fast-in-a-hurry" meals and often uses the convenience foods typical of the time and place. Delphine is dubious about her new stepmother's cooking talents: "I doubted Mrs. could cook like Big Ma, but I knew she could scramble some eggs and fry bacon without burning them" (*PSBE* 213). Marva's contemporary cooking technique is most poignantly shown in marked contrast with the old style of cooking at the end of the book, during the preparation for Christmas breakfast after Big Ma has returned home to Alabama:

> Pa and Mrs. tried to make a Merry Christmas. Pa had Johnny Mathis singing Christmas carols on our deluxe stereo. Mrs. made the kind of biscuits that pop when you twist the can. Not the kind you set on the windowsill to rise the night before you bake them. That was all right. Her biscuits still smelled doughy and buttery and would go great with cheese grits and sausage. While I got the grits boiling, Mrs. kept saying, "No, darling. Christmas is for kids doing kid things." But once I had the cheese grated and the sausage dancing in the frying pan, she was anxious for a taste.
>
> Mrs. meant well, but she didn't understand. I had to make the Christmas cheese grits. I wanted something to taste merry like Christmas morning in Big Ma's kitchen. (*PSBE* 235–36)

Notably, Delphine here validates both the "quick-fast-in-a-hurry" packaged biscuits that Marva resorts to as well as Big Ma's slow cooking: she is happy with the taste of convenience biscuits but insists on replicating her grandmother's special slow-cooked cheese grits and sausage for her sisters and father. She knows the difference between the kind of biscuits her grandmother made and those from her stepmother, evaluating both types in terms of cooking preparation and taste, and finding good in both of them. But for the feast day, she also needs the traditional taste of cooking represented by her grandmother's cooking style and ingredients, and she is old enough and has learned enough to take on that role. Although Delphine does not practice her grandmother's cooking techniques on every occasion she is called on to cook, her grandmother has passed on to her the values of slow cooking, and the holiday calls for the extra time and effort inherent in them. Marva seems to lack the kitchen expertise that Big Ma represents, suggesting the gradual erosion of old-fashioned country cooking in the urban environment.

The Christmas breakfast episode exhibits the central paradox of *P.S. Be Eleven*: the title comes from Cecile's reminder at the end of each letter to her daughter to take the time to be a child, to be eleven rather than an adult, even as Delphine begins to desire more adult responsibility as she steps into adolescence. Cecile wants Delphine to have the childhood that she herself didn't have. Marva as the new stepmother tries to reinforce that too, especially on Christmas morning, which she defines as "for kids doing kid things." But Delphine, now turned twelve at the end of October, as she reminds her mother, insists on taking an adult role to prepare a traditional Christmas breakfast, with foods and techniques learned from her grandmother. She notes her success by her stepmother's reaction: Marva is "anxious for a taste" once she sees and smells the cooking grits and sausages. This cooking scene demonstrates Hinton and Branyon's thesis about the series: Delphine is negotiating her developing identity through all three of the women role models of her life: Cecile, Marva, and Big Ma, each of whom is represented in the pressures that Delphine feels to stay young and the simultaneous pressures to grow up, and all of whom help her develop as a strong Black woman. Moving into adolescence, Delphine embraces a more adult role in her kitchen responsibility at this moment and does so with far greater grace and without the reluctance she felt when pushed into that role a few months earlier in *One Crazy Summer*, the first book of the series.

* * *

Tapping into her own childhood memories of the Black Power movement in Queens, in *One Crazy Summer* Williams-Garcia explores how, in a revolutionary place and time—in this case, Oakland, California in 1968—food can be a way to rethink one's place in the world. Williams-Garcia recalled in the acceptance speech for her Coretta Scott King Author Award for *One Crazy Summer*:

> In my neighborhood I observed the expression of Black Panther ideology in poetry, in music, and on posters. There were free clinics and sickle cell anemia testing. Free breakfast programs. Clothing and shoe give-aways. There were children's programs, although I never attended

any. . . . When I sat down to write *One Crazy Summer*, I chose children and childhood as my entree into the Black Power Movement. Children were being born into the revolution. Children were ever-present and at the heart of the ideals of change and revolution. They were served by the Black Panther Party in community programs and attended Black Panther–run schools, such as the Oakland Community School. They learned to be intellectually curious and aware, and to serve within their communities. ("CSK Author Award Acceptance," 86–93)

In this first novel of the series, Delphine and her sisters visit Oakland to meet their estranged mother for the first time in seven years, and while Delphine has few illusions about Cecile as a mother, feeding children lies at the heart of Delphine's personal definition of motherhood. Cecile, however, confounds Delphine's definition by her reluctance to engage in traditional women's work in the kitchen; she relies on take-out Chinese food and the community program of the Black Panthers to provide most of the girls' meals. Cecile is working out her personal definition of liberation, which to some degree overlaps the Black Panthers' revolutionary political and social aims. In Oakland of 1968, food production and consumption carried political weight. If, in the second and third books in the series Williams-Garcia portrays food and foodways as integral to longstanding social hierarchies and patterns of behavior, expectations, and interactions, in *One Crazy Summer* she uses food and foodways as expressions of a radical moment in history when conventions and hierarchies are questioned, deconstructed, and upset to produce a more egalitarian culture grounded in self-determination, where power and power sharing is negotiated by one and all. Food structures the different paths of discovery that Cecile and her daughters chart. In essence, Cecile's insistent and radical need to (re)make her identity and to ground her power in those acts of self-fashioning motivates and structures the action in *One Crazy Summer*, whose central conflict occurs when Cecile's radical self-possession encounters her daughters' need to be cared for when they come to visit her. Cecile may have made her kitchen into a vehicle of artistic expression, but Big Ma judges Oakland, and thus Cecile, through a much more conservative and conventional cooking metaphor: "Oakland's nothing but a boiling pot of trouble cooking. All them riots" (*OCS* 5).

Williams-Garcia holds back the story of Cecile's personal history until near the end of the novel. Delphine has only fragmentary memories of her mother before she left the family, not surprising given the young child she was at the time. But she remembers conflict between her parents, particularly over Cecile's desire—or need—to write. Before departing for the West Coast seven years earlier, Cecile obsessively wrote poetry on the walls of the kitchen in Louis's apartment in Queens, only to have her writing painted over again and again by Louis and his brother, Darnell. This erasure of her self-expression—her attempt to create a space liberated from conventional gender expectations (woman as cook, cooking for others)—pushed her to flee rather than capitulate, a flight triggered by Louis denying her the ability to name her third daughter Afua when he insists on Fern as the newborn baby's name. Delphine discovers that in her Oakland home Cecile has reconfigured her kitchen into an art, poetry, and print studio, a repurposing that allows her to freely remake her identity as poet and artist, rather than mother and cook. When Cecile tells Delphine of her own childhood and young adulthood, she implicitly reveals reasons behind many of the actions that that puzzle her daughter.

Orphaned at eleven, Cecile lived a Cinderella-like life afterwards when her aunt took her in but made her sleep on the floor. The aunt turned Cecile out of the house at sixteen because she was remarrying and wanted no competition from a teenaged niece with her new husband in the house. Louis, Delphine's father, found Cecile ill and sleeping on a park bench and took her in, offering her a place to stay in exchange for chores. Cecile gave birth to Delphine the next year (*OCS* 207–8). Cecile is a woman who had nothing to call her own throughout her adolescence and was thrust early into adulthood. She faced the choice of living independently but on the streets, or dependently in a house controlled by the man who owned it and fathered her children. Although she does speak well of Louis, the fact they never married and his inability to understand her need to write suggests a basic incompatibility between them. Karen Coats and Lisa Rowe Fraustino posit that motherhood is a role governed by performative expectations, which derive from social texts that "offer scripts for mothers to follow in order to realize a cultural ideal" (108). Rather than conforming to the social scripts dictated for a young mother and needing to find her own identity after so many years of oppression and suppression, Cecile Johnson chooses to leave Louis Gaither and her three young daughters, moving to Oakland, California, where she pursues her vocation as a poet and artist.

Delphine, on the other hand, has bottled up a great deal of resentment at her mother for leaving her and her sisters. Much of her definition of motherhood rests on the mother's responsibility to feed her children. She notes that Cecile's final acts of motherhood before leaving them were to nurse the newborn Fern and give a cookie to toddler Vonetta. Equally, she believes that Cecile fails the three of them as a mother when they first arrive in Oakland by refusing to make a meal for them herself, or even, perhaps, not realizing that providing dinner for the girls is now her responsibility:

> In the animal kingdom the mother bird brings back all she's gathered for the day and drops it into the open mouths of each bird squawking to be fed. Cecile looked at us like it didn't occur to her that we would be hungry and she'd have to do what mothers do: feed their young. I'm no Big Ma in the kitchen, but I would have opened a can of beans and fried up some franks. I can bake a chicken and boil potatoes. I would have never let my long-gone daughters travel three thousand miles without turning on the stove. (30–31)

Cecile not only does not make dinner, she refuses to even let her daughters into the kitchen. Her solution to the problem of dinner is fast food: takeout from Ming's, a local Chinese restaurant. Delphine's anger at her mother is not shared by her sisters, however: "Vonetta and Fern squealed for the shrimp and Pepsi, forgetting that this was wrong. Our mother should have cooked real food for us—at the very least baked a chicken. Made franks and beans" (32). The younger girls are easily seduced by the rare treat of fast food and soda pop and do not feel the emotional deprivation that Delphine attaches to Cecile's refusal to cook a homemade dinner, even one that came from a can and packaged meat. Delphine here echoes her grandmother's resentment of Cecile: Big Ma constantly harps on Cecile's selfishness and cannot forgive her for leaving the family (*OCS* 4, 45), a move that necessitated Big Ma coming to live in Brooklyn and look after the children.

The fast food becomes the normal means of handling dinner while the girls are visiting—until Fern develops constipation and Delphine decides to take matters into her own hands. She has developed an acute craving for a conventional dinner: "All day long at the Center I could think of nothing else but a home-cooked meal. We marched to the Safeway store after playing in the park for an hour. My shopping list was burned into my brain" (*OCS* 103). After purchasing cabbage, onion, potatoes, chicken thighs and wings, and stewed prunes, Delphine demands that Cecile let her inside the kitchen to cook, and she wins by standing her ground despite her mother's anger and by insisting on her own competence:

> "You can't come in my kitchen making a mess. This is my workplace. I don't need you in here turning things upside down."

I said, "I don't make messes," without a lick of sass. I spoke the plain truth. I'd never made a mess in my life. Not even for the fun of it. (*OCS* 106)

Cecile eats Delphine's home-cooked meal with relish—far more than Vonetta and Fern, who pout over losing the nightly fast food treats. In response to their whining question about why they can't have pizza or shrimp lo mein, Delphine responds, "'Because,' I said, enjoying my role as their enemy and big sister, 'that's not food for everyday eating.' I held up the brown Safeway bag with its big red *S* printed right in the center. 'This is'" (*OCS* 103–4). Delphine makes her sisters' health a priority.

In Oakland and her mother's home, Delphine acts as an autonomous agent and learns to negotiate the world around her for her own, her family's, and the community's benefit. In a place where Cecile has successfully redefined herself and taken control of her life, Delphine is motivated by a similar impulse, even if that impulse is shaped by more conventional gender behaviors (that is, inspired by Big Ma) and thus criticized by Cecile as a "yoke" (*OCS* 110). Significant for Delphine's decisions and actions—and Cecile's, for that matter—is the social milieu of west Oakland in the summer of 1968,[5] represented by the Black Panthers' presence in the narrative, particularly the Free Breakfast for Children Program. Motivated by the poverty and political powerlessness of Oakland's African American population, the founding group of the Black Panthers in Oakland became nationally infamous for observing and engaging police to resist and prevent the abuse of Oakland's Black population; however, they also initiated a variety of less-known social programs. These were intended to engage the community and pursue a more thorough and ongoing radical revisioning of the relationship between Oakland's African American population and the city. One of the most ubiquitous effects of poverty is hunger, and the Panthers' most successful community outreach was the Free Breakfast Program. Joshua Bloom and Waldo E. Martin write in *Black against Empire*, "The Party sought meaningful activities for members that would serve the community, strengthen the Party, and improve its image in the public relations battle with the state. In this context, community programs quickly became a cornerstone of Party activity nationwide" (181). The Free Breakfast for Children Program began in Oakland in September, 1968. The Black Panthers prioritized it to make it "the most important Panther activity" (Bloom 182), one of the Panthers' "*programs for survival*" (Patel 1, emphasis in original). Mary Potorti notes in "Feeding Revolution: The Black Panther

Party and the Politics of Food" that "The practical benefits of free breakfasts were great. As *The Black Panther* regularly emphasized, a morning meal worked to silence the hunger pains of Black youth that so often incapacitated them during school hours" (46). Moreover, the program was independent of government aid, relying "entirely on donations from community members, local churches, and most importantly from neighborhood businesses and grocery chains" (45).

If the milieus of *P.S. Be Eleven* and *Gone Crazy in Alabama* are stabilized by longstanding societal norms, the Oakland of *One Crazy Summer* is permeated by a radical push for self-reliance, autonomy, and a mindset both aware and critical of social injustice. In this novel Williams-Garcia forces the girls, especially Delphine, to seriously rethink their expectations of themselves, their mother, and their newfound community. As mentioned above, one of the central tenets of Hinton and Branyon's argument is that "Williams-Garcia places Delphine in a position to push back against myths and interlocking oppressions and gives her role models to consider as she begins to assume the fullness of who she is as an emerging young Black woman" (341). While Hinton and Branyon make this claim about the series as a whole, in this novel the pushback develops most sharply in the challenging milieu that Delphine must navigate in her mother's house in its west Oakland neighborhood and at the People's Center, where the free breakfasts, education, social outreach, and activism constitute one of the structural centers of the novel.

The novel is punctuated by breakfast scenes at the People's Center, followed by lessons or activities to teach the kids about issues of social justice that impact them directly. Williams-Garcia's portrayal reflects what Potorti observes about the actual free breakfast program: "In this way, the breakfast programs had the potential to awaken the revolutionary consciousness of the people to see the interrelatedness of capitalism, social stratification, and their own material deprivation and political marginalization" (46). By sending her daughters to the People's Center for breakfast, Cecile catalyzes their independence and speeds up their integration into the neighborhood community. Delphine is surprised that the breakfast program exists: it does not fit the view of the Oakland Panthers as "militant" that she has absorbed from television news (*OCS* 57, 64). She intuitively understands why the media focus on violence (both real and potential) instead of daily social work, when she notes that "beating eggs never makes the evening news" (*OCS* 64). The girls learn that the breakfast program is feeding not just African American kids but everyone in the neighborhood (Black, white, Hispanic, Chinese). Despite the criticisms of Crazy Kelvin, they eventually realize that the local Panthers recognize them as part of the community because they are "Sister Inzilla's" children (*OCS* 67): they belong because Cecile (Inzilla/Nzila) contributes (albeit reluctantly) to the Panthers' missions by making informational posters and flyers for them. The person who most effectively facilitates their integration is Sister Mukumbu, whom Delphine recognizes as a "true teacher" because "She asked a teacher's type of question. The kind that says: Join in" (*OCS* 71). And while the walls of the room feature posters with titles that reflect the Panthers' activism—"What We Want," "What We Believe"—Sister Mukumbu creates an integrative, cross-disciplinary lesson (combining astronomy and politics) that uses the motion of revolution as a metaphor to broaden the children's understanding of the reach of the concept, a nice example of liberal education. On another day, Delphine watches "the young white guys who delivered bread and orange juice" to the Center talk easily with the Panthers and realizes how skewed the media portrayal of angry "militants" is: the media "never showed anyone like Sister Makumbu or Sister Pat, passing out toast and teaching in classrooms" (*OCS* 87). On another day, the children are served grapes for a snack and learn "how the migrant workers who picked them had to fight for their rights" (*OCS* 87), showing the Panthers' concern for social injustice for all those who suffer from it.

The lessons that the girls absorb at the People's Center along with their breakfasts culminate in two scenes of the novel where the girls autonomously practice the ideology they have learned. When the local Safeway where Delphine shops for their dinners refuses to put up a poster to advertise a "Free Huey" rally in a neighborhood park, Delphine abruptly realizes the political power of food. Although she has introduced herself as a regular store customer, the manager shuts her down with a refusal, as "against store policy." Although he phrases it politely and smiles, Delphine chooses to boycott the store for its unwillingness to support the community: "I had been keeping a list of the no-sayers and put Safeway at the very top of it. My sisters, Cecile, and I would eat egg rolls, white rice, bean pies, and fried fish before we spent another penny in the stores of the no sayers" (*OCS* 184). In other words, Delphine chooses to abandon her position on homemade food vs. fast food in order to not support a business that she perceives as at odds with her own political agenda.

In the second culminating scene, after the police break into Cecile's house, wreck her kitchen/art space, and arrest her, the first thing that the girls do once they return to the house is clean up that space and put it back together the best that they can. In doing so, the daughters manifest their acceptance of the kitchen as their mother's place, defined by Cecile and her vision of herself as poet and artist rather than society's conventional view of that space as gendered and maternal:

> I mopped the floor once the papers, letter blocks, and mess had been cleared away. We brought all the letters and boxes into the living room and spread out the tablecloth. We spent the rest of the afternoon sorting through Cecile's letters. It was like a game. Finding the right letters, the right type, the right size. I put the "Nzila" in one box by themselves. We didn't know if that was the right way, but at least it was a way. (*OCS* 175)

As Delphine's choice to privilege the letters of her mother's chosen name suggests, she has radically revised her ideas about her mother's untraditional life choices from when they arrived in Oakland. At the beginning she was filled with resentment over Cecile's abandonment of herself and her sisters, her rejection of the role of mother, especially as manifested in Cecile's refusal to cook for them. But even early on Delphine was seeking to understand a purpose to her mother's unconventional actions, as she thought when she first got a glimpse of papers hanging in the kitchen Cecile would not allow the girls to enter: "And this, the white wings hanging in her house, wasn't strange at all. It was halfway what I expected. I would hate to think she had left us to lead a normal cookie-baking, pork chop–frying life" (*OCS* 53). Delphine's rejection of a conventional motherly role for Cecile, here defined by cooking and baking, suggests how much she *needs* to understand her mother's radical redefinition of her life after leaving them. To have found out that Cecile embraced a traditional, kitchen-based woman's role but without her children would hurt far worse than discovering that her mother can live a fulfilling life as an artist—a life that is at odds with the orthodox practice of motherhood.

Cecile's life choices work and make sense in radicalized 1968 Oakland in ways that would be far more difficult for her to achieve in conventional Brooklyn. She is part of a community that is finding ways to support its members who need social aid. Not every attempt is completely successful or long term, but the ferment of 1968 manifests in food aid from multiple sources. The Black Panthers' Free Breakfast Program is the most obvious, both historically and within the novel. As Raj Patel observes, it was responsible "for instigating real 'school meal revolutions' . . . and for embarrassing the federal government into taking child nutrition seriously" (3). Its revolutionary purpose and success were noted by Elaine Brown: "Our goal was not feeding breakfast but creating the conditions for revolution. For example, this effort sparked the people to demand that schools throughout the country provide free breakfasts, and the people won" (qtd. in Shih and Williams 98). But the Panthers are not the only ones concerned by hunger in the community. The girls encounter another, more privately based attempt to feed the hungry on their first evening in Oakland. Their mother sends them to Ming's, the local Chinese takeout restaurant. When the proprietor sees the girls arrive, she dismisses them rudely: "The Chinese lady behind the counter said, 'No free egg rolls. No more free egg rolls'" (*OCS* 36). After the girls assert their intention and demonstrate their ability to pay, the proprietor explains: "'Everybody poor. Everybody hungry. I give free egg roll. Feel sorry. Then everyone come for free egg roll.' She muttered on like Cecile did and looked mean and tired like Big Ma looks on washboard days" (*OCS* 37). Delphine unkindly christens her "Mean Lady Ming," failing to note that this woman had established a small social program of her own, trying to ease the problem of hunger in the area around her through providing one small free item. Demand proves to be higher than she can economically sustain through her business, however, and she has been forced to stop giving out free food. Williams-Garcia's choice to include this small scene reinforces the social ill of hunger that the Panthers try to solve and muster greater resources to combat. One final example of concern for food-endangered community members occurs after Cecile is arrested with two other Black Panthers. Mrs. Woods, the mother of Hirohito, a neighborhood boy from the People's Center, brings "a pan with tinfoil over it" that is filled with "fried pork chops, rice, and string beans" (*OCS* 171) so the girls can have dinner—and then takes them in until Cecile is released. While this form of bringing food to a family in crisis is an ancient practice across cultures, the reason Mrs. Woods articulates for stepping forward to help them connects to the political climate of the day: her husband, a Vietnam veteran, was also arrested months ago and is currently in prison for protesting. She says to Delphine, "We know the same things. We have to stick together" (*OCS* 178), a pronouncement that explicitly links her food aid to the girls with the political oppression both families have experienced. On both national and personal levels, *One Crazy Summer* links food with politics to show the possibilities of radical change.

* * *

To adopt the Black Panthers' language, in *One Crazy Summer, P.S. Be Eleven*, and *Gone Crazy in Alabama* Rita Williams-Garcia sketches "programs for survival" for her characters in the urban West, urban North, and rural South. In the context of African Americans' diasporic history, particularly in the twentieth century, each of those milieus requires a distinct set of strategies to navigate the limitations and oppressions imposed on them—whether it is the racially restrictive real estate covenants of the West and the North, or the segregated Jim Crow South—to create a space (neighborhood, home, farm) where a safe, self-affirming existence is possible. In *One Crazy Summer*, Delphine, Vonetta, and Fern find themselves in a place where radical social forces have pushed beyond the envelope of the status quo to demand a civic reorganization where power, responsibility, and governance are shared by all of the citizens of the city. Oakland in 1968 was a place where the profound self-fashioning that Cecile pursues was possible, and in that milieu her daughters begin to discover their own power, what they can make of themselves in a place which, despite longstanding injustices, affords them much freedom and latitude. Having started the series in revolutionary Oakland, Williams-Garcia explores the roots out of which the revolution grew: the more conventional post–Great Migration urban experience that the girls have grown up with, and then the rural south that their father, grandmother, and great grandmother knew. As Williams-Garcia moves forward in her series, she reaches back into the African American experience, and foodways, of the recent and more distant past. Thus, in the subsequent books, the girls find themselves back in more restrictive circumstances than in the first. The freedoms they discovered in Oakland are curtailed, particularly in *Gone Crazy in Alabama*, but those freedoms the girls experienced function as a restless historical telos, a reminder of what is possible when the times permit change. In each novel, as Hinton and Branyon observed, the girls encounter women who model varying paths toward womanhood; close examination reveals how directly tied to food and foodways those paths are, including community breakfasts, convenience foods, and country cooking. Food thus becomes instrumental to understanding how the characters navigate the social landscape, its traps and opportunities, to create for themselves a protected space in which to survive and thrive.

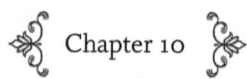

Chapter 10

REFUGEE NARRATIVES, CUISINE CLASH

The Case of Thanhha Lai's *Inside Out & Back Again*

> To truly grieve the loss of a nation and the robbed history of a banished people, that old umbilical cord must be unearthed and, through the task of art, through the act of imagination, be woven into a new living tapestry.
>
> —ANDREW LAM, *PERFUME DREAMS:*
> *REFLECTIONS ON THE VIETNAMESE DIASPORA* (15)

To begin with a sweeping generalization, just as colonialism and its effects have been an integral part of human history, so too have refugees and forced migrations. The Babylonian exile of the seventh century BCE, the 1830 Trail of Tears, or the 2018 refugee crisis in Venezuela (to cite three unrelated examples widely separated by time and geography) all show that history is marked, even structured, by the involuntary displacement of individuals and groups due to war, violence, and politics. As Roger Zetter glosses the history of refugees in the introduction to the first volume of *The Journal of Refugee Studies*:

> Alienation, persecution and forced migration are amongst the most profoundly disturbing human experiences. Documented over many centuries, the traumas of mass exodus confront those who are excluded from societies at times of acute political crises or rapid and fundamental redefinition of their economic, social or ethnic identity. But in the present century it is the word "refugee" which has increasingly been deployed to describe the millions of uprooted people who have been forced into exile or displaced within their own countries because of intolerance, war or other human factors. "Refugee" constitutes one of

the most powerful labels currently in the repertoire of humanitarian concern, national and international public policy and social differentiation. (1)

Of recent crises, one of the most well covered has been the exodus of Vietnamese nationals after the fall of South Vietnam in 1975. Journalists, scholars, authors, and artists have documented, analyzed, theorized, and explored the global migration of the Vietnamese after the end of the Vietnam War. According to Mai-Lin K. Hong, "Southeast Asian war refugees, of whom Vietnamese are the largest subset, have been cataloged, filmed, photographed, psychoanalyzed, studied, and otherwise 'viewed' through lenses of journalism, Hollywood filmmaking, anthropology, policy, social work, and more" (21–22). All of these lenses, however, look at the refugee experience as other, from the perspective of the West, which is narrow, restrictive, and bent on erasure. For Hong, "Vietnamese refugees have appeared in American literature, historiography, and mass media most often as passive, traumatized objects of Western spectatorship, pity, and charity; as reminders (to Americans) of US military failure; or, in positive but no less problematic cases, as grateful, compliant additions to the American national community" (22). Corroborating Hong's point are two articles, one recent and one older. In "'The New Americans': The Creation of a Typology of Vietnamese-American Identity in Children's Literature" from 2010, Subarno Chattarji analyzes a set of nonfiction children's books about the Vietnamese experience written by non-Vietnamese authors for a non-Vietnamese audience. She characterizes the books as flattening "complexities to create a disjunction between two nations, cultures and lives in order to emphasize the successful Americanization of these new people" (419). Chattarji demonstrates the limited, stereotypical portrayals of the tragic war, the hardworking Vietnamese grateful to a magnanimous nation that has saved and redeemed them. Correlatively, other constructions of Vietnamese American identity, such as the more complex realities of the war and the refugee crisis, and the United States's complicity in creating that crisis, are absent from these portrayals. In a 1991 article, Jan Susina reviews a set of children's fiction, written by non-Vietnamese for a non-Vietnamese audience, all of which work with reductive stereotypes of the refugees facing intolerant Americans. These paint a picture of the difficulties of settlement and assimilation while encouraging acceptance but without exploring the historical, ideological, or material complexities on either side of the conflict and, in the end, focusing more on "the various responses of the native-born Americans to these recent immigrants" (59) rather than on the immigrants themselves. Both types of books are clearly inadequate to meet the contemporary call for books, especially for young readers, that portray authentic experiences of minority peoples with well-developed subjectivity.

In *Body Counts: The Vietnam War and Militarized Refuge(es)*, Yén Lê Espiritu praises the development of the field of Vietnamese Studies beyond its initial focus on a set of stereotypes of Vietnamese refugees as tragic, passive, in need of salvation, grateful, and hardworking ("a model minority") and, instead, has begun to "provide us a rare glimpse into how Vietnamese have created their worlds and made meaning for themselves" (15). In concert with Espiritu's observation, Vietnamese immigrants have taken up agency and produced texts about the experience of violence in the war, displacement in its aftermath, assimilation (and resistance to that) within American culture, and even, at this historical moment, the return to and rediscovery of Vietnam both by those who fled it and their descendants. Such texts have also won awards, signifying the willingness of contemporary culture to engage with a past that is difficult for both Vietnamese and Americans: examples include Viet Thanh Nguyen's *The Sympathizer: A Novel*, which won the 2016 Pulitzer Prize, and—the focus of our study—Thanhha Lai's *Inside Out & Back Again*, winner of the 2011 National Book Award for Young People's Literature and a Newbery Honor book in 2012. Lai's autobiographical novel, based on her own experiences immigrating to the United States during her childhood in the wake of the Vietnam War, offers a complex view of the immigrant experience. She constructs a portrait of the Vietnamese immigrant agenda that shows the need to adapt to a new culture, the pressing desire to maintain original cultural identity, and the various means by which the family members seek and achieve agency in their new lives, what writer and journalist Andrew Lam calls "that adding on of identity, that effort to adjust" (*East Eats West* 3). Food consistently serves as a cornerstone in the family's efforts, from their pleasure in the foods of their homeland before they leave, to their puzzlement over the strange new foods of the alien new land, and their adaptation of food traditions to maintain their cultural identity as they acclimate to American culture.

In terms of food and the maintenance of a diasporic, transnational Vietnamese identity (Viet Kieu), Jennifer Howell's analysis of Vietnamese French graphic novelist Clément Baloup's use of Vietnamese food and foodways in *Quitter Saigon* (2012) and *Little Saigon* (2013) presents a useful correlation. She notes that "Vietnamese foodways . . . transcend geographical regions and can transplant ethnicity beyond the point of origin

... maintain[ing] links to a past whose physical traces were lost during forced migrations" (33–34). In Baloup's two books, learning, preparing and eating Vietnamese dishes in France produce cross-generational bonding in the form of a father–son cooking lesson. Food is a memory trigger and catalyst for storytelling, for "the majority of Baloup's protagonists recount their experiences of war and displacement while sharing a Vietnamese meal" (36). Food is a means through which trauma is processed while keeping a familial and cultural history alive within another language, culture, and set of foodways in an evolving present. As Howell puts it,

> It should be noted that what, when, and how we eat—or what are commonly referred to as "foodways"—are closely related to ethnic identity. . . . Food becomes an external stimulus for memory (external to the memory of war and migration). . . . Food, specifically Vietnamese food, thus emerges as the apex of the transnational triangle, creating a tangible or perhaps edible link between past and present, between country of origin and host country. (37–38)

Using Susan Kalcik's essay "Ethnic Foodways in America: Symbol and the Performance of Identity," Howell makes the claim for foodways as a particularly strong cultural anchor "because they are the earliest-formed layers of culture and therefore are the last to erode" (41). For Howell, "Clément Baloup's highlighting of foodways surfaces as an efficient way to navigate the transnational triangle and to resist historical amnesia" (48–50).

Within an American context, Thanhha Lai adopts a similar use of food in *Inside Out & Back Again*, signaling a recovery and maintenance of the past as well as an active engagement with the present, both in terms of time and place. Lai uses food and foodways in a variety of ways to capture the refugee arc, from waiting for the North Vietnamese army to enter Saigon and trigger the departure of Hà and her family, to the period of deprivation and uncertainty on the South Vietnamese navy ship and the refugee camp in Guam, to initial settlement in the United States, to the slow integration into the community in Alabama where their sponsor has brought them.[1]

The book begins and ends with the celebration of the Lunar New Year (Tết) and the special ceremonial foods which reinforce Vietnamese culture. As Nicole Routhier notes in *The Foods of Vietnam*,

> Festivals and holidays, always an integral part of Vietnam's culture, are celebrated with banquets that feature special foods. Tet, the Lunar New

Year, is the most important of the holidays. . . . Families gather to prepare and feast on traditional dishes, such as abalone soup (*sup bao ngu*), fried spring rolls (*cha gío*), glutinous rice cakes filled with meat and beans and boiled in banana leaves (*banh trung*), and candied fruit (*mut*). (13)²

At the beginning of the book, Há's mother prepares *báhn chúng* (which *The Foods of Vietnam* transliterates as *banh trung*) in the face of the coming disaster, despite the prophecy that the *báhn chúng* would be "smeared with blood" (4). At the end of the book, a year later, as the family has begun to settle into their new life, the mother makes a version of *báhn chúng* adapted to available ingredients, which Há declares "Not the same, / but not bad" (258), after having spent their first five months in the United States feeling disgusted by most American foods. In essence, what the mother manages at the end of the book is to produce a transnational food that reflects the family's transformation from Vietnamese to Viet Kieu (foreign settled). In the introduction to *Into the Vietnamese Kitchen: Treasured Foodways, Modern Flavors*, chef, food, and cookbook writer Andrea Nguyen speaks to a similar hybrid food experience when her family settled in Southern California after the fall of Saigon:

> Times were tough, but our family always enjoyed satisfying meals. At first, we made do on what we could afford to spend and what was locally available. That meant Americanizing Vietnamese food. Mom and Dad hunted down substitutes for key ingredients, such as fish sauce, that were unknown in supermarkets. But as diligent as they were, the food wasn't the same because we had to rely on unremarkable rice and soy sauce. (4)

Just as Clément Baloup and Andrea Nguyen show "how Vietnamese have created their worlds and made meaning for themselves" (Espiritu 15), so too does Tranhha Lai in *Inside Out & Back Again*.

Lai begins her narrative by showing conditions in Saigon near the end of American occupation. As the North Vietnamese approach the city and food becomes scarce and expensive, Há ingeniously manages the money her mother gives her for supplies to buy sweets for herself. When her mother sends her to the market to buy food, Há shaves down the amounts from a hundred grams to ninety-nine grams of pork, seven-eighths of a bushel of water spinach rather than a bushel, and four and three-fourths cubes of tofu instead of five. Although the merchants grumble about the odd amounts, the slight differences in price create a small surplus of change that Há can use for the sweets she craves: "a pouch of toasted coconut / one sugary fried dough / two crunchy mung bean cookies" (20). A few months later, when the political situation is more dire and prices have doubled, Há still manages to shave a little off the pork and buys just the fried dough as her treat, feeling both sacrificial in giving up the other sweets and clever in her ability to still be able to manage a little treat for herself in this period of deprivation without her mother's or brothers' knowledge.

After fleeing their home in Saigon as boat refugees in the early part of the novel, when the family is beset by scarce supplies, shortages and hunger, and no one on board can cook for fear of being detected by the North Vietnamese, food becomes for the refugees a means of survival and an insecure source of nutrition, yet even in such strained circumstances Há maintains a sense of the pleasure food creates. Although she receives a very small portion of rice, she still savors its flavor and remembers another flavor from home:

> The first hot bite
> Of freshly cooked rice
> Plump and nutty
> Makes me imagine
> The taste of ripe papaya
> Although one has nothing
> To do with the other. (78)

Homesickness takes the form of food longings for Há: her mother gives her paper to write on, but Há prefers to draw the foods she misses, especially in her hunger:

> Pouches of pan-fried shredded coconut
> Tamarind paste on banana leaf
> Steamed corn on the cob
> Rounds of fried dough
> Wedges of pineapple on a stick
> And of course
> cubes of papaya tender and shiny. (81)

Há is aware of other families' food hoarding: although everyone hides the supplies they brought and she does not see others eating, she nonetheless smells "sardines, dried durian, / salted eggs, toasted sesame" (75). Hungry, Há cannot stop herself from leaning toward the family on the neighboring mat, but her mother, too proud to beg and more aware of the social mores than her daughter, shakes her head, insisting that Há too ignore the unoffered food. The refugees have no idea, of course, how long they will be at sea before finding help; such hoarding by individual families is the logical recourse for survival by those who have limited resources which must last for an undetermined amount of time.

The material recovery of food as cultural signifier begins when they are rescued by an American ship and start to feel more secure; all the refugee families bring out their hidden food resources from below deck: "ramen noodles, beef jerky / dried shrimp, butter biscuits, / tamarind pods, canned fish," all shared among the refugees in a party atmosphere (93). But it is in the refugee camp in Guam when cases of fish sauce (*nước mắm*) arrive that Vietnamese foodways more fully recover. With fish sauce, the refugees begin to cook again rather than simply eat from the cans of strange foods supplied to them in the camp:

> Everything is
> more edible
> with *nước mắm*.
>
> Brother Vũ
> sautés the beef-and-potato goo
> with onions
> and sprinkles on the magic sauce
> before serving the mess with rice.
>
> Lines extend to the beach. (100–102)

Há is so enraptured with it that she drinks a cup of it straight, ecstatic over its "salty . . . bitter . . . fishy" taste:

> My head whirls
> and my breath stinks
> for days
>
> I do not mind. (100–102)

Refugee Narratives, Cuisine Clash: Lai's *Inside Out & Back Again*

Routhier notes that fish sauce is "the one most characteristic element in virtually every Vietnamese dish . . . a salty, pungent sauce derived from fermented anchovies. *Nuoc mam* is to the Vietnamese what soy sauce is to the Chinese" (9). As the refugees depart from their homeland and begin the process of integrating into the larger world, especially given that most everything has been stripped from them, food remains a viable, accessible, material, and sensual marker of their Vietnamese identity. Food becomes the locus for a developing a transnational identity, an evolving present, which Howell notes "creat[es] a tangible or perhaps edible link between past and present" (38).

In the camp, no longer starving, Há's attitude toward the food available to them is initially marked by alienation and abjection. The canned beef and potatoes taste "like salty vomit" (96). Once they have fish sauce, the "magic sauce," the hybrid results are palatable, because they taste—they trigger the senses as—Vietnamese. In the United States, as they transition toward integration, Há and her family must once again move from experiencing food as abject to palatable. The chicken that their sponsor usually provides them from the grocery store, "chopped and frozen" (119), is, like the rest of the food he brings, strange. One day, as a treat he brings them a bucket of fried chicken that initially smells quite promising, but the first bite is disgusting:

> The skin tastes as promised,
> crunchy and salty,
> hot and spicy.
>
> But
> Mother wipes
> the corners of her mouth
> before passing her piece
> into her napkin.
>
> Brother Vũ gags. (120)

Back in Vietnam the family was accustomed to eating freshly slaughtered free-ranging chicken fed on a natural diet of self-foraged insects, resulting in a "tight" muscle texture to the meat when it was chewed (121). The industrially raised and processed chicken their sponsor has offered them cannot compete: its loose, soggy consistency quite literally turns their stomachs.

Há's experience with school lunches is also marked by alienation and abjection. A stranger in a school filled with children who have been classmates for years, unable to speak English, racially different from the black and white children who self-segregate in the lunchroom, and confronted with an unfamiliar and unappetizing hot dog for lunch, Há does not know how to insert herself into the social landscape in which she finds herself on her first day at school. Unable to integrate, instead she simply retreats from the lunchroom. Her solution is to save rolls from dinner and eat them in the bathroom during lunch period each day rather than revisit "the noisy room / full of mouths / chewing and laughing" (181). When her tutor and family friend, Mrs. Washington, discovers this is Há's daily routine, she is horrified and vows to improve her young pupil's experience. The next day, Há's teacher, Miss Scott, allows her to stay at her desk and eat the lunch that Mrs. Washington has packed: a sandwich, potato chips, an apple, and a cookie. Há lacks the vocabulary for several of the American foods, but the combination pleases her Vietnamese-shaped palate: "Something salty, / something sweet, / perfect" (183). Two of her classmates come in as she is eating, red-haired Pam and African American Steven: the only two who seem willing to cross color lines with each other are likewise willing to welcome their new Asian classmate. Their offer of friendship allows her to escape the abject, isolated space of the bathroom and makes the social landscape less to be feared. Although Há's school experience improves once she has friends, other classmates continue to persecute her. Her particular bully, whom she never calls by name but refers to merely as "Pink Boy," frequently calls her "pancake face" as a racial slur. When both of them are angered in a confrontation, she notices that "No longer pink, / he's red, / blood-orange red / like a ripe papaya," and she calls him "Đu đủ Face," using the Vietnamese word for papaya. His friends, however, misunderstand her, hearing "Doo-doo Face," and laugh at him (220). Há thus turns the tables on her tormentor: he attempts to render her abject by comparing her to food, which is what she does to him with the papaya comparison; the pun she cleverly creates allows her to publicly abjectify him by comparing him to excrement. She empowers herself not only by standing up to him, but by showing her mastery of two languages—a particularly satisfying experience given how she has struggled with the new language and often felt inadequate in the face of it.

More than any other food in the book, the papaya is the overarching, multivalent symbol of *Inside Out & Back Again*. It is present throughout the book, from beginning to end; its memory is present through long stretches of its physical absence; it is material, imaginary, and a key marker of memory for Há. It grounds her identity as Vietnamese. In Saigon, she plants and cultivates the papaya tree in spite of the coming disaster. She values its fruits, which serve as a measure of her love for her mother, whom she says she loves "even more than I love / my papaya tree" as she plans to give the first fruit to her mother (7). She watches with excitement as the fruit grows, looking forward to its ripening and the sensual delight it will bring:

> Middle sweet
> between a mango and a pear.
>
> Soft as a yam
> gliding down
> after three easy,
> thrilling chews. (21)

But the date for that desire is April 5, 1975, and Saigon falls on April 30. The family eats the largest still unripe papaya from the tree just before leaving: "Mother says yellow papaya / tastes lovely / dipped in chili salt" and urges her children to eat fresh fruit while they can. Há projects her grief over their departure onto the unripe papaya fruit: "Black seeds spill / like clusters of eyes, / wet and crying," while her brother cuts down the tree as they flee so as not to give the invading army any help or sustenance (60). The abandoned, unripe papaya clearly serves as a symbol for Há's own childhood in her homeland of Vietnam.

Há does not get the chance to harvest or eat the ripe fruits from the tree, but, more importantly, she takes the memory of them on her journey, a memory which becomes emblematic of her lost home. On the ship, she savors the nutty flavor of her ration of rice while remembering her papaya tree, as referenced above. Observing her mother's suffering because of the loss of her husband, Há feels compassion for her mother because of her own sense of loss over her papaya tree (176). In Alabama, Há's teacher introduces Vietnam—and thus, Há herself—solely through a set of pictures of the war and its devastations. Shocked by this reductive view of her country and herself, although she is still too shy to protest, Há wonders why there could not be other, more representative pictures of Vietnam: "She should have shown / something about / papayas and Tết" (195). For Há, the papaya has become a metonym for her home culture.

The papaya eventually also provides an empowering link to her new culture. Fortuitously, when she meets with her neighbor Mrs. Washington, who lost her son in the war, Há gets the visual portrait of her homeland that she had longed for through the son's photographs of Vietnam as a green and verdant land. One picture of a papaya tree excites Há and creates her first compassionate tie with someone in the United States outside her family: "Excited I yell, / Đu đủ! / I'm stabbing at the image. / *Best food*" (202). The interchange with Mrs. Washington, who laughs about the similar sound to the American euphemism for excrement, gives Há the inventive, linguistic power to assert herself later to defeat the bully who has been harassing her. Finally, at the climax of the novel, Mrs. Washington gives Há a package of dried, sugar-coated papaya slices for Christmas, a gift that should signal a bridge between her home country and the new one. Há, however, is angered rather than pleased:

> Three pouches of
> dried papaya
>
> Chewy
> Sugary
> Waxy
> Sticky
>
> Not the same
> at all. (232)

She rejects the overprocessed fruit for its taste and texture, throwing it into the garbage as abject, unwilling to accept any substitute for the delicious fresh fruit from her backyard tree in Saigon. She "stare[s] at the photograph of a real papaya tree, / wonder[s] if [she']'ll ever taste sweet, tender, orange flesh / again" (233). But Há's mother recovers the fruit, washes off the sugar coating, and rehydrates the slices, after which Há finds them acceptable:

> The sugar has melted off
> leaving
> plump
> moist
> chewy
> bites.
>
> Hummm...

Not the same,
but not bad
at all. (234)

Há's willingness to see the connection between her memory of fresh papaya and the reconstituted fruit foreshadows her acceptance of her mother's adapted *báhn chúng*—"Not the same, / but not bad" (258)—for their Tết celebration at the end of the novel. Perhaps most effectively through the papaya, Lai makes the point that remembered, reconstituted, and adapted foods are fundamental symbols for transnational identity.

In *Nothing Ever Dies: Vietnam and the Memory of War*, Viet Thanh Nguyen makes the point that "minority writers are most easily heard in America when they speak about the historical events that defined their population" (201). As such, they can give aesthetic voice—represent memory—in particular ways: "Each racially defined ethnic group gets its own notable history for which it is remembered by Americans. . . . *Vietnamese Americans get the war*. Any ethnically defined literature is bound up with that ethnic group's history in America, because so-called ethnic literatures are forms of memory . . ." (200–201, emphasis ours). Nguyen, however, sees this role as a trap. Vietnamese American writers could simply reproduce the given history and its conventions (tragic loss, grateful refugees, assimilating to American life as a "model minority"). But Nguyen claims that the ethical minority writer has the responsibility of writing beyond those conventions: "While a minority's power is not equal to the majority's power, the minority must claim responsibility for the power it does possess, the power it must have if it can resist and ultimately, liberate itself" (197). Per our chapter's epigraph, for Andrew Lam such liberation comes about for Vietnamese American authors when their "art, through the act of imagination, [is] woven into a new living tapestry" (*Perfume Dreams* 15). Hong's analysis of Lai's accomplishments in *Inside Out & Back Again* shows how Lai's novel is congruent with Nguyen and Lam's aesthetic call to action:

> Lai's text does not advocate solutions to, or even overtly criticize, the structural dilemmas its characters face. But it does enable the reader to observe, with Hà's critical gaze, the intersecting social, political, and economic pressures that contour refugee experiences. In doing so, the text gently disrupts the dominant narratives of rescue, gratitude, and private hospitality that frequently structure popular narratives about Vietnamese refugees that are told from non-Vietnamese perspectives. (34–35)

Lai thus successfully writes against the flattened complexities that Chattarji criticized in American portrayals of the Vietnamese refugee diaspora. Although Hong does not refer specifically to the representations of food in Lai's narrative, food nonetheless serves as a prominent mediator of the clash and connection between cultures that Lai's protagonist Há experiences throughout the novel and becomes a primary form through which Há and her family experience Lam's "adding on of identity, that effort to adjust" (*East Eats West* 3). The preservation and practice of specific foods and foodways provide comfort in recreating traditions in a strange and new land; other newer foods, such as the chocolate chip cookies and pancakes which Mrs. Washington makes for Há to reward her success in learning English, help provide entrance to a new society.[3] Food provides one of the primary means through which Lai achieves the disruption of "the dominant narratives of rescue, gratitude, and private hospitality" for which Hong commends her (Hong 34–35). It is through food that Lai complicates the experience of Vietnamese immigration and the resulting transnational shift in sense of identity. Her portrayals of unpalatable fried chicken or dried papaya upset the expected "gratitude" narrative; her depiction of refashioned traditional foods such as the *báhn chúng* for Tết made in the form of a log with regular rice and black beans wrapped in cloth, rather than in a square with glutinous rice and mung beans wrapped in banana leaves, shows the satisfaction in learning to adapt to new conditions while preserving old foodways. Such techniques empower Lai's immigrant characters to create a bridged sense of personal and national identity—as she no doubt had to create for herself.

NOTES

Chapter 1: An Invitation to the Table: The Tastes of Children's Literature

1. Although we have not included a chapter on Latinx literature, we refer interested readers to our 2016 article, "Privilege and Exploitation: Food as Dual Signifier in Pamela Muñoz Ryan's *Esperanza Rising*."

Chapter 2: American Children's Cookbooks as Scenes of Instruction: Tracking Historical Shifts of Work, Play, Pleasure, and Memory

1. A virtue exemplified by one of the most popular of nineteenth-century American cookbooks, Lydia Marie Child's *The Frugal [American] Housewife*, which went through "33 editions in the United States, 12 in England, and 9 in Germany" (Holland 46).

2. With the recipes organized in categories (for example, Sandwiches and Canapes, Soups, Eggs, Soufflés, and Timbales), Rombauer's *Cooking for Boys and Girls* reflects the organization of late nineteenth- and twentieth-century adult cookbooks, like *The Joy of Cooking* or *The Boston Cooking School Cookbook*, rather than serving as a cumulative guide to domestic mastery. Moreover, reflecting what Susan Leonardi esteems in *The Joy of Cooking, Cooking for Boys and Girls* is chatty and interactive. Along with instruction on utensils, ingredients, and method, Rombauer intercuts narratives, stories that are meant to entertain and instruct (much like Aunt Jane's stories in *Six Little Cooks*). Most important, and what distinguishes it from the majority of children's cookbooks of the era, *Cooking for Boys and Girls* focuses on from-scratch cooking. Rombauer's children's cookbook had some success since it went through nine printings between 1946 and 1952, but it did not achieve the long publishing history of *The Joy of Cooking* and was displaced in the 1950s by children's cookbooks focused on convenience foods.

3. The commercial tie-in is acknowledged on the copyright page. Tacoma Metal Products began making the Little Chef Oven in 1945; the deluxe version had elements that would actually heat up (Haley).

4. For those who doubt the feasibility of persuading a small American child to enjoy a wide variety of global cuisines, see also *Hungry Monkey: A Food-Loving Father's Quest*

to *Raise an Adventurous Eater*, by Matthew Amster-Burton, food critic for the *Seattle Times*. He chronicles the adventure of raising his daughter to share all meals with him and his wife, eating the same food they consumed. By age one Iris happily consumed minced "endive gratin, salmon, pasta with arugula, barbequed ribs" (23), as well as sushi, bibimbap, dim sum, and both Thai and Szechuan food. Although she became pickier around age three, many of these continued to be favorites as she grew, although she eventually lost the taste for spicy food (53).

5. This national picnic happened on Bastille Day 2000 to commemorate the millennium (Lichfield).

6. Other types of texts within this group would include hobby and craft books, which also contain directions for children to carry out to produce real-world objects.

7. Although Barbara Wall focuses primarily on fiction in *The Narrator's Voice: The Dilemma of Children's Fiction*, we find her definition of the narrative format of "double address" appropriate for describing how the writers of children's cookbooks, as a genre, address both a child and adult audience: "narrators will address child narratees overtly and self-consciously, and will also address adults . . . as the implied author's attention shifts away from the implied child reader to a different older audience. . ." (178). Wall speaks of other narrative formats—single address, dual address, even covert double address—but it is the overt form of double address that is most applicable to children's cookbooks.

Chapter 3: Puddings and Pies: Meat Pastries in the Tales of Beatrix Potter

1. Peter Rabbit is the counterexample, because he rejects his mother's safe and comfortable prepared foodways to pursue the dangerous, raw food in the paradoxically wild space of Mr. McGregor's garden. Peter Rabbit is the exception, along with the lettuce-munching bunnies in *The Tale of the Flopsy Bunnies*, to the norm of civilized cooking among Potter's characters who desire to eat.

2. Linda Lear notes in her biography of Potter that "Her gardens, her house and her animals—even the rats—were to figure in the books she produced over the next several years" (218).

3. In "Good Taste and Sweet Ordering: Dining With Mrs Beeton," Margaret Beetham calls *Mrs Beeton's Book of Household Management* "the bible of the Victorian domestic manager" (394), the leading cookbook "of a vast array of books and articles which advised the Victorian reader on how to manage dining in the middle-class home" (393). Because of the work of a very active publishing industry, *Mrs. Beeton's* became omnipresent in middle-class British homes from its first publication in 1861 to well into the twentieth century.

4. The title references Alice Walker's famous essay, "In Search of Our Mother's Gardens," which plots and restores a forgotten history of African American women artists by questioning and then erasing the boundary between high and low art. We wanted to have Peter's quest—a telemachiad—resonate with Walker's search for a past.

5. As Burchardt and Conford note in their book on rural England, *The Contested Countryside*, farmers are not alienated from the means of production: they know the land and will kill rabbits, pigeons and other pests to survive economically (9).

6. For further discussion of the many forms of this complicated food genre, see Alan Davidson's entry in *The Oxford Companion to Food* (638–39). An example of how pudding figures in national identity comes from Samuel Johnson, who cites in the *Dictionary* this verse from Matthew Prior as a source for his definition: "Pudding and beef make Britons fight."

7. Please see Janet Theophano's *Eat My Words: Reading Women's Lives Through the Cookbooks They Wrote*, Palgrave, 2002.

8. For details, please see chapters 7 and 8 of *The Pudding Lady*, pp. 26–74.

9. For recipes, please see pp. 81–82.

10. See Davidson's definition of the roly-poly pudding on pp. 668–69 of *The Oxford Companion to Food*.

11. A breadcrumb pudding requires a pan or mold. For an example, please see the recipe for Baked Bread Pudding on p. 633 of *Mrs. Beeton's*.

12. For further corroboration of how clothing reflects the rats' class aspiration, see Carole Scott's two essays, "Clothed in Nature or Nature Clothed: Dress as Metaphor in the Illustrations of Beatrix Potter and C. M. Barker" and "Between Me and the World: Clothes as Mediator between Self and Society in the Work of Beatrix Potter."

13. Hill Top, Potter's farm in the Lake District village of Near Sawrey, suffered a serious infestation of rats early on in Potter's ownership. Mrs. Cannon, part of the tenant family that ran the farm, reported to Potter that she had seen "a rat 'sitting up eating its dinner under the kitchen table in the middle of the afternoon'" (Lear 211, 217).

14. Such soot smuts would not have surprised Potter's original audience. Judith Flanders, in her discussion of kitchen stoves in *Inside the Victorian Home: A Portrait of Domestic Life in Victorian England*, notes the frequent presence of soot in food of the period, and the improvements that new stove technology offered: "One of the major advantages . . . was that soot no longer fell into the food that was in the oven, although it could still come down the chimney and fall in the saucepans. Soot in food remained a major problem" (105).

15. To understand the ubiquity of the blue willow china pattern in Britain from the Victorian era into the twentieth century, please see the introductory section of Patricia O'Hara's article in *Victorian Studies*, "'The Willow Pattern That We Knew': The Victorian Literature of Blue Willow."

16. Tommy Brock's name, consistently used with its diminutive first name, denotes the lower-class status of the badger, compared to the upper-class status of the eponymous fox Mr. Tod, who is called consistently by the title "Mister" within the story. Potter likewise suggests upper-class status for her other fox character, in *The Tale of Jemima Puddle-Duck*: although lacking a name, he is always referred to as a "gentleman" by the narrator. Potter also uses dialectal terms as surnames for the characters: a "brock" is a badger and a "tod" is a fox (*Oxford English Dictionary*).

17. Potter makes a neat food-based pun in using a magpie for the doctor: Duchess even claims that since "he is a Pie himself, he will certainly understand" (47–48). Presumably, she means he will understand that there must have been a patty-pan in the pie. Potter undercuts this with verbal irony by making the "doctor" spout only nonsense (he seems to understand nothing) and with situational irony by having him leave the patty-pan behind at the end of the story, rather than steal the shiny object as a magpie traditionally would.

18. In the Whiskerses' hasty move to Farmer Potatoes's barn, where they and their descendants down to the fourth generation live, they lose their middle-class aspirations and become ordinary country rats, living on chicken feed and stolen oats and bran—not cooked meals (*Samuel Whiskers* 77).

19. Two examples of such sentimentalized rhetoric: 1) "From her first book, *The Tale of Peter Rabbit*, Beatrix Potter went on to create a series of stories and lovable characters that have charmed and enchanted children for generations" (https://www.peterrabbit.com/books/—official Penguin/Frederick Warne website). 2) "Beatrix Potter, the writer of one of the most beloved children's books of all time, *The Tale of Peter Rabbit* (1902), was a woman of immense talent, indefatigable spirit, and generous heart" (https://beatrixpottersociety.org.uk/about-beatrix/, The Beatrix Potter Society).

20. In his classic essay, "Excessively Impertinent Bunnies: The Subversive Element in Beatrix Potter," Humphrey Carpenter highlights the role Potter "played in shaping the modern literary sensibility" (Reynolds 10) of authors like W.H. Auden, George Orwell, and Graham Greene. In "Radical Qualities of *The Tale of Peter Rabbit*," Eliza Dresang speaks to Potter's explicit use of death, particularly linked with food, as a break with the conventions of children's literature (109).

Chapter 4: "A Little Smackerel of Something": Food and the *Künstlerroman* in the Winnie-the-Pooh Books

1. What Connolly describes as "a pastoral world of innocence, play, and peace" (104).

2. In his hunt for honey in this chapter, Pooh reenacts the behavior of early hunter-gatherers who, before the innovation of domesticated hives, would climb trees to raid bees' nests of honeycombs and honey. In *Sweetness & Light*, Hattie Ellis discusses ancient rock and cave paintings that portray this practice (37–42).

3. Extending Douglas's discussion of meal structure, it is important to explore a slightly larger metonymic structure—sociability, creativity, *and* food in *Winnie-the-Pooh* and *The House at Pooh Corner*. Douglas substantiates this broader view in her essay, "Cultural Bias": "Among all living beings, humans are the only ones who actively make their own environment, the only ones whose environment is a cultural construct" (6).

4. Jam, originally a means of preserving fruit, occupies a central place in the British diet, especially at breakfast and as a snack on bread or toast, as well as a filling or layer in cakes, tarts, and some puddings. "Per capita, consumption was around 10 lb per year" in late nineteenth-century Britain (Davidson 415).

5. As Pooh notes in conversation with Piglet at the end of *Winnie-the-Pooh*, food and daily adventures are essentially synonymous:

> "When you wake up in the morning, Pooh," said Piglet at last, "what's the first thing that you say to yourself?"
> "What's for breakfast?" said Pooh. "What do *you* say, Piglet?"
> "I say, I wonder what's going to happen exciting today?" said Piglet.
> Pooh nodded thoughtfully.
> "It's the same thing," he said.

Chapter 5: Food of the Woods and Plains: Two Visions of Food, Culture, Land, and History in Laura Ingalls Wilder's Little House Books and Louise Erdrich's Birchbark Series

1. For further analysis of Wilder's cultural erasure, please see Elizabeth Jameson, "Unconscious Inheritance and Conscious Striving: Laura Ingalls Wilder and the Frontier Narrative"; Frances W. Kaye, "Little Squatter on the Osage Diminished Reserve: Reading Laura Ingalls Wilder's Kansas Indians"; John E. Miller, *Laura Ingalls Wilder and Rose Wilder Lane: Authorship, Place, Time, and Culture*; Ann Romines, *Constructing the Little House: Gender, Culture, and Laura Ingalls Wilder*; Sharon Smulders, "'The Only Good Indian': History, Race, and Representation in Laura Ingalls Wilder's *Little House on the Prairie*."

2. Our understanding of structure as cultural and historical force and its applicability to food comes from Jean-Louis Flandrin and Massimo Montanari's introduction to *Food: A Culinary History from Antiquity to the Present*. They write, "The routines of daily life have a structure, and within that structure even the most insignificant events have a necessary place and a precise significance" (2). Flandrin and Montanari derive their understanding of structure from French historian Fernand Braudel's work, *The Structure of Everyday Life*.

3. Although Erdrich's series is set before Wilder's, our discussion follows the chronological order of the authors' composition instead, given that Erdrich is aware of and to some degree writing against Wilder's view of the nineteenth-century encroachment of European peoples on the lands of the indigenous peoples of the American West.

4. Please see our article, "Privilege and Exploitation: Food as Dual Signifier in Pamela Muñoz Ryan's *Esperanza Rising*," for a fuller discussion of the cultural significance of food as both produced and consumed.

5. Please see our discussion of how Ma's cheese-making reflects Wisconsin dairy culture in "Utilizing Food Studies with Children's Literature and its Scholarship: Laura Ingalls Wilder's Little House Books as Case Study," in *Food in Literature* (206).

6. In *History of Food*, Maguelonne Toussaint-Samat offers similar assessments of dairy (113–24) and wheat (128–38) but focuses on the mythical (for example, Demeter and wheat) rather than the magical.

7. Capudo, Michael J., and Joseph Bruchac. *Keepers of the Earth: Native Stories and Environmental Activities for Children*. Fifth House Publishers, 1989.

8. Original quotation from *Natural Wild Rice in Minnesota*. Minnesota Department of Natural Resources, 2008, p. 5.

9. Sean Sherman is founder and CEO Chef of The Sioux Chef, whose mission statement is "We are committed to revitalizing Native American Cuisine and in the process we are re-identifying North American Cuisine and reclaiming an important culinary culture long buried and often inaccessible" (http://sioux-chef.com/). Karlos Baca networks through the Taste of Native Cuisine Facebook page (https://www.facebook.com/TasteofNativeCuisine/), whose purpose is "helping to bring a sense of place and time to Indigenous Culinary History."

Chapter 6: "A Profound Love for Luscious Things": Food as Symbolism and History in Maurice Sendak's *In the Night Kitchen*

1. In "Betrayed by Chicken Soup: Judaism, Gender and Performance in Maurice Sendak's *Real Rosie*," Leslie Tannenbaum offers a lengthy discussion of Sendak as a Jewish American writer, particularly of the post–World War II generation, for whom she offers the following description: "The '50s and '60s thus saw Jewish writers turning inward and focusing on such themes as the struggles and ambivalences about success and the identity problems created by the lure of integration into American culture, all of which was framed as a more general existential angst" (371). Although, as Joyce Antler claims, this generation may have moved beyond the earlier generation of Jewish American writers' focus on narratives of immigration and acculturation to pursue more universal themes of alienation (205), Sendak still grounds much of his writing and art—as well as so many of the personal stories he tells in interviews—in the specifics of his family's history in Poland and the United States.

2. Reference is based on the twenty-ninth edition (1949).

3. Page numbers are for the tenth edition (1920).

4. The Sunshine Bakery's East Coast commercial site was not for away in Long Island City. The factory of one thousand windows was built in 1912 and was the largest production bakery until 1955. It closed in 1965 ("Throw-back Thursdays").

5. The two buildings where Sendak grew up in Brooklyn that he references in *In the Night Kitchen* by including their addresses—1717 West 6th St. and 1756 58th St.—were both built in 1931, according to realtor.com.

6. In *Nothing but Trouble* (1944), Oliver Hardy plays a character dressed in a chef's outfit, complete with toque, just as the bakers wear in *In the Night Kitchen*.

7. For more complete descriptions of the kitchen implements and food containers that Sendak uses, please see Cech 196, Bodmer 275, and Cott 50. For further discussion of the friends and family to whom the labels refer, see Lane 182–83 and Cech 197–98.

8. Mickey's adventure in a cake-dough onesie seems to derive visually from Wilhelm Busch's *Max and Moritz (A Story of Seven Boyish Pranks)* (1865). In their sixth trick, the two mischievous boys fall first into flour and then into dough. Caught by the baker, who rolls them out and bakes them in the oven (the fate Mickey escapes), Max and Moritz

eat their way out of their baked shells headfirst (looking remarkably like Mickey in his dough suit) and escape. Sendak is on record in several interviews as owning copies of Busch's work and thinking highly of it (Hentoff 6, Haviland 29, Harris 38).

9. John Cech discusses the label of the Merita Bakery's Mickey Snacks; it seems quite similar to the last image of *In the Night Kitchen* (198–99).

10. There is a correlative reading of Peter Rabbit, who, although in bed, resists the chamomile tea his mother would dose him with (see p. 37 of this volume).

Chapter 7: *Dangerous Angels: The Weetzie Bat Books*: Food, Place, and Sparkly Glam Slinkster Cool Vegetarianism in Los Angeles

1. Except for two years (1999–2001) as a restaurant critic for *Gourmet* in New York City, Gold lived out his journalistic career in Los Angeles.

2. *Los Angeles and Hollywood Map*. Global Graphics, 2016.

3. The characters actually spend very little time on the freeways (e.g., only when Dirk drives to San Francisco on I-5 in search of Duck in *Weetzie Bat* and when Dirk and Duck drive the US 101 to visit Duck's family in Santa Cruz in *Witch Baby*). In Block's *Los Angeles Times Book Review* article, "Punk Pixies in the Canyon," she notes that she was driving around Laurel Canyon—not the LA freeways—when she saw the "punk princess" who inspired the protagonist of the first book.

Chapter 8: *Ratatouille* and Restaurants: A Portrait of the Artist as a Young Rat

1. Mice occupy leading roles in stories from Aesop's "The Town Mouse and the Country Mouse" to E. T. A. Hoffmann's "The Nutcracker and the Mouse King," Disney's Mickey Mouse, E. B. White's *Stuart Little*, and Brian Jacques's Redwall novels. For a longer (but not complete) list of fictional mice and rat characters in literature (many of whom are in children's books), see Wikipedia's list at https://en.wikipedia.org/wiki/List_of_fictional_rodents_in_literature.

2. See also our discussion of Beatrix Potter's *The Tale of Samuel Whiskers, or the Roly-Poly Pudding* (1908), with its eponymous rat character and his wife Anna Maria, in chapter 3 of this volume.

3. See the recent studies of chefs as creative artists: Katharina Balazs, "Some Like It Haute: Leadership Lessons from France's Great Chefs"; Bénédict Beaugé, "On the Novelty in Cuisine: A Brief Historical Insight"; Vanina Leschziner, *At the Chef's Table: Culinary Creativity in Elite Restaurants*.

4. Rats in general possess highly developed senses of taste and smell. Sullivan notes that "They have an excellent sense of taste, detecting the most minute amounts of poison, down to one part per million" (6). Remy's talent thus mirrors his species's capabilities.

5. The relevant quotation from *An Introduction to the Principles of Morals and Legislation* (1789): "The day may come, when the rest of the animal creation may acquire those rights which never could have been withholden from them but by the hand of

tyranny. The French have already discovered that the blackness of skin is no reason why a human being should be abandoned without redress to the caprice of a tormentor. It may come one day to be recognized, that the number of legs, the villosity of the skin, or the termination of the *os sacrum*, are reasons equally insufficient for abandoning a sensitive being to the same fate. What else is it that should trace the insuperable line? Is it the faculty of reason, or perhaps, the faculty for discourse? . . . the question is not, Can they *reason?* nor, Can they *talk?* but, Can they *suffer?*" (311)

6. The *confit byaldi* was originated by nouvelle cuisine chef Michel Guerrard and adapted by the film's culinary advisor, Thomas Keller (Cloake).

7. The exterminator's shop is based on Julien Aurouze, a real-life pest-control shop founded in Paris in 1872. "The shop is on a busy commercial street leading to the Les Halles shopping center, the former site of Paris's wholesale food market. Rat infestation was one of several reasons the market was moved out to the suburbs in 1971" (Viscusi). The film faithfully reproduces the taxidermy rats in the window of the traditional Parisian storefront, hanging by their necks from traps. They date from a particularly bad infestation in 1925.

8. It is worth noting that Colette as a woman lacks the opportunities to advance that Remy gains in the film. She asks Linguini, "How many women do you see in this kitchen? Only me! Why do you think that is? Because haute cuisine is an antique hierarchy built on rules invented by stupid old men who designed them to make it impossible for women to enter this world. But still I am here. How did this happen? Because I am the toughest cook in this kitchen, and I've worked too hard for too long, and I am not going to jeopardize it for some garbage boy who got lucky." And yet she does exactly that: she gives up her hard-won position and future career in the finest haute cuisine restaurant in Paris because she falls in love with the garbage boy. The end of the film shows her as Remy's sous chef in the bistro—a position that is in one sense a move up from her job as *rotisseur* at Gusteau's, although the promotion is undercut by her shift to a far less prestigious (though popular) restaurant. Rats may escape their marginalization to a degree in this film, but Disney•Pixar still expects a woman to give up her best career prospects for her man.

Chapter 9: "Beating Eggs Never Makes the Evening News": Politics and Kitchens in Rita Williams-Garcia's *One Crazy Summer* and Its Sequels

1. *One Crazy Summer* takes place during the summer of 1968. The Black Panthers did not initiate their Free Breakfast for Children Program in Oakland until September of that year (Bloom 182).

2. A concise comparative analysis of the systematic nature of these restrictions can be found in Douglas Flamming's *African Americans in the West*, pp. 102–4.

3. Williams-Garcia does not use the term "soul food" in the novels. In an interview in *Southern Living*, the renowned African American chef and cookbook writer, Edna Lewis identifies soul food as urban, "hard times food in Harlem," and not accurate enough to

describe the food and foodways of her rural Virginia home: "When I grew up, everyone had a garden, and we ate bountiful food—vegetables, fruits, grains, beans, and more fish than meat. People didn't know any better than to be good cooks, and good food bonded us together" (Gee 128). It is worth noting that, cognizant of Edna Lewis, food studies scholars use "soul food" and "country cooking" as contested, non-synonymous descriptors for African American food and foodways. As Adrian Miller diplomatically puts it, Edna Lewis "serves . . . as a referee on the boundaries between soul food and southern food" (7). The scholarly discussions are fascinating but far beyond the scope of this chapter. Given Edna Lewis's childhood remembrance above and its coincidence with Williams-Garcia's descriptions of food and farms in *Gone Crazy in Alabama*, it is most accurate to label the food in the novel—as well as Big Ma's food in *P.S. Be Eleven*—as country, not soul food.

4. For an excellent discussion of the Second Great Migration and its roots in the First, please refer to James N. Gregory's "The Second Great Migration: A Historical Overview" in *African American Urban History Since World War II*, edited by Kenneth L. Kusmer and Joe W. Trotter, U of Chicago P, 2009, pp. 19–38.

5. According to Chris Romberg in chapter 7 of *No There There: Race, Class, and Political Community in Oakland*, in the 1960s manufacturing moved out of Oakland, leaving the African American population feeling ignored as money and manufacturing settled into other cities around the Bay Area. The businessmen—primarily white—who ran the city believed that capitalism would save Oakland, but it had not, particularly for the African American population living in west Oakland. At the time, the Oakland Economic Development Council (OEDC) represented an African American voice in an otherwise white city government, and it asked for economic development opportunities for the poorer areas of Oakland as well as a police review board to handle community problems (that is, police violence). The city government rejected OECD's proposals, enlarging the rift between the city government and the African American population. The Black Panthers then stepped into that rift to actively challenge the status quo and shift the political balance of power in the city. (145–72)

Chapter 10: Refugee Narratives, Cuisine Clash: The Case of Thanhha Lai's *Inside Out & Back Again*

1. In choosing Alabama as the primary United States setting for *Inside Out & Back Again*, Lai not only replicates her own experience as a refugee, since her family was resettled in Montgomery, Alabama (261), but also accurately reflects general refugee settlement practices at the time: "In many ways the sponsorship program contributed to the dispersal of the Vietnamese across America. Because few individuals could afford to act as sponsors and the number of organizations willing to act as sponsors within a given community was limited, the Vietnamese were scattered across the country by their assignment of sponsors" (Montero 28).

2. Nicole Routhier was born in Saigon to a Vietnamese mother and a French father. She says, "I learned about cooking from my nanny, a native of Hue [Central Vietnam], and my mother from Haiphong [Northern Vietnam]; both were home cooks of the first order" (Routhier, "Preface"). Although not a refugee of the Vietnam War, she experienced a transnational life at an early age, moving to Laos with her mother, who ran a restaurant that served Vietnamese food there between 1967 and 1970 (Claiborne 54) before moving on to Brussels, France, and then to New York in 1981. In 1989, *The Foods of Vietnam* won the Julia Child Award for Best American Cookbook from the International Association of Culinary Professionals (Schrader 20).

3. Lai reverses the immigrant arc in her second novel, *Listen, Quietly* (2015). In doing so, she follows the authorial arc set out by Viet Thanh Nguyen: "The movement from the homeland to the adopted land, as refugees and exiles, and finally the return and reconciliation, marks much of the [Vietnamese American] literature" (206). The main character, Mai, is a second generation Vietnamese American teenager who accompanies her grandmother back to Vietnam to bring to closure the unresolved fate of her long-missing grandfather. The novel's backstory shows how Mai's parents successfully transitioned from refugees to the role of "model minority": the father becoming a doctor and the mother a lawyer, living in the wealthy enclave of Laguna Beach, California. Mai grows up as a very Americanized child, but her parents and grandmother have kept her knowledge of her culture and history alive in part through family stories and connections and in part through the Vietnamese food they prepare at home. *Listen, Quietly* is a cultural (re)immersion tale for Mai. To introduce Mai to the family, geography, rural and urban life, the wars, and the culture and history of both the old and new Vietnam, Lai structures the novel's narrative arc—and thus also Mai's experiences—intensively through food, foodways, and meals. These function as mediators through which Mai gains access to a broader cultural landscape, which allows her to discover her roots and herself by bridging back to the time before the refugee experience of her parents and grandmother. In *Inside Out & Back Again*, Lai uses food to access the particular refugee experience of the Vietnamese who came to the United States, whereas in *Listen, Quietly* she uses food as signifier for self-discovery.

WORKS CITED

Chapter 1: An Invitation to the Table: The Tastes of Children's Literature

Barthes, Roland. "Towards a Psychosociology of Contemporary Food Consumption." *Annales E. S. C.*, vol. 16, no. 5, 1961, pp. 977–86.
Barthes, Roland. *Mythologies.* Hill and Wang, 1972.
Block, Francesca Lia. *Dangerous Angels: The Weetzie Bat Books.* HarperCollins, 1998.
Brillat-Savarin, Jean Anthelme. *The Physiology of Taste: Or, Meditations on Transcendental Gastronomy.* 1825. Translated by M. F. K. Fisher, Knopf, 1971.
Brown, Rebecca A. "Please Don't Cook Those Sweet Potatoes: Race, Labor, Food, and Subterfuge in Mercer Mayer's *Liza Lou and the Yeller Belly Swamp.*" *Children's Literature Association Quarterly*, vol. 41, no. 4, 2016, pp. 420–42.
Carrington, Bridget, and Jennifer Harding, editors. *Feast or Famine? Food and Children's Literature.* Cambridge Scholars, 2014.
Carroll, Lewis. *Alice in Wonderland: Authoritative Texts of Alice's Adventures in Wonderland, Through the Looking-Glass, The Hunting of the Snark, Backgrounds, Essays in Criticism,* edited by Donald J. Gray, Norton, 1971. Norton Critical Edition.
Douglas, Mary. "Deciphering a Meal." *Myth, Symbol, and Culture,* special issue of *Daedalus,* vol. 101, no. 1, 1972, pp. 61–81.
Everett, James. "Oranges of Paradise: The Orange as Symbol of Escape and Loss in Children's Literature." *Critical Approaches to Food in Children's Literature,* edited by Kara K. Keeling and Scott T. Pollard, Routledge, 2009, pp. 193–206.
Gigante, Denise. *Taste: A Literary History.* Yale UP, 2005.
Susan Honeyman, *Consuming Agency in Fairy Tales, Childlore, and Folk Literature.* Routledge, 2010.
Katz, Wendy R. "Some Uses of Food in Children's Literature." *Children's Literature in Education,* vol. 11, no. 4, 1980, pp. 192–99.
Keeling, Kara K, and Scott T. Pollard. "Power, Food and Eating: An Intertextual Reading of Maurice Sendak and Henrik Drescher." *Children's Literature in Education,* vol. 30, no. 2, 1999, pp. 127–43.
Keeling, Kara K, and Scott T. Pollard. "In Search of his Father's Garden." *Beatrix Potter's Peter Rabbit: A Children's Classic at 100,* edited by Margaret Mackey, Children's Literature Association and Scarecrow Press, 2002, pp. 117–30.

Keeling, Kara K, and Scott T. Pollard, editors. *Critical Approaches to Food in Children's Literature.* Routledge, 2009.

Keeling, Kara K, and Scott T. Pollard. "The Key Is in the Mouth: Orality in *Coraline.*" *Children's Literature,* vol. 40, 2012, pp. 1–27.

Keeling, Kara K, and Scott T. Pollard. "Gazing Forward, Not Looking Back: Comfort Food without Nostalgia in the Novels of Polly Horvath." *Consumption,* special issue of *Jeunesse: Young People, Texts, Culture,* vol. 6, no. 1, 2014, pp. 56–76.

Keeling, Kara K, and Scott T. Pollard. "Privilege and Exploitation: Food as Dual Signifier in Pamela Muñoz Ryan's *Esperanza Rising.*" *The Lion and Unicorn,* vol. 40, no. 3, 2016, pp. 280–99.

Keeling, Kara K, and Scott T. Pollard. "Utilizing Food Studies with Children's Literature and its Scholarship: Laura Ingalls Wilder's Little House Books as Case Study." *Food and Literature,* edited by Gitanjali Shahani, Cambridge UP, 2018, pp. 200–219.

Korsmeyer, Carolyn. *Making Sense of Taste: Food & Philosophy.* Cornell UP, 1999.

Kristeva, Julia. *Powers of Horror: An Essay on Abjection.* Columbia UP, 1982.

Lai, Thanhha. *Inside Out & Back Again.* Harper, 2011.

Leonardi, Susan J. "Recipes for Reading: Summer Pasta, Lobster à la Riseholme, and Key Lime Pie." *PMLA,* vol. 104, no. 3, 1989, pp. 340–47.

Lévi-Strauss, Claude. "The Culinary Triangle." *Partisan Review,* vol. 33, 1966, pp. 586–95.

Lévi-Strauss, Claude. *The Raw and the Cooked.* Harper and Row, 1969.

Milne, A. A. *The House at Pooh Corner.* E. P. Dutton, 1928.

Milne, A. A. *Winnie-the-Pooh.* E. P. Dutton, 1926.

Nikolajeva, Maria. *From Mythic to Linear: Time in Children's Literature.* Scarecrow Press, 2000.

Perrot, Jean. "Maurice Sendak's Ritual Cooking of the Child in Three Tableaux: The Moon, Mother, and Music." *Children's Literature,* vol. 18, 1990, pp. 68–86.

Potter, Beatrix. *The Tale of Mr. Tod.* Frederick Warne, 1912.

Potter, Beatrix. *The Tale of Peter Rabbit.* Frederick Warne, 1902.

Potter, Beatrix. *The Tale of the Pie and the Patty-Pan.* Frederick Warne, 1905.

Potter, Beatrix. *The Tale of Samuel Whiskers, Or, the Roly-Poly Pudding.* Frederick Warne, 1908.

Ratatouille. Directed by Brad Bird and Jan Pinkava, Disney•Pixar, 2007.

Sendak, Maurice. *In the Night Kitchen.* Harper and Row, 1970.

Sendak, Maurice. *Where the Wild Things Are.* Harper and Row, 1963.

Vallone, Lynne. "'What Is the Meaning of All This Gluttony?' Edgeworth, the Victorians, C.S. Lewis and a Taste for Fantasy." *Papers: Explorations into Children's Literature,* vol. 12, no. 1, 2002, pp. 47–54.

Williams-Garcia, Rita. *Gone Crazy in Alabama.* HarperCollins, 2015.

Williams-Garcia, Rita. *One Crazy Summer.* HarperCollins, 2011.

Williams-Garcia, Rita. *P.S. Be Eleven.* HarperCollins, 2013.

Chapter 2: American Children's Cookbooks as Scenes of Instruction: Tracking Historical Shifts of Work, Play, Pleasure, and Memory

Amster-Burton, Matthew. *Hungry Monkey: A Food-Loving Father's Quest to Raise an Adventurous Eater.* Mariner Books–Houghton Mifflin Harcourt, 2009.

Works Cited

Bedford, Annie North. *Susie's New Stove: The Little Chef's Cookbook*. Illustrated by Corinne Malvern, Simon and Schuster, 1950. A Little Golden Book.

Beim, Jerrold. *The First Book of Boys' Cooking*. Franklin Watts, 1957.

Belasco, Warren J. *Appetite for Change: How the Counterculture Took on the Food Industry*. Cornell UP, 2007.

Child, Lydia M. *The Frugal Housewife: Dedicated to Those Who Are Not Ashamed of Economy*. Marsh and Capen, and Carter and Hendee, 1829.

De Certeau, Michael, Luce Girard, and Pierre Mayol. *The Practice of Everyday Life, Volume 2: Living and Cooking*. Translated by Timothy J. Tomisik, U of Minnesota P, 1998.

Haley, Andrew. "The 'Little Chef' Stove." *H-PCAACA*. H-net. Humanities and Social Sciences Online. https://networks.h-net.org/node/13784/discussions/49774/14-little-chef-stove. October 22, 2014. Accessed 4 November 2017.

Holland, Patricia G. "Lydia Maria Child (1802–1880)." *Legacy: A Journal of Nineteenth Century Women's Writers*, vol. 5, no. 2, 1988, pp. 45–53.

Inness, Sherrie. *Dinner Roles: American Women and Culinary Culture*. U of Iowa P, 2001.

Ireland, Corydon. "Getting Fresh with Mollie: Harvard Hosts Famed Cookbook Author Katzen." *Harvard Gazette*, 21 October 2010. https://news.harvard.edu/gazette/story/2010/10/getting-fresh-with-mollie/. Accessed 17 November 2017.

Judson, Clara Ingram. *Cooking Without Mother's Help: A Story Cook Book for Beginners*. Nourse, 1920. What I Can Do with My Hands Books.

Katzen, Mollie. *Honest Pretzels: And 64 Other Amazing Recipes for Cooks Ages 8 & Up*. Tricycle Press, 1999.

Katzen, Mollie. *Salad People and More Real Recipes*. Tricycle Press, 2005.

Katzen, Mollie, and Ann Henderson. *Pretend Soup and Other Real Recipes: A Cookbook for Preschoolers & Up*. Tricycle Press, 1994.

Kirkland, Elizabeth Stansbury. *Six Little Cooks or Aunt Jane's Cooking Class*. Jansen, McClurg, 1877.

Leonardi, Susan J. "Recipes for Reading: Summer Pasta, Lobster à la Riseholme, and Key Lime Pie." *PMLA*, vol. 104, no. 3, 1989, pp. 340–47.

Lichfield, John. "France Prepares for Its National Picnic 'sur l'herbe.'" *The Independent*, 13 July 2000, http://www.independent.co.uk/news/world/europe/france-prepares-for-its-national-picnic-sur-lherbe-5369842.html. Accessed 3 November 2017.

Little Golden Books: 75 Years of Timeless Publishing. Random House Children's Books, 2017, www.littlegoldenbooks.com/about/. Accessed 19 November 2017.

Longone, Jan. "'As Worthless as Savorless Salt'? Teaching Children to Cook, Clean, and (Often) Conform." *Gastronomica*, vol. 3, no. 2, 2003, pp. 104–111.

Neuhaus, Jessamyn. *Manly Meals and Mom's Home Cooking: Cookbooks and Gender in Modern America*. Johns Hopkins UP, 2003.

Rombauer, Irma S. *A Cookbook for Girls and Boys*. Bobbs-Merrill, 1952.

Shapiro, Laura. *Something from the Oven: Reinventing Dinner in 1950s America*. Penguin, 2004.

Slothower, Jodie, and Jan Susina. "Delicious Supplements: Literary Cookbooks as Additives to Children's Texts." *Critical Approaches to Food in Children's Literature*, edited by Kara K. Keeling and Scott T. Pollard, Routledge, 2009, pp. 21–38.

Wall, Barbara. *The Narrator's Voice: The Dilemma of Children's Fiction*, St. Martin's Press, 1991.

Waters, Alice, Bob Carrau, Patricia Curtan. *Fanny at Chez Panisse*. Illustrated by Ann Arnold, Harper Collins, 1992.

Waters, Alice, and Bob Carrau. *Fanny in France*. Illustrated by Ann Arnold, Viking, 2016.

Chapter 3: Puddings and Pies: Meat Pastries in the Tales of Beatrix Potter

Acton, Eliza. *Modern Cookery for Private Families: Reduced to a System of Easy Practice, in a Series of Carefully Tested Receipts, in Which the Principles of Baron Liebig and Other Eminent Writers Have Been as Much as Possible Applied and Explained*. Longman, Green, Longmans, and Roberts, 1860.

Beatrix Potter's Peter Rabbit. Frederick Warne, 2016, www.peterrabbit.com/books/. Accessed 19 May 2018.

Beetham, Margaret. "Good Taste and Sweet Ordering: Dining with Mrs Beeton." *Victorian Literature and Culture*, vol. 36, no. 2, 2008, pp. 391–406.

Bibby, M. E. *The Pudding Lady: A New Departure in Social Work*. National Food Reform Association, 1916.

"brock, n.1." *OED Online*, Oxford University Press, March 2018, www.oed.com/view/Entry/23562. Accessed 13 May 2018.

Burchardt, Jeremy, and Philip Conford. *The Contested Countryside: Rural Politics and Land Controversy in Modern Britain*. London: I. B. Taurus, 2008.

Carpenter, Humphrey. "Excessively Impertinent Bunnies: The Subversive Element in Beatrix Potter." *Children and Their Books: A Celebration of the Work of Iona and Peter Opie*, edited by Gillian Avery and Julia Briggs, Clarendon, 1989, pp. 271–98.

Daley, Suzanne and Ross D. Formam. "Cooking Culture: Situating Food and Drink in the Nineteenth Century." *Victorian Literature and Culture*, 2008, vol. 36, no. 2, pp. 363–73.

Davidson, Alan, and Tom Jaine. *The Oxford Companion to Food*. Oxford UP, 2006.

Davies, Sue. "The St. Pancras School for Mothers." 30 May 2014. Wellcome Library. http://blog.wellcomelibrary.org/2014/05/the-st-pancras-school-for-mothers/. Accessed 19 May 2018.

Davin, Anna. "Loaves and Fishes: Food in Poor Households in Late Nineteenth-Century London." *History Workshop Journal*, No. 41, Spring 1996, pp. 167–92.

Dresang, Eliza, "Radical Qualities of *The Tale of Peter Rabbit*." *Beatrix Potter's Peter Rabbit: A Children's Classic at 100*, edited by Margaret Mackey, Children's Literature Association and the Scarecrow Press, 2002, pp. 99–110.

Evans, Heather A. "Food, Gender, and 'The Tale of Samuel Whiskers.'" *Victorian Literature and Culture*, vol. 36, no. 2, 2008, pp. 603–23.

Flanders, Judith. *Inside the Victorian Home: A Portrait of Domestic Life in Victorian England*. W. W. Norton, 2004.

Fromer, Julie E. "'Deeply Indebted to the Tea-plant': Representations of English National Identity in Victorian Histories of Tea." *Victorian Literature and Culture*, vol. 36, no. 2, 2008, pp. 531–47.

Works Cited

Johnson, Samuel. "Pudding." *A Dictionary of the English Language: A Digital Edition of the 1755 Classic by Samuel Johnson*, edited by Brandi Besalke. 6 Dec. 2012, johnsonsdictionaryonline.com/?page_id=7070&i=1598. Accessed 19 May 2018.

Kristeva, Julia, and Leon S. Roudiez. *Powers of Horror: An Essay on Abjection*. Columbia UP, 1982.

Lavelle, Marie. "A Storm in a Tea-Cup? 'Making a Difference' in Two Sure Start Children's Centres." *Children & Society*, vol. 29, no. 6, 2015, pp. 583–92.

Lear, Linda. *Beatrix Potter: A Life in Nature*. St. Martin's, 2007.

Lévi-Strauss, Claude. *The Raw and the Cooked*. Harper and Row, 1969.

Mennell, Stephen. "On the Civilizing of Appetite." *Food and Culture: A Reader*, edited by Carole Counihan and Penny van Esterik, Routledge, 1997, pp. 315–37.

Miller, Ian. "'A Dangerous Revolutionary Force Amongst Us': Conceptualizing Working-Class Tea Drinking in the British Isles, C. 1860–1900." *Cultural & Social History*, vol. 10, no. 3, 2013, pp. 419–38.

O'Hara, Patricia. "'The Willow Pattern That We Knew': The Victorian Literature of Blue Willow." *Victorian Studies*, vol. 36, no. 4, 1993, pp. 421–42.

Pollard, Scott, and Kara Keeling. "In Search of his Father's Garden." *Beatrix Potter's Peter Rabbit: A Children's Classic at 100*, edited by Margaret Mackey, Children's Literature Association and the Scarecrow Press, 2002, pp. 117–30.

Potter, Beatrix. *The Complete Tales of Beatrix Potter: The 23 Original Peter Rabbit Books*. Frederick Warne, 1989.

Potter, Beatrix. *The Tale of Mr. Tod*. Frederick Warne, 1912.

Potter, Beatrix. *The Tale of the Pie and the Patty-Pan*. Frederick Warne, 1905.

Potter, Beatrix. *The Tale of Samuel Whiskers, Or, the Roly-Poly Pudding*. Frederick Warne, 1908.

Reynolds, Kimberley. *Radical Children's Literature: Future Visions and Aesthetic Transformations in Juvenile Fiction*. Palgrave Macmillan, 2007.

Scott, Carole. "Between Me and the World: Clothes as Mediator between Self and Society in the Work of Beatrix Potter." *The Lion and the Unicorn*, vol. 16, no. 2, 1992, pp. 192–98.

Scott, Carole. "Clothed in Nature or Nature Clothed: Dress as Metaphor in the Illustrations of Beatrix Potter and C. M. Barker." *Children's Literature*, vol. 22, 1994, pp. 70–89.

Sendak, Maurice. *Where the Wild Things Are*. Harper and Row, 1963.

Spencer, Colin. *British Food: An Extraordinary Thousand Years of History*. Columbia UP, 2003.

The Beatrix Potter Society. https://beatrixpottersociety.org.uk/about-beatrix/. Accessed 19 May 2018.

Theophano, Janet. *Eat My Words: Reading Women's Lives Through the Cookbooks They Wrote*. Palgrave, 2002.

"tod, n.1." *OED Online*, Oxford UP, March 2018, www.oed.com/view/Entry/202809. Accessed 13 May 2018.

Walker, Alice. *In Search of Our Mothers' Gardens: Womanist Prose*. Harcourt Brace Jovanovich, 1983.

Walvin, James *Fruits of Empire: Exotic Produce and British Taste, 1660–1800*. Macmillan, 1997.

Chapter 4: "A Little Smackerel of Something": Food and the *Künstlerroman* in the Winnie-the-Pooh Books

Berenstain, Stan, and Jan Berenstain. *The Big Honey Hunt.* Beginner Books, 1962.
Bond, Michael, and Peggy Fortnum. *A Bear Called Paddington.* Houghton Mifflin, 1960.
Connolly, Paula T. *Winnie-the-Pooh and The House at Pooh Corner: Recovering Arcadia*, edited by Robert Lecker, Twayne, 1995. Twayne's Masterwork Studies, No. 156.
Crittenden, Alyssa N. "The Importance of Honey Consumption in Human Evolution." *Food and Foodways*, vol. 19, no. 4, 2011, pp. 257–73.
Ellis, Hattie. *Sweetness & Light: The Mysterious History of the Honeybee.* Harmony Books, 2004.
Douglas, Mary. "Deciphering a Meal." *Myth, Symbol, and Culture*, special issue of *Daedalus*, vol. 101, no. 1, 1972, pp. 61–81.
Douglas, Mary. *Cultural Bias.* Royal Anthropological Institute of Great Britain and Ireland. Occasional Paper No. 35. 1978.
Hemmings, Robert. "A Taste of Nostalgia: Children's Books from the Golden Age—Carroll, Grahame, and Milne." *Children's Literature*, vol. 35, 2007, pp. 54–79.
Kipling, Rudyard. *The Jungle Book.* Century Company, 1920.
Lukanuski, Mary. "A Place at the Counter: The Onus of Oneness." *Eating Culture*, edited by Ron Scapp and Brian Seitz, State U of New York P, 1998, pp. 112–20.
Marx, Steven. *Youth against Age: Generational Strife in Renaissance Poetry: With Special Reference to Edmund Spenser's "The Shepheardes Calender."* Peter Lang, 1986.
Milne, A. A. *The House at Pooh Corner.* E. P. Dutton, 1928.
Milne, A. A. *Winnie-the-Pooh.* E. P. Dutton, 1926.
Nodelman, Perry. *The Pleasures of Children's Literature.* 3rd ed., Allyn and Bacon, 2003.
Snyder, Susan. *Pastoral Process: Spenser, Marvell, Milton.* Stanford UP, 1998.
Virgil, and David Ferry. *The Georgics of Virgil: A Translation.* Farrar, Straus and Giroux, 2005.
Ward, Lynd. *The Biggest Bear.* Houghton Mifflin, 1952.
Wilder, Laura Ingalls. *Little House in the Big Woods.* 1932. Illustrated by Garth Williams, Harper Trophy, 1971.

Chapter 5: Food of the Woods and Plains: Two Visions of Food, Culture, Land, and History in Laura Ingalls Wilder's Little House Books and Louise Erdrich's Birchbark Series

Berry, Wendell. *Bringing It to the Table: On Farming and Food.* Counterpoint, 2009.
Berzok, Linda M. *American Indian Food.* Greenwood, 2005.
Braudel, Fernand. *The Structures of Everyday Life: The Limits of the Possible.* Harper and Row, 1981.
Brillat-Savarin, Jean Anthelme. *Physiologie du goût: Ou, méditations de gastronomie transcendante.* Vol. 1. 4th ed. Just Tessier, 1834.
Brillat-Savarin, Jean Anthelme. *The Physiology of Taste: Or, Meditations on Transcendental Gastronomy.* 1825. Translated by M. F. K. Fisher, Knopf, 1971.
Butler, Kristin. "Chef Karlos Baca, Founder of Taste of Native Cuisine, Talks Decolonizing Foodways and Waking Up the Indigenous Consciousness." *Indian Country Today*, 8 August 2017, newsmaven.io/indiancountrytoday/archive/chef-karlos-baca-founder-of-taste-of-native-cuisine-KdjpcMUR30K4hlbzTUzt3w/. Accessed 26 January 2019.

Works Cited

Capudo, Michael J. and Joseph Bruchac. *Keepers of the Earth: Native Stories and Environmental Activities for Children*. Fifth House, 1989.

Chang, Li Ping. "(Re)location of Home in Louise Erdrich's *The Game of Silence*." *Children's Literature in Education*, vol. 42, no. 2, 2011, pp. 132–47.

Davidson, Alan, and Tom Jaine. *The Oxford Companion to Food*. Oxford UP, 2006.

Erdrich, Louise. *The Birchbark House*. Hyperion Books for Children, 1999.

Erdrich, Louise. *The Game of Silence*. HarperCollins Publishers, 2005

Erdrich, Louise. *The Porcupine Year*. HarperCollins Publishers, 2008.

Erdrich, Louise. *Chickadee*. HarperCollins Publishers, 2012.

Erdrich, Louise. *Makoons*. HarperCollins Publishers, 2016.

Fernández-Armesto, Felipe. *Near a Thousand Tables: A History of Food*. The Free Press, 2002.

Flandrin, Jean L., Massimo Montanari, and Albert Sonnenfeld. *Food: A Culinary History from Antiquity to the Present*. Columbia UP, 1999.

Fraser, Caroline. *Prairie Fires: The American Dreams of Laura Ingalls Wilder*. Metropolitan–Henry Holt, 2017.

Gargano, Elizabeth. "Oral Narrative and Ojibwa Story Cycles in Louise Erdrich's *The Birchbark House* and *The Game of Silence*." *Children's Literature Association Quarterly*, vol. 31, no. 1, pp. 27–39.

Halliday, Lisa. "The Art of Fiction, No. 208: Louise Erdrich." *Paris Review*, Issue 195, 2010, pp. 132–66.

Jameson, Elizabeth. "Unconscious Inheritance and Conscious Striving: Laura Ingalls Wilder and the Frontier Narrative." *Laura Ingalls Wilder and the American Frontier: Five Perspectives*, edited by Dwight M. Miller, UP of America, 2002, pp. 69–94.

Limerick, Patricia Nelson. *The Legacy of Conquest: The Unbroken Past of the American West*. W. W. Norton, 1987.

Kaye, Frances W. "Little Squatter on the Osage Diminished Reserve: Reading Laura Ingalls Wilder's Kansas Indians," *Great Plains Quarterly*, vol. 20, no. 2, 2000, pp. 123–40.

Keeling, Kara and Scott Pollard. "Privilege and Exploitation: Food as Dual Signifier in Pamela Muñoz Ryan's *Esperanza Rising*." *The Lion and the Unicorn*, vol. 40 no. 3, 2016, pp. 280–99.

Keeling, Kara and Scott Pollard. "Utilizing Food Studies with Children's Literature and its Scholarship: Laura Ingalls Wilder's Little House Books as Case Study." *Food in Literature*, edited by Gitanjali Shahani, Cambridge UP, 2018, pp. 200–219.

"Louise Erdrich: In-Depth Written Interview." Minneapolis, Minnesota on October 23, 2009. *Teachingbooks*. www.teachingbooks.net/interview.cgi?id=63&a=1. Accessed 18 July 2018.

Miller, John E. *Becoming Laura Ingalls Wilder: The Woman Behind the Legend*. U of Missouri P, 1998.

Miller, John E. *Laura Ingalls Wilder and Rose Wilder Lane: Authorship, Place, Time, and Culture*. U of Missouri P, 2008.

Minnesota Department of Natural Resources. *Natural Wild Rice in Minnesota*. Minnesota Department of Natural Resources, 2008.

Murphy, Andi. *Toasted Sister* Podcast. Retrieved from toastedsisterpodcast.com/about/.

Nearing, Helen, and Scott Nearing. *The Maple Sugar Book: Together with Remarks on Pioneering as a Way of Living in the Twentieth Century*. Schocken Books, 1970.

Norrgard, Chantal. "From Berries to Orchards: Tracing the History of Berrying and Economic Transformation among Lake Superior Ojibwe." *American Indian Quarterly*, vol. 33, no. 1, 2009, pp. 33–61.

Phillips, John. "Building on Tradition," *Tribal College: Journal of American Indian Higher Education*, vol. 22, no. 3, 2011, pp. 14–20.

Raster, Amanda, and Christina Gish Hill. "The Dispute over Wild Rice: An Investigation of Treaty Agreements and Ojibwe Food Sovereignty." *Agricultural and Human Values*, vol. 34, no. 2, 2017, pp. 267–81.

Ray, Lana, and Paul Nicolas Cormier. "Killing the Weendigo with Maple Syrup: Anishinaabe Pedagogy and Post-Secondary Research." *Canadian Journal of Native Education*, vol. 35, no. 1, 2012, pp. 163–76.

Schlebecker, John T. *Why We Thrive: A History of American Farming, 1607–1972*. Iowa State UP, 1975.

Smulders, Sharon. "'The Only Good Indian': History, Race, and Representation in Laura Ingalls Wilder's *Little House on the Prairie*." *Children's Literature Association Quarterly*, vol. 27, no. 4, 2002, pp. 199–202.

Sorenson, Barbara Ellen. "Wild Food Summit: Anishinaabe Relearning Traditional Gathering Practices." *Tribal College: Journal of American Indian Higher Education*, vol. 22, no. 3, 2011, pp. 32–34.

Spaeth, Janet. *Laura Ingalls Wilder*. Twayne, 1987.

Standage, Tom. *An Edible History of Humanity*. Walker and Company, 2009.

Stewart, Michelle Pagni. "'Counting Coup' on Children's Literature about American Indians: Louise Erdrich's Historical Fiction." *Children's Literature Association Quarterly*, vol. 38, no. 2, 2013, pp. 215–35.

Tannahill, Reay. *Food in History*. Stein and Day, 1973.

Toussaint-Samat, Maguelonne. *History of Food*. Translated by Anthea Bell, Barnes and Noble, 1992.

Vennum, Thomas. *Wild Rice and the Ojibwe People*. Minnesota Historical Society Press, 1988.

Walker, Barbara. *The Little House Cookbook: Frontier Food from Laura Ingalls Wilder's Classic Stories*. Harper and Row, 1979.

Wilder, Laura Ingalls. *By the Shores of Silver Lake*. 1939. Illustrated by Garth Williams, Harper Trophy, 1971.

Wilder, Laura Ingalls. *Little House in the Big Woods*. 1932. Illustrated by Garth Williams, Harper Trophy, 1971.

Wilder, Laura Ingalls. *Little House on the Prairie*. 1935. Illustrated by Garth Williams, Harper Trophy, 1971.

Wilder, Laura Ingalls. *Little Town on the Prairie*. 1941. Illustrated by Garth Williams, Harper Trophy, 1971.

Wilder, Laura Ingalls. *The Long Winter*. 1940. Illustrated by Garth Williams, Harper Trophy, 1971.

Wilder, Laura Ingalls. *On the Banks of Plum Creek*. 1937. Illustrated by Garth Williams, Harper Trophy, 1971.

Chapter 6: "A Profound Love for Luscious Things": Food as Symbolism and History in Maurice Sendak's *In the Night Kitchen*

Antler, Joyce. "Sleeping with the Other: The Problem of Gender in Jewish-American Literature." *Feminist Perspectives on Jewish Studies*, edited by Lynn Davidman and Shelly Tenenbaum. Yale UP, 1994, pp. 191–223.

"Author and Illustrator Maurice Sendak." *Now with Bill Moyers*, 12 March 2004, billmoyers.com/content/author-and-illustrator-maurice-sendak/. Accessed 30 July 2018.

Bodmer, George R. "Max-Mickey-Ida: Sendak's Underground Journey." *Journal of Evolutionary Psychology*, vol. 7, nos. 3–4, 1986, pp. 271–84.

Braun, John. "Sendak Raises the Shade On Childhood." *New York Times*, 7 June 1970, pp. 216–26.

Busch, Wilhelm. "Max und Moritz / Max and Moritz (1865)." *19th-Century German Stories: Web Editions for Language Learning & Literary Study*, edited by Robert Godwin-Jones, School of World Studies, Virginia Commonwealth University, 1999. germanstories.vcu.edu/mm/mmmenu.html. Accessed 30 July 2018.

Carlisle, Nancy and Melinda Talbot Nasardinov. *America's Kitchen*. Historic New England, 2008.

Cech, John. *Angels and Wild Things: The Archetypal Poetics of Maurice Sendak*. Pennsylvania State UP, 1995.

Chertoff, Emily. "The Surprising History of the Milk Carton." *The Atlantic*, 1 Aug. 2012. https://www.theatlantic.com/national/archive/2012/08/the-surprising-history-of-the-milk-carton/260587/. Accessed 30 July 2018.

Cohen, Patricia. "Concerns Beyond Just Where the Wild Things Are." *New York Times*, late ed., 10 September 2008, p. E1.

Cott, Jonathan. *There's a Mystery There: The Primal Vision of Maurice Sendak*. Doubleday, 2017.

Diner, Hasia R. *Hungering for America: Italian, Irish, and Jewish Foodways in the Age of Migration*. Harvard UP, 2001.

Douglas, Mary. "Deciphering a Meal." *Myth, Symbol, and Culture*, special issue of *Daedalus*, vol. 101, no. 1, 1972, pp. 61–81.

Gabaccia, Donna R. *We Are What We Eat: Ethnic Food and the Making of Americans*. Harvard UP, 1998.

"Getting to Know Maurice Sendak." *The Maurice Sendak Library*. Morton Schindel, producer. Weston Woods, 1985.

Harris, Muriel. "Impressions of Sendak." *Conversations with Maurice Sendak*, edited by Peter Kunze, UP of Mississippi, 2016, pp. 36–46. Originally published in *Elementary English*, vol. 48, no. 7, 1971, pp. 825–32.

Haviland, Virginia. "Questions to an Artist Who Is Also an Author: A Conversation between Maurice Sendak and Virginia Haviland." *Conversations with Maurice Sendak*, edited by Peter Kunze, UP of Mississippi, 2016, pp. 21–35. Originally published in the *Quarterly Journal of the Library of Congress*, vol. 28, no. 4, October 1971, pp. 262–80.

Hentoff, Nat. "Among the Wild Things." *Conversations with Maurice Sendak*, edited by Peter Kunze, UP of Mississippi, 2016, pp. 3–20. Originally published in *The New Yorker*, 22 January 1966.

Kander, Mrs. Simon. *The Settlement Cookbook*. 10th edition, The Settlement Cookbook, 1920.

Kander, Mrs. Simon. *The Settlement Cookbook*. 29th edition, The Settlement Cookbook, 1949.

Keeling, Kara, and Scott Pollard. "Power, Food, and Eating in Maurice Sendak and Henrik Drescher: *Where the Wild Things Are, In the Night Kitchen*, and *The Boy Who Ate Around*." *Children's Literature in Education*, vol. 30, no. 2, 1999, pp. 127–43.

Levinson, Julian. *Exiles on Main Street: Jewish American Writers and American Literary Culture*. Indiana UP, 2008.

Liebs, Chester H. *Main Street to Miracle Mile: American Roadside Architecture*. Little Brown, 1985.

Nothing But Trouble. Directed by Sam Taylor, performances by Stan Laurel, Oliver Hardy, and Mary Boland, Metro-Goldwyn-Mayer, 1944.

Perrot, Jean. "Maurice Sendak's Ritual Cooking of the Child in Three Tableaux: The Moon, Mother, and Music." *Children's Literature*, vol. 18, 1990, pp. 68–86.

Potter, Beatrix. *The Tale of Peter Rabbit*. Frederick Warne, 1902.

Ravage, M. E. *An American in the Making: The Life Story of an Immigrant*. Harper and Brothers, 1917.

Roskolenko, Harry. *The Time That Was Then: The Lower East Side, 1900–1914, an Intimate Chronicle*. Dial Press, 1971.

Sendak, Maurice. *In the Night Kitchen*. Harper and Row, 1970.

Sendak, Maurice. *Where the Wild Things Are*. Harper and Row, 1963.

Sternlicht, Sanford. *The Tenement Saga: The Lower East Side and Early Jewish American Writers*. U of Wisconsin P, Terrace Books, 2004.

Symons, Michael. *A History of Cooks and Cooking*. U of Illinois P, 2004.

Tannenbaum, Leslie. "Betrayed by Chicken Soup: Judaism, Gender and Performance in Maurice Sendak's *Real Rosie*." *The Lion and the Unicorn*, vol. 7, no. 3, 2003, pp. 362–76.

"Throwback Thursdays—Sunshine Bakery, Long Island City." *The Queens Tribune*. Focus section. 30 June 2016.

Wald, Priscilla. "Of Crucibles and Grandfathers: The East European Immigrants." *The Cambridge Companion to Jewish American Literature*, edited by Hana Wirth-Nesher and Michael P. Kramer, Cambridge UP, 2003, pp. 50–70.

Chapter 7: *Dangerous Angels: The Weetzie Bat Books*: Food, Place, and Sparkly Glam Slinkster Cool Vegetarianism in Los Angeles

Belasco, Warren J. *Appetite for Change: How the Counterculture Took on the Food Industry*. Cornell UP, 2007.

Block, Francesca Lia. *Dangerous Angels: The Weetzie Bat Books*. HarperCollins, 1998.

Block, Francesca Lia. "Punk Pixies in the Canyon." *Los Angeles Times (pre-1997 Fulltext)*, 26 July 1992, *ProQuest*, https://o-search-proquest-com.read.cnu.edu/docview/281713388?accountid=10100.

Banham, Reyner. *Los Angeles: The Architecture of Four Ecologies.* U of California P, 1971.
Brady, Jean and Merle Miller. *The Ultimate L.A. Food Guide: Shopping for Quality Ingredients and Prepared Foods.* Jeremy P. Tarcher, 1983.
Brillat-Savarin, Jean Anthelme. *The Physiognomy of Taste: Or, Meditations on Transcendental Gastronomy.* Translated by M. F. K. Fisher, Counterpoint, 1949.
Campbell, Patricia J. "People Are Talking About Francesca Lia Block." *The Horn Book Magazine*, vol. 69, no. 1, 1993, pp. 57–64.
Davidson, Alan, and Tom Jaine. *The Oxford Companion to Food.* Oxford UP, 2006.
Davis, Mike. *City of Quartz: Excavating the Future in Los Angeles.* Verso, 1990.
Geary, George. *L.A.'s Legendary Restaurants: Celebrating the Famous Places Where Hollywood Ate, Drank, and Played.* Santa Monica Press, 2016.
Gold, Jonathan. *Counter Intelligence: Where to Eat in the Real Los Angeles.* LA Weekly Book, 2000.
Klein, Norman M. *The History of Forgetting: Los Angeles and the Erasure of Memory.* Verso, 1998.
Los Angeles and Hollywood Map. Global Graphics, 2016.
The Mamas and the Papas. "Twelve Thirty." *The Papas & the Mamas.* MCA Records, 1968.
Raksin, Alex. "On the Wrong Road to Paradise: *City of Quartz: Excavating the Future in Los Angeles* by Mike Davis with Photographs by Robert Morrow (Verso/Routledge: $29.95; 440 pp.)." *Los Angeles Times (pre-1997 Fulltext)*, 9 Dec. 1990, ProQuest, https://0-search-proquest-com.read.cnu.edu/docview/281234083?accountid=10100.
Saxena, Anand M. *The Vegetarian Imperative.* Johns Hopkins UP, 2011.
Stuart, Tristram. *The Bloodless Revolution: A Cultural History of Vegetarianism from 1600 to Modern Times.* W. W. Norton, 2007.
Susina, Jan. "The Rebirth of the Postmodern Flaneur: Notes on the Postmodern Landscape of Francesca Lia Block's *Weetzie Bat*." *Marvels and Tales*, vol. 16, no. 2, 2002, pp. 188–202.
Tuan, Yi-fu. *Space and Place: The Perspective of Experience.* U of Minnesota P, 1977.

Chapter 8: *Ratatouille* and Restaurants: A Portrait of the Artist as a Young Rat

Balazs, Katharina. "Some Like It Haute: Leadership Lessons from France's Great Chefs." *Organizational Dynamics*, vol. 30, no. 2, 2001, pp. 134–48.
Bentham, Jeremy. *An Introduction to the Principles of Morals and Legislation: Printed in the Year 1780, and Now First Published.* T. Payne, 1789.
Beaugé, Bénédict. "On the Novelty in Cuisine: A Brief Historical Insight." *International Journal of Gastronomy and Food Science*, vol. 1, 2012, pp. 5–14.
Blount, Margaret J. *Animal Land: The Creatures of Children's Fiction.* W. Morrow, 1975.
Brillat-Savarin, Jean Anthelme. *The Physiology of Taste: Or, Meditations on Transcendental Gastronomy.* 1825. Translated by M. F. K. Fisher, Knopf, 1971.
Cloake, Felicity. "How to Make Perfect Ratatouille." *The Guardian*, 15 Jul. 2010, US edition, www.theguardian.com/lifeandstyle/wordofmouth/2010/jul/15/how-to-make-perfect-ratatouille. Accessed 26 July 2017.
Elias, Norbert. *The Civilizing Process.* Urizen Books, 1978.
Elick, Catherine. *Talking Animals in Children's Fiction: A Critical Study.* McFarland, 2015.

Ferguson, Priscilla P. *Accounting for Taste: The Triumph of French Cuisine.* U of Chicago P, 2004.

Ferguson, Priscilla P. *Word of Mouth: What We Talk about when We Talk about Food.* U of California P, 2014.

Ferguson, Priscilla, and Gary Alan Fine. "Sociology at the Stove." Review of *Ratatouille*, directed by Brad Bird and Jan Pinkava. *Contexts*, vol. 1, no. 7, 2008, pp. 59–61.

Grahame, Kenneth. *The Wind in the Willows.* Illustrated by Michael Hague, Ariel Books, 1980.

Herhuth, Eric. "Cooking like a Rat: Sensation and Politics in Disney-Pixar's *Ratatouille*." *Quarterly Review of Film and Video*, vol. 31, 2014, pp. 468–85.

Johnson, Kathleen R. *Understanding Children's Animal Stories.* Edwin Mellen, 2000. Studies in Comparative Literature, vol. 33.

Leschziner, Vanina. *At the Chef's Table: Culinary Creativity in Elite Restaurants.* Stanford UP, 2015.

O'Brien, Robert C. *Mrs. Frisby and the Rats of Nimh.* Illustrated by Zena Bernstein, Atheneum, 1971.

Proust, Marcel. *Remembrance of Things Past.* Vol. 1: *Swann's Way; Within a Budding Grove*, translated by C. K. Scott Moncrieff and Terrence Kilmartin, Random House, 1981.

Rao, Hyagreeva, Philippe Monin, and Rodolphe Durand. "Institutional Change in Toque Ville: Nouvelle Cuisine as an Identity Movement in Gastronomy." *American Journal of Sociology*, vol. 108, no. 4, 2003, pp. 795–843.

Ratatouille. Directed by Brad Bird and Jan Pinkava, Disney•Pixar, 2007.

"Ratatouille Edit Bay Visit!" *ComingSoon.net*, 25 Apr. 2007, www.comingsoon.net/movies/features/19939-ratatouille-edit-bay-visit. Accessed 26 July 2017.

Singer, Peter. *Practical Ethics.* Cambridge UP, 1979.

Spang, Jessica. *The Invention of the Restaurant: Paris and Modern Gastronomic Culture.* Harvard UP, 2000.

Sullivan, Robert. *Rats: Observations on the History and Habitat of the City's Most Unwanted Inhabitants.* Bloomsbury, 2004.

Trubek, Amy. *Haute Cuisine: How the French Invented the Culinary Profession.* U of Pennsylvania P, 2000.

Viscusi, Gregory. "'Ratatouille' Makes Star of Rat-Trap Shop." *Los Angeles Times*, 17 August 2007. http://articles.latimes.com/2007/aug/17/entertainment/et-ratatouille17. Accessed 26 July 2017.

White, E. B. *Charlotte's Web.* Harper and Row, 1980.

Chapter 9: "Beating Eggs Never Makes the Evening News": Politics and Kitchens in Rita Williams-Garcia's *One Crazy Summer* and Its Sequels

Bloom, Joshua and Waldo E. Martin Jr. *Black Against Empire: The History and Politics of the Black Panther Party.* U of California P, 2013.

Bower, Anne L. "Introduction: Watching Soul Food." *African American Foodways: Explorations of History and Culture*, edited by Anne L. Bower, U of Illinois P, 2007, pp. 1–14.

Coats, Karen, and Lisa Rowe Fraustino. "Performing Motherhood: Introduction to a Special Issue on Mothering in Children's and Young Adult Literature." *Children's Literature in Education*, vol. 46, no. 2, 2015, pp. 107–9.

Flamming, Douglas. *African Americans in the West.* ABC-CLIO, 2009.

Gee, Denise. "The Gospel of Great Southern Food." *Southern Living*, June 1996, pp. 126–28.

Gregory, James N. "The Second Great Migration: A Historical Overview." *African American Urban History Since World War II*, edited by Kenneth L. Kusmer and Joe W. Trotter, U of Chicago P, 2009, pp. 19–38.

Hinton, KaaVonia, and Angela Branyon. "'Your Hair Ain't Naughty:' Representations of Women in Rita Williams-Garcia's Novels." *The Lion and the Unicorn*, vol. 41, no. 3, 2017, pp. 327–43.

Joyner, Charles. *Down by the Riverside: Slave Folk in a South Carolina Slave Community.* U of Illinois P, 1984.

Lewis, Edna. *The Taste of Country Cooking.* Alfred A. Knopf, 1976.

Miller, Adrian. *Soul Food: The Surprising Story of an American Cuisine, One Plate at a Time.* U of North Carolina P, 2013

Patel, Raj. "Survival Pending Revolution: What the Black Panthers Can Teach the US Food Movement." *Food First Backgrounder: Institute for Food and Development Policy*, vol. 18, no. 2, 2012, pp. 1–3.

Potorti, Mary. "Feeding Revolution: The Black Panther Party and the Politics of Food." *Radical Teacher*, no. 98, 2014, pp. 43–50.

Romberg, Chris. *No There There: Race, Class, and Political Community in Oakland.* U of California P, 2004.

Shih, Bryan and Yohuru Williams, editors. *The Black Panthers: Portraits from an Unfinished Revolution.* Nation Books, 2016.

Shapiro, Laura. *Something from the Oven: Reinventing Dinner in 1950s America.* Penguin, 2004.

Whit, William C. "Soul Food as Cultural Creation." *African American Foodways: Explorations of History and Culture*, edited by Anne L. Bower, U of Illinois P, 2007, pp. 45–58.

Whitehead, Tony. "In Search of Soul Food and Meaning: Culture, Food, and Health." *African Americans in the South: Issues of Race, Class, and Gender*, edited by H. A. Baier and Yvonne Jones, U of Georgia P, 1982, pp. 94–110.

Williams-Garcia, Rita. "Between Delphine and a Hard Place." *Language Arts*, vol. 94, no. 3, 2017, pp. 211–12.

Williams-Garcia, Rita. "CSK Author Award Acceptance: One Crazy Road to Here." *The Horn Book Magazine*, vol. 87, no. 4, 2011, pp. 86–93.

Williams-Garcia, Rita. *Gone Crazy in Alabama.* HarperCollins, 2015.

Williams-Garcia, Rita. *One Crazy Summer.* HarperCollins, 2011.

Williams-Garcia, Rita. *P.S. Be Eleven.* HarperCollins, 2013.

Yentsch, Anne. "Excavating African American Food History." *African American Foodways: Explorations of History and Culture*, edited by Anne L. Bower, U of Illinois P, 2007, pp. 59–98.

Chapter 10: Refugee Narratives, Cuisine Clash: The Case of Thanhha Lai's *Inside Out & Back Again*

Baloup, Clément. *Little Saigon.* La Boîte à Bulles, 2012.

Baloup, Clément. *Quitter Saigon.* La Boîte à Bulles, 2013.

Baloup, Clément, Olivia Hanks, and Pierre Daum. *Vietnamese Memories: Book 1*. Humanoids, 2018.

Baloup, Clément, Olivia Hanks, and Pierre Daum. *Vietnamese Memories: Book 2*. Humanoids, 2018.

Chattarji, Subarno. "'The New American': The Creation of a Typology of Vietnamese-American Identity in Children's Literature." *Journal of American Studies*, vol. 44, no. 2, 2010, pp. 409–28.

Claiborne, Craig. "The Flavors of Vietnam Re-Created in America." *New York Times*, 27 Feb. 1985, pp. 45, 54.

Espiritu, Yén Lê. *Body Counts: The Vietnam War and Militarized Refuge(es)*. U of California P, 2014.

Hong, Mai-Lin K. "Reframing the Archive: Vietnamese Refugee Narratives in the Post–9/11 Period." *Melus*, vol. 41, no. 3, 2016, pp. 18–41.

Howell, Jennifer. "Vietnamese Foodways and Viet Kieu Postmemory in Clément Baloup's Graphic Narratives." *European Comic Art*, vol. 8, no. 1, 2015, pp. 25–51.

Kalcik, Susan. "Ethnic Foodways in America: Symbol and the Performance of Identity." *Ethnic and Regional Foodways in the United States: The Performance of Group Identity*, edited by Linda Keller Brown and Kay Mussell, U of Tennessee P, 1984, pp. 37–65.

Lai, Thanhha. *Inside Out & Back Again*. Harper, 2011.

Lai, Thanhha. *Listen, Quietly*. HarperCollins, 2015.

Lam, Andrew. *Perfume Dreams: Reflections on the Vietnamese Diaspora*. Heyday Books, 2005.

Lam, Andrew. *East Eats West: Writing in Two Hemispheres*. Heyday Books, 2010.

Montero, Darrel. *Vietnamese Americans: Patterns of Resettlement and Socioeconomic Adaptation in the United States*. Westview Press, 1979.

Nguyen, Andrea. *Into the Vietnamese Kitchen: Treasured Foodways, Modern Flavors*. Ten Speed Press, 2006.

Nguyen, Viet Thanh. *The Sympathizer: A Novel*. Grove Press, 2015.

Nguyen, Viet Thanh. *Nothing Ever Dies: Vietnam and the Memory of War*. Harvard UP, 2016.

Routhier, Nicole. *The Foods of Vietnam*. Stewart, Tabori and Chang, 1989.

Schrader, Michael. "Routhier Wins IACP Award for Foods of Vietnam." *Nation's Restaurant News*, vol. 24, no. 27, 1990, p. 20.

Susina, Jan. "'Tell him about Vietnam': Vietnamese-Americans in Contemporary American Children's Literature." *Children's Literature Association Quarterly*, vol. 16, no. 2, 1991, pp. 58–63.

Zetter, Roger. "Refugees and Refugee Studies—A Label and an Agenda." *The Journal of Refugee Studies*, vol. 1, no. 1, 1988, pp. 1–7.

INDEX

abjection, 48, 127, 129–30, 131–32, 134, 135, 173, 174, 176
activism, 26, 30, 87, 161, 162–64
Acton, Eliza, 38, 39, 40
adaptation, 66, 84, 137; of foods, 40, 43, 77, 91, 126, 144, 149, 150, 154, 168, 170, 176–77, 178; of people, 9, 81, 168, 177, 178
advertising, 20, 97, 98, 100, 101, 148, 162
African Americans, 142, 144, 146, 147, 149, 160, 161, 174, 180n4, 187n5; and food, 150, 152, 186n3; children's literature, 7; diasporas of, 9, 152, 154, 165
agency, 4, 6, 13, 26, 30, 31, 32, 85, 92, 102–3, 104, 105, 127, 128, 140, 158, 168, 170–71, 174; through cooking, 16, 18–19, 25, 28–29, 34, 130–31, 135, 159–60; lack of, 13, 20, 22–24, 98, 104, 158
agriculture, 6, 51, 67, 68–70; plows, 70; Western, 8, 66, 75, 82, 83, 86, 89
Alabama, 9, 144, 146, 147, 148, 150, 152, 153, 154, 155, 169, 175, 187n1
alcohol, 116
Alice's Adventures in Wonderland, 3–4, 10, 99
alienation, 92, 114, 151, 166, 173, 174
Alligators All Around, 90
alterity. *See* Other
American Indian Movement (AIM), 87
angel of the house, 15, 17, 29
animal fantasy, 36, 123, 126, 127, 128, 129, 140, 141, 142, 143
animal/human relationships, 44, 45, 124, 128, 129–30, 134–36, 140, 141, 142–43; hybridity, 126, 135–36, 140

animals, 51, 68, 74, 87, 107, 114, 115–16, 122, 151, 159, 180n1; as analogs for children, 37, 46, 142; as characters, 35, 36, 37, 43, 44, 45, 46, 54, 55, 57, 59, 123, 127, 128, 130, 135, 141
animals, game, 36, 66, 67, 82, 83; antelope, 67; bear, 67, 80, 82, 83; beaver, 82; buffalo, 80, 82, 83; deer, 67, 82, 83, 146, 148; ducks, 67; fish, 35, 67, 78, 82, 87, 88, 187n3; geese, 67; moose, 80, 82, 83, 85; prairie chicken, 67; rabbit, 67, 82; squirrel, 67; turkey (wild), 67
animals, livestock, 82; cattle, 67, 68, 69, 71, 146, 147, 148–49, 150–51, 152, 153; chickens and poultry, 67, 68, 146–48, 149, 152, 173; pigs, 47, 67, 147
Anishinaabe. *See* Ojibwe
anorexia, 114, 116, 117–18
appetite, 41, 53, 59, 78, 112, 134
assimilation, 9, 92, 93, 95, 102, 105, 167, 168, 169, 173, 184n1; resistance to, 92, 168, 173, 175, 177–78
Association for the Study of Food and Society, 5
autonomy, 16, 19, 29–30, 104, 126, 147, 158, 160, 161, 162
aversion. *See* disgust
awards, for children's literature: Coretta Scott King, 144, 152, 156–57; National Book Award for Young People's Literature, 144, 168; Newbery Honor Award, 144, 168; Scott O'Dell Award for Historical Fiction, 144

Baca, Karlos, 88, 184n9
bakeries, 29, 94, 95, 96, 97, 98, 99, 100, 103, 107, 108, 149, 184n4, 185n9
bakers, 97, 99, 100, 102–3, 104, 105, 108, 184n8
Bakhtin, Mikhail, 124, 127, 130, 143
baking, 15, 39, 42, 48, 73, 95, 97, 100, 103, 119, 163
Balazs, Katherina, 125, 133, 137, 138, 185n3
Baloup, Clément, 168–69, 170
Banham, Reyner, 107, 110, 113–14
Barthes, Roland, 5
Bataille, George, 48
bears, 51–52, 56, 58, 62, 67, 68, 80, 82, 83
Beard, James, 19, 26
Beaugé, Bénédict, 126, 185n3
Bedford, Annie North, 20–23, 25, 27, 29, 33, 34
Beecher, Catherine, 15
bees, 8, 51, 52, 56–57, 182n2
Beim, Jerrold, 24–25, 27, 33, 34
Belasco, Warren, 13, 26, 32, 113
Bellow, Saul, 96
Benjamin, Walter, 109
Bentham, Jeremy, 134, 185n5
Berenstain Bears, 51
Berry, Wendell, 67
Berzok, Linda, 75, 77, 80, 82, 83, 87–88
Bibby, M. E., 40
Birchbark House, The, 74, 76, 77–78, 81, 84
Birchbark series, 8, 9, 65–67, 74–76, 77–78, 80, 81, 82, 84, 86, 87, 88, 89
Black Panthers, 9, 153, 156–57, 160–61, 164, 187n5; and breakfast program, 9, 145, 156, 160–61, 162, 163, 186n1
Black Power movement, 9, 144, 152, 156–57
Block, Francesca Lia, 7, 9, 106, 107, 108, 109, 110, 111, 113, 114, 116, 120, 121, 185n3
Bloom, Joshua, 160
Blount, Margaret, 123
blue willow dish pattern, 44–45, 181n15
Bodmer, George, 103, 184n7
Bond, Michael, 52
bourgeois. *See* class: middle
Bower, Anne, 152

Boy Who Ate Around, The, 4, 91
Brady, Jean, 108
Branyon, Angela, 146, 149, 156, 161, 165
Braun, John, 96, 105
Brillat-Savarin, Jean Anthelme, 3–4, 6, 10, 67, 112–13, 122, 143
Brooklyn, 91, 92, 102, 105, 144, 148, 151, 152, 153, 154, 159, 163, 184n5
Brown, Elaine, 163–64
Brown, Rebecca A., 5
Bruchac, Joseph, 76
Busch, Wilhelm, 184n8
By the Shores of Silver Lake, 67, 72

Campbell, Patricia J., 107, 109
Canning Season, The, 6
capability. *See* agency
Capudo, Michael J., 76
Carême, Marie-Antoine, 125–26, 127
Carlisle, Nancy, 98
Carrington, Bridget, 5
Carroll, Lewis, 3–4, 108
cautionary tale, 37
Cech, John, 90, 91, 92, 96, 98, 100, 184n7, 185n9
Chang, Li Ping, 66
Charlie and the Chocolate Factory, 100
Charlotte's Web, 122, 123, 148
Chattarji, Subarno, 167, 178
chefs, 9, 20, 22, 26, 29, 30, 34, 99, 123, 125, 126, 127, 128, 131, 132, 134, 135, 136, 137, 170; as artists, 125, 126, 128, 130–31, 132, 133, 136, 139, 140, 141, 185n3
Cherokee Bat and the Goat Guys, 108, 115–16
Chez Panisse, 26, 30–31, 34
Chickadee, 76, 77, 81, 83
Chicken Soup with Rice, 90
Child, Julia, 19, 26
Child, Lydia Marie, 179n1
child and childhood, 4, 6, 7, 11, 13, 16, 20, 21, 22, 24, 26, 27, 28, 29, 33, 34, 41, 46, 53, 55, 62, 64, 66, 88, 90, 91, 92, 93, 96, 97, 98, 99, 100, 105, 109, 126, 138–39, 150, 156, 157, 158, 163, 168, 175, 179n1, 180n7, 186n3, 188n3; and innocence, 46, 148, 182n1

child cooks, 11, 12, 13–17, 21–23, 24–25, 26, 28–30, 33, 145, 154–56, 159–60
child readers, 14, 15, 17, 23, 24–25, 29, 33, 34, 36, 38, 44, 46, 58, 64, 75, 86, 88, 97–98, 123, 124, 126, 128, 129, 130, 168, 180n7
children's literature, 4, 5, 6, 7, 10, 11, 12, 33, 46, 51
Children's Literature Association, 4
Children's Literature in Education, 4
Cinderella, 158
civility, 35–36, 42, 45, 47–49
class, 13, 25, 37, 38, 39, 42, 68–69, 142, 161, 181n12, 181n16; lower, 40–42, 46, 94, 142, 164, 181n16; middle, 13, 17, 36, 38, 39, 40, 41–42, 45, 46, 47, 49, 50, 180n3, 182n18; upper, 181n16
Coats, Karen, 158
Cohen, Patricia, 102
colonialism, 8, 66, 69, 77, 166
comedy, 113, 121
comfort, 6, 9, 34, 42, 50, 52, 58, 76, 112, 113, 114, 117, 121, 137, 178, 180n1
commerciality, 22, 50, 91, 98, 100, 101, 102, 103, 105, 179n3, 184n4
community, 17, 23, 25, 26, 28, 29–30, 33, 68, 76, 79, 82, 103, 109, 120, 165, 167, 187n5; boundaries, 29, 53–55, 105, 142; ethnic enclaves, 91, 92, 94, 95, 96, 105, 106, 149, 160, 187n5; global, 28, 32, 34; hierarchies within, 53–55, 105, 141–42; inclusion/ exclusion of, 53–55, 60, 92, 105, 113, 114, 121, 141–43, 152, 161, 162, 163–64, 169, 174; local, 28, 30, 31–32, 34, 107, 112, 157, 160, 161, 162–64; sociability, 43, 47, 49, 52–53, 56–58, 60–61, 63, 107, 112, 113, 116, 137, 141, 143, 182n3
Connolly, Paula T., 52–53, 61–62, 182n1
consumerism, 19, 20, 22, 24, 33, 94, 98, 154
consumption of food. *See* eating
cookbooks, 5, 7, 11–12, 16, 19, 23, 24, 26, 28, 36, 39, 123, 179n1, 179n2; African American, 9, 186n3; boys', 24–25; children's, 7, 11–34, 179n2, 180n7; French, 126, 127, 128, 130; instructional, 14, 16, 18–19, 20, 21–22, 31, 32, 33, 34, 38, 40, 179n2; Jewish American, 8, 95; literary, 12–13, 64, 86; receipt books, 13, 15, 16, 17–18, 27, 30; Vietnamese American, 9, 170, 188n2; as writing, 17–19, 27, 30, 38
cookery, 5, 13, 16, 17, 20, 25, 39, 42, 95
cooking, 5, 10, 11, 13, 14, 15, 16, 17, 19, 23, 30, 36, 37, 38, 43, 49, 76–77, 86, 97, 98, 102, 138, 145, 157, 163, 165; attitudes about, 12, 15, 20, 23, 24–27, 29, 30–33, 34, 40, 50, 154–56, 159–60; children cooking (*see* child cooks); creativity of, 27, 31, 112, 113, 125, 126, 128–33, 134, 139, 149–50, 185n3; frugal, 17, 19, 40, 42; as gendered (*see* gender); learning, 14–17, 18, 21–22, 23, 24–25, 28–30, 40, 128, 129, 136, 188n2; pedagogy, 13, 15–19, 20, 21–22, 25, 28–29, 31–32, 33, 40, 169 (*see also* didacticism; cookbooks: instructional); as play, 14, 20–23, 25, 34; providing agency (*see* agency: through cooking); real, 20, 21, 23, 25, 26, 28, 29, 108, 112, 154–56, 159; restaurant, 30–31, 34, 95, 99, 111, 117, 119, 125, 131–34, 137, 139, 140; from scratch, 19, 145, 154–56, 179n2, 186n3; as service, 15–17, 18, 24, 25–26, 27, 28, 33, 34, 142, 145, 158; as sign of civilization, 36, 39, 41–42, 44–46, 58, 70–72, 91, 135, 139–40, 141–43, 180n1, 182n18; as transforming ingredients, 43–44, 72; utensils, 18, 20, 32, 37, 40, 42, 44–46, 90, 99, 100, 102, 134, 179n2, 184n7
Cooking without Mother's Help, 16–19, 20, 21, 23, 27, 28, 30, 31, 32
Coraline, 6
Cormier, Paul Nicolas, 76
Cott, Jonathan, 90, 91, 97, 98, 184n7
counting coup, 74–75, 77, 80, 81
creativity, 53, 56, 57, 58, 91, 113, 130–31, 133, 150, 158, 163, 182n3; in cooking, 27, 31, 112, 129, 130, 131, 132, 149, 150; lack of, 58; in writing, 13, 18
Critical Approaches to Food in Children's Literature, 4, 6
Crittenden, Alyssa N., 51

crops, 64, 67, 69–70, 73, 82, 86, 87, 103; corn, 69, 73, 81; rice, 147; wheat, 69–71, 72, 73, 83, 86, 183n6; wild rice, 8, 83–85, 86–87

cuisine and culinary heritage, 11, 30, 32–33, 48, 54, 66, 68, 107, 116, 120, 141, 179n4; African American, 9, 149, 150, 152, 153, 186n3; American, 9, 11, 12, 13, 14, 16, 17, 18, 19, 20, 29, 34, 66, 68, 80, 87, 92, 100, 102, 103, 105, 113, 154, 170, 174, 179n1, 179n4; British, 36, 37, 38, 39, 40, 41, 42, 43, 47, 50, 58, 182n4; countercuisine, 26, 32, 113; erosion of, 19, 22, 25, 27, 156, 169; French, 125, 126, 129, 138, 139; haute, 9, 19, 125–26, 127, 137, 139, 186n8; indigenous, 87–89, 184n9; Jewish, 8, 90, 91, 94, 95, 102, 103, 107; nouvelle, 30, 138, 139, 185n3, 186n6; Ojibwe, 66, 78, 80, 83–85, 87; soul food, 9, 117, 150, 186n3; southern or country, 9, 148, 152, 153, 154, 156, 165, 186n3; Vietnamese, 9, 168–70, 172, 173, 174, 175, 188n2, 188n3; West African, 149; Western, 72; vegetarian, 26, 28, 29, 35, 66, 107, 112, 113–14, 115, 116, 117, 118, 120, 121, 148

culture, 9, 10, 11, 12, 15, 19, 25, 33, 50, 54, 60, 67, 68, 91, 101, 103, 104, 142, 152, 158, 164, 169, 182n3, 183n5; African American, 7, 9, 142, 144, 146, 147, 149, 150, 152, 153, 154, 157, 160, 165, 180n4, 187n5; American, 8, 15, 29, 64, 65, 92, 93, 94, 96, 97, 100, 101, 102, 105, 167–68, 169, 177, 178, 184n1, 188n3; Anglo/European American, 5, 6, 8, 15, 64, 66, 68, 69–72, 75, 77, 80, 81, 83, 86, 87, 88, 89; British, 5, 7, 36, 38, 40, 42, 47; children's, 11, 12; clashes among, 8, 9, 65, 66, 74–77, 80, 82, 86–89, 142, 149–50, 167–68, 174, 178; counter, 113; definition of, 149; erasures of, 65, 74, 88–89, 102, 167, 183n1; French culinary, 125, 126, 127, 133, 138, 140; Jewish, 7, 8, 91–96, 102, 103, 105, 184n1; Los Angeles, 9, 106–10; Ojibwe, 7, 8, 66, 76, 77, 78, 80, 81, 84, 85, 86, 87, 88; popular, 5, 102, 109, 186n3; rural, 7, 9, 43, 47, 127–28, 131, 134, 137, 138, 139, 141, 144, 147–48, 150–51, 152, 153, 154, 156, 165, 181n5, 182n18, 185n1, 186n3, 188n3; urban, 7, 9, 19, 40, 41, 69, 92, 93–94, 95–97, 98, 99–102, 106–9, 111, 117, 128, 138, 144–45, 148, 150, 151, 153, 154, 156, 160, 165, 170, 184n4, 186n3, 187n5, 188n3; Vietnamese, 7, 167, 168, 169, 173, 175, 188n3

dairying, 69, 71–72, 147–49, 150–51, 183n5, 183n6
Dangerous Angels series, 9. *See also* Weetzie Bat series
Daley, Suzanne, 37
Daniel, Carolyn, 5
Davidson, Alan, 43, 47, 58, 119, 181n6, 182n4
Davin, Anna, 40, 42
Davis, Mike, 109, 110
desire, 15, 16, 17, 19, 24, 25, 42, 53, 56, 58, 60, 61, 69, 93, 99, 100, 105, 113, 130, 152, 156, 158, 168, 180n1; for food(s), 4, 8, 35, 36–37, 40, 45, 46, 53, 56, 57, 58, 60, 61, 63, 78, 92, 103, 118, 120, 148, 151, 175, 180n1
diasporas, 9, 152, 165, 166, 168, 178, 187n1
didacticism, 33, 37. *See also* cooking: pedagogy
diet, 36, 40, 43, 66, 67, 69, 71, 72, 73, 80, 82, 83, 142, 182n4
Diner, Hasia, 94, 95
disgust, 47–49, 128, 129, 132, 136, 139, 142, 148, 170, 173
Disney•Pixar, 9, 123, 124, 125, 126, 138, 141, 186n8
displacement, 65, 66, 77, 86, 166, 168, 169. *See also* migration: forced
doing-cooking, 27, 29, 31, 32
domesticity, 13, 15, 21, 22, 24, 25, 28, 29, 30, 31, 32, 33, 34, 37, 39, 40, 42, 46, 99, 179n2, 180n3
double address, 28, 33–34, 180n7
Douglas, Mary, 5, 8, 53–54, 58, 60, 91, 105, 182n3
dream, 93, 99, 100, 101, 102, 104
Drescher, Henrik, 4, 91
drugs, 116, 119, 151

eating, 3, 4, 5, 6, 10, 19, 33, 35, 36, 37, 39, 44, 48, 49, 51, 52, 53, 54, 55, 56, 57, 58, 59, 60, 66, 67, 68, 69, 71, 72, 73, 77, 78, 81, 84, 87, 88, 94, 98, 100, 103, 104, 106, 118, 120, 122, 123, 129, 132, 139, 143, 145, 146, 148, 154, 157, 160, 169, 172, 175, 180n1, 182n4, 183n4, 184n8; carnivorous, 36, 43, 44, 45, 46, 48, 49, 114, 118–19, 173; children, 3–4, 10, 11, 20, 21, 22, 23, 24, 25, 41, 79, 80, 90, 92, 96, 97, 98, 103, 105, 111, 114, 115, 117–19, 148, 150–51, 158, 159, 160, 162, 170–72, 174, 175, 179n4; in a civilized manner, 36, 46, 48, 58, 122, 127, 137, 143; danger of being eaten, 4, 35, 37–38, 44, 49, 90, 92, 103, 105; overeating, 52, 57, 58, 78–79, 129; predator vs. prey relationship, 35, 36, 43–44, 46, 47, 49, 105; in restaurants, 95, 96, 110–12, 117, 118–19, 137, 140, 141; restraint in, 15, 30, 41–42, 58, 78–79; as social occasion, 32, 48, 52, 54, 55, 112, 113, 114, 115, 117, 141, 169, 174

egalitarianism, 68, 127–28, 141–43, 157

Elias, Norbert, 139, 140

Elick, Catherine, 123, 124, 127, 128, 130, 135, 141, 143

Ellis, Hattie, 51, 62, 182n2

embedded discourse, 11, 13, 34

Escoffier, Auguste, 126, 127, 133, 137

Espiritu, Yén Lê, 168, 170

Erdrich, Louise, 7, 8, 9, 64, 65–66, 74–85, 86, 87, 88–89, 183n3

ethnicity, 13, 92, 94, 102, 106, 150, 166, 168, 169, 177

Evans, Heather A., 38–39, 41, 42, 44

Everett, James, 5–6

Everything on a Waffle, 6

expansion, westward (US), 6, 8, 13, 64, 65, 66, 69, 70, 74, 77, 81–82, 86, 88, 89, 183n3

family, 23, 29, 34, 45, 90, 104, 124, 187n1; as audience for cooking, 15–16, 19, 21, 25, 129, 155–56, 160; as eating and cooking unit, 38, 39, 40, 48, 67, 69, 70–73, 81, 95, 96, 98–99, 102, 106, 111, 112, 113, 143, 148, 149, 150–52, 153–55, 159–60, 168, 170–73; as emotional support and outlet, 74, 101, 107, 112, 114–16, 120, 142, 152, 176–77; group need vs. individual desire, 78–79, 145, 150–52, 157–59; as setting for emotional crises, 50, 85, 114–15, 140, 144, 145, 150–52, 157–60, 163, 175; as source of identity, history, and traditions, 9, 13, 17–18, 20, 21, 27, 28, 30, 66, 70–71, 79, 81, 85, 92–93, 119, 149, 153, 155–56, 162, 169–70, 178, 184n7, 188n3; as unit for food production, 8, 65–73, 75–85, 86, 88–89, 128–29, 130, 141, 142, 143, 146–52, 154

Fanny at Chez Panisse, 26, 30–33

Fanny in France, 26, 30, 32–33

farmers' markets, 9, 29, 107, 108, 110, 122

farming, 6, 31, 34, 35, 37, 43, 65, 66, 67, 68–73, 75, 108, 148, 165, 181n5, 181n13, 186n3; African American, 144, 145, 146, 147, 149; factory, 148, 150–51; family, 146–52, 154; sharecropping vs. ownership, 147; subsistence, 67, 71, 72, 80, 146–47

fathers, 16, 21, 23, 35, 36–37, 43, 44, 45, 82, 85, 111, 117, 126, 128, 136, 140, 141, 142, 144, 151, 155, 158, 165, 169

feminism, 4, 7, 12, 21, 38–39

Ferguson, Priscilla, 125–26, 128, 138, 140, 141

Fernández-Armesto, Felipe, 70, 72

Fine, Gary Alan, 126

First Book of Boys' Cooking, The, 24–25

Fisher, Carol, 12, 14, 20

Flandrin, Jean-Louis, 73, 183n2

flavor, 3, 4, 38, 80, 112, 118, 125, 128, 129, 154, 171, 175

food (types): canned, 19, 20, 24, 101, 145, 154, 172, 173; comfort, 6, 9, 52, 76, 112, 113, 114, 117, 137, 178; convenience, 19, 20, 23, 24, 25, 27, 29, 34, 105, 144, 145, 154, 155, 159, 165, 179n2; dessert, 14, 15, 24, 29, 39, 41, 103, 147 (*see also* sweets); fast, 154, 159–60, 162; frozen, 6, 19, 20, 22, 24, 145, 154, 173; global, 28, 34, 70, 71, 108, 125, 139, 179n4; healthy, 26, 29, 107, 112–21, 160; home cooking, 13, 91–92,

107, 111, 112, 115, 116, 117, 145, 148, 153–56, 159–60, 162, 186n3; industrialized, 6, 8, 19, 20, 25, 34, 91–92, 98, 99, 100, 102–3, 113, 148, 150–51, 154, 173, 184n4; junk, 115, 118–19, 154, 159–60, 162; local, 8, 26, 28, 30, 31, 32, 34, 71, 88, 107, 149, 150, 170; novelty food, 20; organic, 26, 30; produce (garden), 29, 30, 34, 67, 69, 71, 72, 73, 80, 108, 146, 147, 152, 154, 186n3; raw vs. cooked, 19, 36, 43–44, 66, 87, 119, 142, 148, 154, 180n1; "real," 19, 20, 29, 83, 159; sacred, 84, 94; seasonal, 30, 66, 67, 69, 75, 76, 77, 80, 88, 147, 150–51; vegetarian, 26, 28, 29, 35, 66, 107, 112, 113–18, 120, 121, 148. *See also* cuisine and culinary heritage

food, as signifier, 4, 5, 6, 7, 9, 10, 11, 12, 35, 36, 37, 45, 49–50, 52, 53, 60, 62, 65, 73, 80, 81, 84, 91, 94, 96, 97, 104, 106, 109, 114, 119, 120, 121, 149, 152, 172, 188n3

food, as social code, 53–54, 58, 91, 92, 104–5

food, as structuring narrative, 8, 11, 21, 32, 34, 53, 56, 58–59, 60, 65–66, 67, 80, 82, 84–85, 91, 101, 111–12, 120–21, 127, 131, 153, 157, 161, 164, 177, 182n3, 183n2, 188n3

food, as structuring society, 30, 54–55, 58, 60, 66, 68–69, 70, 71, 72–73, 75, 76, 77, 126, 141, 143, 156, 157, 164, 183n2

food, ethical practices of, 78–79, 84–85, 87–88, 107, 109, 112–14, 117–21, 127, 132, 143, 150–51

food, manufactured, 8, 19, 91–92, 98, 105, 148–51, 154, 184n4

food, preparation of, 5, 6, 14, 17, 18, 19, 23, 24, 28, 29, 31, 32, 33, 34, 36, 37, 39, 40, 44, 45, 46, 48, 66, 67, 68, 84, 87, 88, 91, 98, 106, 112, 121, 125, 127, 128, 134, 136, 137, 141, 143, 146, 149, 154, 169, 170, 180n1, 188n3; whole meals, 15, 16, 21, 22, 24, 27, 33, 47, 155–56

Food and Literature, 8

food and sexuality, 53, 97, 115–16, 118–19

food genocide, 88–89

food (in)security, 40–41, 46, 82–83, 86–87, 88–89, 94, 160–61, 163–64, 170–72

food preservation, 38, 47, 66, 67, 72, 73, 77, 87, 113, 119, 182n4; canning, 19, 20, 24, 73, 101, 145, 147, 154, 172, 173; drying, 19, 68, 73, 77, 78–80, 87, 115, 118, 154, 172, 176, 178; freezing, 6, 19, 20, 22, 24, 83, 145, 154, 173; pickling, 73, 100; smoked, 42, 87

food production. *See* farming; hunting and gathering

food sovereignty, 86–89

food studies, 4–5, 12, 13, 39, 65, 186n3

foods (specific): apples, 43, 112, 122, 127, 174; *bánh chúng*, 170, 177, 178; baked goods, 47, 95; beans, 28, 31, 73, 81, 101, 106, 110, 118, 122, 128, 145, 154, 159, 162, 164, 170, 171, 178, 187n3; beef, 24, 67, 108, 172, 173, 181n6; berries, 37, 68, 77–80, 82, 110, 112, 116, 117, 127; biscuits, 15, 19, 97, 155, 172; breads, 24, 58, 69, 70–72, 76, 94, 96, 98, 101, 103, 115, 116, 117, 118, 148, 162, 182n4; butter, 4, 39, 41, 71–72, 94; cabbages, 72, 148, 159; cake, 15, 18, 45, 93, 95, 96, 97, 100, 101, 102–3, 104, 105, 115, 116, 118, 128; candy, 94, 108, 115; carrots, 72, 73, 112, 118, 127, 145, 148, 154; cheese, 28, 31, 32, 71–72, 106, 108, 110, 112, 115, 118, 127, 129–30, 132, 155, 183n5; chicken, 90, 145, 146, 148, 154, 159, 173, 178; coffee, 94, 95, 101, 117; condensed milk, 52, 58; cookies, 28, 103, 112, 118, 158, 163, 171, 174, 178; corn, 69, 73, 81, 151, 171; cream, 73, 101; egg rolls, 118, 162, 164; eggs, 18, 45, 68, 94, 117, 128, 146, 147, 148, 150, 152, 155, 161, 172, 179n2; fish, 6, 19, 31, 67, 82, 87, 94, 108, 122, 162, 172, 187n3; fish sauce (*nước mắm*), 170, 172, 173; flour (wheat), 18, 41, 43, 70–71, 76, 80, 97, 128, 184n8; fruit, 15, 28, 77, 78, 79, 94, 118, 147, 170, 175, 176, 177, 182n4; honey, 8, 51–53, 56, 57, 58, 59, 60, 61, 62, 68, 182n2; jam, 41, 58, 95, 100, 101, 182n4; lettuce, 73, 119, 180n1; maple sugar, 52, 68, 75–77, 78, 79, 80, 84; maple syrup, 8, 68, 75–76, 77, 116; meat, 35, 36, 44, 48, 64, 66, 67–68, 80, 82, 83, 87, 94, 110, 114, 118–19, 122, 145, 146, 148, 151, 154, 159, 170, 173, 187n3;

milk, 55, 68, 71–72, 97, 102–3, 104, 105, 112, 117, 118–19, 146, 147, 148–49, 150–52; oranges, 5–6, 19, 95, 162, 174; nuts, 36, 51, 68, 95, 118, 147; onions, 72, 115, 117, 119, 132, 159, 172; papaya, 171, 174–77, 178; pastry, 38, 39, 41, 42, 43, 44, 95; pemmican, 77, 80; pie, 35–36, 37, 38, 43–49, 68, 80, 112, 117, 147, 162, 182n17; pie, meat, 35, 37, 43–44, 47–49, 50; pie, rabbit, 5, 35–37, 43, 44–46, 49; pizza, 31, 112, 115, 145, 154, 160; pork, 37, 67, 108, 145, 148, 154, 163, 164, 170, 171; potatoes, 72–73, 81, 106, 107, 145, 154, 159, 173, 174, 182; pudding, meat, 37, 41; pudding, roly-poly, 39, 41, 46; pudding, suet, 40, 41; puddings, 31, 38–42, 43, 46, 49–50, 118, 181n6, 181n11; ratatouille, 131, 137, 138, 139; rice, 90, 112, 114, 117, 118, 119, 147, 162, 164, 170, 171, 172, 175, 178; salads, 24, 25, 31, 35, 47, 112; salt, 45, 67, 101, 102, 122, 132, 172, 173, 174, 175; sandwiches, 24, 52, 72, 105, 112, 114, 117, 174, 179n2; sausage, 64, 74, 94, 155, 156; soup, 22, 24, 31, 78, 131–35, 170; spinach, 115, 118, 170; squash, 72, 73, 81, 122; sugar, 18, 29, 39, 40, 73, 115, 118, 119, 122, 128, 176; tomatoes, 73, 101, 104, 115, 119, 122, 137, 147; vegetables, 19, 22, 24, 28, 29, 35–37, 66, 67, 69, 72–73, 94, 108, 112, 114, 117, 147, 187n3; venison, 146, 148; wild rice (*manoomin*), 8, 83–85, 86–87

foodways, 7, 9, 10, 51, 146, 157, 165, 169, 178, 180n1; African American, 9, 144, 146, 152, 157, 165, 186n3; British, 7, 36, 38; definition of, 5, 169; European American, 8, 68, 69–71, 77, 80; French, 128; industrial, 19, 92, 100, 102–3, 113, 144, 154–56, 173; Jewish, 8, 92, 94; Ojibwe, 8–9, 65–66, 68, 74–77, 79–80, 83, 86–89; pioneer (US), 6, 8, 9, 64–66, 75, 76, 86; southern or country (US), 9, 144, 150, 152; Vietnamese, 9, 106, 168–69, 170, 172, 178, 188n3

Forman, Ross D., 37

France, 32, 34, 125, 126, 127, 128, 131, 133, 137, 138, 139, 142, 168–69
Fraser, Caroline, 74
Fraustino, Lisa Rowe, 158
French Revolution, 125, 126, 127
Freudian theory, 25, 100, 104
Fromer, Julie E., 47
frontier, 64, 65, 66, 69, 71, 81

Gabaccia, Donna, 94, 95
Gaiman, Neil, 6
Game of Silence, The, 76, 81, 82, 84–85
garbage, 123, 129, 134, 141, 143, 176
gardens, 26, 29, 31, 35–37, 69, 70, 71, 72–73, 75, 80–81, 146, 147, 152, 180n1, 180n2, 186n3
Gargano, Elizabeth, 84, 87
Gastronomica: The Journal of Food and Culture, 5, 12
Geary, George, 111
Gelman, Woody, 102
gender, 4, 12, 13, 28, 29, 30, 32, 38, 39, 74, 82–83, 84, 146, 158, 160, 165, 186n8; aprons, 22, 23, 24, 41; feminine roles in cooking and food preparation, 14–17, 19, 23–25, 38–39, 83, 84–85, 99, 112, 145, 156, 157, 158, 160, 163, 165, 186n8; masculine roles in cooking, 23, 24–25, 34, 84, 99, 112; strong Black woman archetype, 146, 149, 156, 161; women's writing, 14, 16–19, 20, 21, 27, 30, 38, 39, 158
Giard, Luce, 26–27, 29
Gigante, Denise, 5
gluttony, 51, 52, 53, 57, 78–80, 122, 129
Glynn, Eugene, 101–2
Gold, Jonathan, 106, 107, 108, 109, 110–11, 112, 120, 185n1
Gone Crazy in Alabama, 9, 144, 146–53, 161, 164, 165, 187n3
gourmandism, 59, 112–13, 120
gourmet, 19, 20, 26, 108
grain. *See* crops
grandmothers, 13, 27, 84, 85, 95, 112, 144–45, 146, 147, 148, 149, 150–51, 153–54, 155, 156, 157, 159, 160, 164, 165, 188n3

Great Plains, 65, 66, 68, 69, 74, 76, 78, 79–80, 82, 83, 86
greed. *See* gluttony
grocery store, 29, 94, 108, 149, 150–51, 154, 159, 160, 161, 162, 173
Guam, 169, 172

Hansel and Gretel, 119
Harding, Jennifer, 5
Hardy, Oliver, 99, 184n6
harvest, 6, 8, 56, 68, 69, 73, 75, 76, 77, 84–85, 87, 103, 116, 154, 175
Haviland, Virginia, 90, 93, 96, 98, 185n8
Hector Protector and As I Went over the Water, 90, 104
Hemmings, Robert, 53, 55, 56, 59
Herhuth, Eric, 127, 136, 139–40
hero, 7, 36, 53, 56, 61, 62, 90, 92, 93, 95, 99, 100, 102–3, 105, 130–31, 136
Higglety Pigglety Pop!, 90, 104
Hill, Christina Gish, 83, 86–87
Hinton, KaaVonia, 146, 149, 156, 161, 165
holidays, 156, 169–70; Christmas, 73, 155–56, 176; Tết (Vietnamese Lunar New Year), 169–70, 175, 177, 178; Thanksgiving, 67, 73
home, 46, 57, 72, 77, 79, 80, 94, 99, 110, 112, 113, 118, 121, 131, 151, 152, 153, 155, 165, 180n3, 186n3; comforts of, 52, 71, 91, 95, 121; cooking at, 16, 28, 34, 40, 71, 91–92, 106, 107, 121, 126, 148, 159–60, 188n3; leaving, 63, 96; loss of, 61, 62, 65, 66, 76, 81, 171, 175, 176; as private space, 96, 98, 102, 104, 111, 158; repressions of, 36–37; returning, 52, 104, 113, 115, 120, 138, 147
homosexuality, 101–2, 112, 117
Honest Pretzels and 64 Other Amazing Recipes for Kids Who Love to Cook, 26, 29, 30, 33
Honeyman, Susan, 5
Hong, Mai-Lin K., 167, 177, 178
Horvath, Polly, 6
hospitality, 14, 27, 45, 49, 57, 60, 177, 178
host(ess), 20, 45, 47–48
House at Pooh Corner, The, 8, 52, 54, 56, 59–61, 62, 182n3
Howell, Jennifer, 168–69, 173

hunger, 42, 45, 50, 53, 57, 58, 67, 71, 78, 94, 116–19, 159, 160–61, 164, 171–72, 173
hunting and gathering, 36, 51, 52, 64, 66, 67–69, 75, 76, 81–85, 87–88, 146, 159, 182n2; berrying, 8, 37, 68, 75, 77–80, 82, 86, 87; buffalo, 8, 79–80, 82, 83; maple sugaring, 8, 68, 75–78, 80, 84, 86; ricing, 83–85, 86, 87

identity, 13, 36, 59–60, 61, 126, 128, 130, 132, 136, 139, 157, 158, 166, 169; African American, 146, 149, 150, 156, 161, 165; British, 38, 40, 42; French, 125, 138; Jewish American, 92, 93, 96, 102, 105; Native/Ojibwe, 77, 83, 85, 86, 87; Vietnamese, 168, 170, 175; Vietnamese American, 9, 167, 168, 177, 178, 188n3; Vietnamese transnational (Viet Kieu), 168, 169, 170, 173, 177, 178
ideology, 6, 7, 11, 12, 13, 15, 23, 24, 33, 65, 74, 86, 139, 146, 156, 162, 167; food ideology, 13, 23, 24, 26, 28, 29, 30, 33, 86, 149, 154
immigration, 6, 69, 89, 142; Jewish, 8, 91–94, 95, 96, 105, 184n1; Vietnamese, 7, 9, 167–68, 169, 173–78, 188n3
imperialism, 13
Indians. *See* Native Americans; Ojibwe
injustice, social, 161, 162, 165
Inness, Sherrie, 12, 16, 19, 22, 23, 24, 25
Inside Out & Back Again, 9, 168, 169–78, 187n1, 188n3
In the Night Kitchen, 7, 90–93, 95, 96, 97–100, 101, 102–3, 104–5, 184n5, 184n6, 184n7, 185n9
Ireland, Corydon, 26

Jewish Americans, 7, 8, 91, 92, 102; artists, 102, 105; writers, 92–93, 96, 184n1. *See also* immigration: Jewish
Jim Crow period of American South, 144, 145, 147, 149, 165
Johnson, Kathleen, 124
Johnson, Samuel, 40, 181n6
Joyner, Charles, 149
Joy of Cooking, The, 25, 179n2

Judson, Clara Ingram, 16–17, 21, 25, 27, 29, 33, 34

Kalcik, Susan, 169
Kander, Mrs. Simon, 95
Kansas, 64, 67, 68, 69, 71, 88
Katz, Wendy, 5
Katzen, Mollie, 26–30, 33, 34
Kazin, Alfred, 95
Keeling, Kara, and Scott Pollard, 4, 5, 6, 7, 8, 36–37, 65, 91, 183n4, 183n5
Kipling, Rudyard, 51
Kirkland, Elizabeth Stansbury, 14–17, 21, 25, 27, 29, 33, 34
kitchen, 14, 15, 16, 17, 18, 19, 23, 24, 25, 28, 29, 33, 34, 37, 38, 39–42, 44, 96–99, 100, 102, 117, 121, 123, 124, 125, 126, 127–29, 130–31, 132, 133–37, 139, 140, 141, 154, 155, 156, 157, 159, 181n13, 181n14, 186n8; deconstruction of, 145, 158, 159, 162–63; lack thereof, 40–42, 46, 98; Night Kitchen, 90, 91, 92, 98, 99, 100, 101, 102, 105
Klein, Norman, 111
Korsmeyer, Carolyn, 5, 10
Kristeva, Julia, 5, 48–49, 91
Künstlerroman, 8, 53, 61, 125, 128, 131, 140

labor. *See* work
labor relations, 13
Lai, Thanhha, 7, 9, 168, 169, 170, 177–78, 187n1, 188n3
Lam, Andrew, 166, 168, 177, 178
landscape, 26, 53, 59, 62, 86–87, 138; social, 26, 33, 50, 60, 107, 165, 174, 188n3; urban, 100, 101, 107, 109–10, 111
Lane, Selma, 93, 102, 184n7
Lavelle, Marie, 47, 49
Lear, Linda, 38, 180n2, 181n13
Leonardi, Susan J., 5, 7, 11–12, 25, 34, 179n2
Leschziner, Vanina, 134, 185n3
lessons. *See* cooking: pedagogy
Levinson, Julian, 93, 102
Lévi-Strauss, Claude, 5, 36, 53, 91
Liebs, Charles, 101

Limerick, Patricia Nelson, 69–70
Lionni, Leo, 122
Listen, Quietly, 188n3
literacy, 13, 130
Little Chef (toy stove), 20, 22, 179n3
Little Golden Books, 20, 22
Little House in the Big Woods, 51, 64, 68, 71, 72, 73, 76
Little House on the Prairie, 64, 67, 68, 71, 74, 75, 88–89
Little House series, 6, 8, 12, 64–67, 69, 70, 72, 74, 75, 77, 80, 81, 82, 86, 89
Little Town on the Prairie, 67, 68, 70, 71, 72, 73
locus amoenus, 53, 81
Longone, Jan, 11, 12–13, 14, 16, 19, 22, 30, 32, 34
Long Winter, The, 70, 73
Los Angeles, 7, 9, 106–12, 113, 120–21, 185n1; food culture, 9, 106–8, 110; food writing, 9, 107–8, 120; geography of, 9, 107–9, 110, 112; Hollywood, 9, 106, 108, 109, 110, 111, 114, 167; inhabitants/Angelenos, 107, 109, 112; Laurel Canyon, 9, 107, 109, 110, 117, 120, 185n3; restaurant culture, 9, 106, 107, 110–12, 120
love, 107, 112, 114, 115, 116, 117, 120, 137, 139, 175, 186n8

Mackey, Margaret, 4, 38
Makoons, 76, 79–80, 81, 83
Mamas and the Papas, 107, 109
Manhattan, 91, 92, 96–97
manners, 32, 36, 41, 45, 47, 54, 55, 58
marginalization, 68, 74, 105, 127, 142–43, 161, 186n8
Martin, Waldo E., 160
Marx, Steven, 62
material culture, 4, 5, 6, 7, 36, 55, 68, 161, 167; food as, 43, 53, 61, 65–66, 81, 91, 100, 172–73, 174–77
Max and Moritz (A Story of Seven Boyish Pranks), 184n8
meals, 8, 11, 14, 17, 19, 20, 21, 22, 24, 27, 33, 41, 45, 46, 47, 58, 71, 72, 94, 103, 105, 106, 111,

117, 118, 119, 121, 142, 145, 148, 150, 154, 155, 157, 159–60, 163, 170, 182n18, 182n3, 188n3; banquets, 54, 55–56, 60, 169; breakfast, 9, 15, 45, 52, 57, 58, 59, 60, 90, 93–94, 98, 103, 105, 117, 145, 148, 155–56, 160, 161, 162, 163, 164, 165, 182n4, 183n5, 186n1; dinner, 16, 17, 19, 21, 23, 31, 35, 38, 40, 45, 73, 95, 117, 131, 136, 152, 154, 155, 159, 162, 164, 174, 181n13; elevenses, 52, 57, 58; feasts, 56, 76, 78, 83, 113, 114, 115, 116, 120, 152, 155, 170; lunch, 52, 60, 72, 174; Sabbath, 95; as site of social relations, 32, 34, 53–55, 57, 58, 59–60, 121, 169; snacks, 33, 56, 58, 147, 162, 182n4, 185n9; supper, 16, 45, 70, 93, 98–99; tea, 15, 36, 47–49, 52, 56, 58, 60

medicine, 14, 37, 60, 79

memory, cultural, 18, 20, 27, 28, 64, 76, 90, 92, 93, 97, 99, 100, 102, 105, 106, 109, 110, 111, 116, 138, 139, 156, 166, 169, 173, 174, 175, 177

Mennell, Stephen, 41–42, 45, 91

menu, 15, 23, 31, 40, 134

metonymy, 10, 54, 57, 60, 99, 102, 104, 110, 175, 182n3

mice, 35, 37, 43, 47, 48, 54, 122, 123, 130, 134–35, 185n1

migration, 8, 9, 13, 75, 167; forced, 9, 78, 80, 166, 169 (*see also* displacement); Great, 144, 145, 152, 154, 165, 187n4

Milne, A. A., 7, 52, 53, 54–55, 57, 59, 60, 61, 62–63

Miller, Adrian, 152, 187n3

Miller, Ian, 47

Miller, John E., 69

Miller, Merle, 108

Minnesota, 64, 65, 69, 71, 73, 86, 88

minority. *See* ethnicity

Missing Angel Juan, 113, 115, 116–20

mobility, social, 39, 40–41, 127

Modern Language Association, 4

Montanari, Massimo, 70, 73, 183n2

Moosewood Cookbook, The, 26

Moosewood Restaurant, 26

mothers, 14, 15, 19, 23, 25, 31, 67, 68, 71, 96, 99, 113, 114, 146, 151, 152, 156, 157, 158, 160, 161, 163, 164, 171, 173, 175; as authority figures, 33, 34, 37, 44, 50, 78–79, 104, 150, 172, 185n10; as cooks and providers of food, 28, 40, 42, 50, 73, 97, 105, 115, 137, 139, 163, 170, 175, 176, 177, 180n1, 188n2; estranged, 115, 144, 157; maternal relationship with children, 98, 105, 137, 138, 152, 163; as models and teachers of cooking, 13, 16, 17, 18, 21–22, 27, 30; and motherhood, 152, 157, 158, 159, 163; refusal to cook, 158–59, 163; as role models for daughters, 145, 146, 163; as signifier of food, 104–5; as unable to cook, 95, 98–99, 115, 155–56

mouth, 3, 56, 57, 63, 72, 76, 78, 79, 108, 159, 173, 174

Moyers, Bill, 98

Mrs. Beeton's Book of Household Management, 5, 36, 38, 39, 41, 42, 43, 44, 180n3, 181n11

Mrs. Frisby and the Rats of NIMH, 122, 123

Murphy, Andi, 88

myth, 43, 51, 76, 79, 81, 83–84, 103, 183n6

narrator, 25, 30, 31, 33, 34, 45, 109, 123, 138, 180n7, 181n16; heterodiegetic, 14, 22; homodiegetic, 17

Nasardinov, Melinda Talbot, 98

Native American children's literature, 7

Native American Renaissance, 66, 87

Native Americans, 64, 65, 66, 74–89, 184n9

Nearing, Helen and Scott, 77

Neuhaus, Jessamyn, 13, 14, 15, 20, 22

New Western history, 8, 69–70

New York City, 92, 93–94, 95, 96, 110, 113, 117, 120, 185n1

Nguyen, Andrea, 170

Nguyen, Viet Thanh, 168, 177, 188n3

Nikolajeva, Maria, 5

Nodelman, Perry, 55

Norrgard, Chantal, 79, 87

North Dakota, 81, 86, 88

nostalgia, 6, 50, 53, 64, 89, 98, 111, 112, 120, 138, 152

Oakland, 9, 144, 145, 151, 152, 153, 156–61, 163, 164, 165, 186n1, 187n5
O'Brien, Robert, C., 122, 123
Ojibwe, 7, 8, 65, 66, 68, 74–89
One Crazy Summer, 9, 144, 145, 153, 156–65, 186n1
On the Banks of Plum Creek, 69, 72, 73
Osage, 88
Other, the, 9, 75, 123, 124–25, 126, 135, 142
Outside Over There, 91
oven, 28, 42, 46, 48, 95, 100, 103, 104, 119, 148, 181n14, 184n8; toy, 20, 22, 179n3
Oxford Symposium on Food and Cookery, 5

palate, 31, 59, 79, 125, 128, 174
paradigmatic, 54, 59, 60
Paris, 9, 32, 125, 126, 128, 131, 133, 137, 138, 186n7, 186n8
party, 15, 35, 36, 47–48, 49, 55, 112, 115, 116, 172
pastoral, 8, 53, 59, 61–63, 182n1
Patel, Raj, 160, 163
Perrot, Jean, 5, 91
pests, 35, 37, 44, 73, 81, 181n5, 186n7
Peter Pan, 62
Phillips, John, 88
picnic, 17, 32, 112, 116, 180n5
Pierre, 90, 104
pioneers, 6, 64, 65, 81–82, 86, 89
Pixar. *See* Disney•Pixar
place, 36, 53, 62, 66, 75, 81, 92, 93, 96, 97, 106–11, 116, 120–21, 144, 145, 153, 155, 156, 160, 163, 165, 169, 184n9
play, 14, 21, 22, 23, 25, 34, 55, 62, 108, 159, 182n1
pleasures, 62–63, 109, 116; of cooking, 16, 26, 27, 30, 32, 97; of food, 9, 15, 19, 22, 25–26, 78–79, 88, 91, 113, 114, 117–18, 139, 168, 171; of mouth, 3, 63; of table, 11, 13, 63; of taste, 4, 10, 32, 34, 112
poet, 8, 53, 56–57, 59, 61, 158, 163
poetry, 53, 56–57, 59–60, 61, 63, 156, 158
poison, 119, 129, 143
Porcupine Year, The, 76, 78, 82
postcolonialism, 4, 87, 142

postmodernism, 75, 87, 109, 110
Potorti, Mary, 160–61
Potter, Beatrix, 4, 7, 35, 36, 37, 38, 39, 41, 42, 43, 44, 45, 46, 47, 49, 50, 180n1, 180n2, 181n13, 181n16, 182n17, 182n19, 182n20, 185n2
poverty, 7, 40, 41–42, 46, 50, 69, 93–94, 160, 161, 164, 187n5
power, 50, 54, 56, 62, 109, 127, 128, 130, 145, 149, 157, 165, 177, 178; for African Americans, 144, 152, 156–57, 160, 187n5; for children, 4, 21, 28, 34, 104, 105, 165, 174–76; of food, 26, 28, 60, 63, 65, 76, 91, 138, 162; lack of, 24, 50, 98, 105, 109, 160; for women, 23, 38, 39, 157
Pretend Soup and Other Real Recipes, 26, 28, 29, 33
processed food. *See* food (types): industrialized
product placement, 20
programmatic architecture, 8, 100, 101
protein, 48, 51, 67
Proust, Marcel, 137, 138
P.S. Be Eleven, 9, 144, 153–57, 161, 164, 187n3
Pudding Lady, The, 40, 41, 42, 46, 50

racism, 74, 75, 145, 147, 149, 165, 174
Rainwater, Catherine, 74–75
range. *See* oven; stove
Raksin, Alex, 109
Rao, Hyagreeva, 126
Raster, Amanda, 83, 86–87
Ratatouille, 9, 123–43
rats, 9, 35, 39, 41–42, 46, 49, 122–43, 181n13, 182n18, 185n1, 185n2, 185n4; extermination of, 49, 124, 129, 130, 134–35, 140, 141, 142, 186n7
Ravage, Marcus, 93–94, 95, 103
Ray, Lana, 76
receipt books. *See* cookbooks
recipe, 5, 7, 11–34, 36, 39, 40, 43, 72, 95, 96, 125, 126, 128, 130, 133–34, 136, 137, 179n2, 181n11
refugees, 166; Vietnamese, 167, 168, 169, 171–73, 177–78, 187n1, 188n2, 188n3

refugee studies, 9, 166
regionalism, 7, 9
restaurants, 9, 26, 30–31, 34, 95, 96, 101, 106, 107, 110, 111–12, 117, 118–19, 120–21, 125–27, 131, 132, 133–34, 136, 140–43, 159, 164, 186n8, 188n2; critics of, 132, 133, 136–39, 179n4, 185n1
Revel, Jean François, 126
revulsion. *See* disgust
roadside architecture, 8, 101
Rombauer, Irma, 20, 179n2
Roth, Philip, 96
Routhier, Nicole, 169–70, 173, 188n2
Rowan, Jan, 107
Ryan, Pam Muñoz, 6, 179n1, 183n4

Saigon, 169, 170, 171, 175, 176, 188n2
Salad People and More Real Recipes, 26, 28, 29, 33
savories, 4, 17, 38, 39, 40, 41, 43, 174
Saxena, Anand, 114
Schlebecker, John T., 69, 70
seeds, 45, 69, 81, 82, 95, 118, 175
self-sufficiency, 64, 67, 146, 147, 149
Sendak, Maurice, 4, 7–8, 50, 90, 91, 92, 93, 96–105, 184n1, 184n5, 184n7, 185n8
Sendak, Philip, 101
Sendak, Sadie, 96, 97, 99, 101
Settlement Cookbook, The, 95
Shahani, Gitanjali G., 8
Shapiro, Laura, 19, 154
Shepard, Ernest, 54, 55, 58
Sherman, Sean, 88, 184n9
Shih, Bryan, 164
silverware. *See* table settings
Singer, Peter, 134–35
Six Little Cooks, or, Aunt Jane's Cooking Class, 12, 14–16, 17, 18–19, 20, 21, 23, 27, 28, 30, 31, 32, 179n2
Slothower, Jodie, 12–13
Snyder, Susan, 53, 61–62
sociability. *See* community
social work theory, 7, 40
Sorenson, Barbara Ellen, 88
South Dakota, 64, 67, 69, 70, 71, 73, 86

Spaeth, Janet, 65
Spencer, Colin, 39, 43
Standage, Tom, 68–69
starvation. *See* hunger
Sternlicht, Sanford, 94, 95
Stewart, Michelle Pagni, 74, 75
stove, 22, 34, 131, 132, 159, 181n14; toy, 20–23
St. Pancras School for Mothers, 40, 42
Stuart, Tristram, 114
Stuart Little, 130, 185n1
subjectivity, 17, 46, 47, 57, 60, 74, 124–25, 129–30, 134–35, 139, 142, 168
Sullivan, Robert, 122–23, 124, 128, 140, 141, 185n4
Sunshine Bakery, 97–98, 99, 100, 103, 184n4
Susie's New Stove: The Little Chef's Cookbook, 20–24, 31, 32
Susina, Jan, 12–13, 109–10, 167
sweets, 4, 15, 17, 38, 39, 40, 41, 43, 51, 58, 95, 97, 100, 105, 119, 170–71, 174, 175, 176
Symons, Michael, 99
synecdoche, 110
syntagmatic, 54, 58, 60

table(s), 10, 11, 13, 21, 23, 32, 34, 37, 38, 39, 54–55, 63, 94, 104, 141, 152, 181n13
table settings, 23, 29, 32, 37, 45, 46, 47, 54, 55, 57, 93
tableware. *See* table settings
Tale of Benjamin Bunny, The, 35, 37, 44
Tale of Jemima Puddle-Duck, The, 35, 37, 181n16
Tale of Jeremy Fisher, The, 35
Tale of Mr. Tod, The, 7, 35, 37, 43, 44–46, 49, 181n16
Tale of Peter Rabbit, The, 4, 5, 7, 35, 36–37, 43, 44, 104, 180n1, 182n19, 182n20, 185n10
Tale of Samuel Whiskers, or, the Roly-Poly Pudding, The, 7, 35, 37, 39, 41–42, 46, 49, 182n18, 185n2
Tale of Squirrel Nutkin, The, 36
Tale of the Flopsy Bunnies, The, 35, 37, 44, 180n1
Tale of the Pie and the Patty-Pan, The, 7, 35–36, 37, 43, 47–49

Tannahill, Reay, 69
taste, 3, 4, 10, 16, 19, 35, 36, 41, 47, 48, 51, 53, 67, 78, 112, 120, 128, 129, 152, 155, 156, 173, 185n4; of food, 53, 59, 67, 71, 79, 118, 119, 132, 155, 171, 172, 173, 175, 176
Theophano, Janet, 17–18, 21, 28, 181n7
These Happy Golden Years, 68, 71, 72, 73
Thick, Malcolm, 72
Toussaint Samat, Maguelonne, 69, 183n6
trauma, 155, 166, 167, 169
Trubek, Amy, 125, 127, 137, 140
Tuan, Yi-Fu, 120
Turner, Frederick Jackson, 6, 66, 89

Vallone, Lynn, 5
values. *See* ideology
Vennum, Thomas, 83–84
vermin, 123, 126, 127, 129–30, 131–32, 134–36, 140, 141, 143
Vietnam, 168, 175, 188n3
Vietnam, North, 169, 170, 171, 188n2
Vietnam, South, 167, 169, 175, 188n2
Vietnamese foodways. *See* foodways: Vietnamese
Vietnamese immigrants. *See* immigrants: Vietnamese
Vietnamese refugees. *See* refugees: Vietnamese
Vietnamese studies, 9, 168
Vietnam War, 164, 167, 168, 169, 170, 175, 176, 177, 188n2
violence, 43–44, 50, 143, 161, 166, 168, 187n5
Virgil, 8, 51, 117
visual text vs. verbal text, 55

Wald, Priscilla, 92, 93, 102
Walker, Alice, 180n4
Walker, Barbara M., 12, 64, 86
Wall, Barbara, 180n7
Walvin, James, 39
Ward, Lynd, 51
Waters, Alice, 26, 27–28, 30–34
Weetzie Bat, 106, 107, 109–10, 111, 112–13, 115, 185n3

Weetzie Bat series, 9, 106, 107, 108, 109, 110, 114, 120
Where the Wild Things Are, 4, 7, 50, 90, 91, 92, 93, 97, 98, 104–5
Whit, William C., 150
White, E. B., 122, 130, 185n1
Whitehead, Tony, 149
Wilder, Laura Ingalls, 6, 7, 8–9, 12, 51, 64, 65–66, 67, 69–73, 74–75, 76, 77, 80, 81, 86, 88–89, 183n1, 183n3
Williams, Yohuru, 164
Williams-Garcia, Rita, 7, 9, 144–46, 149, 150, 152, 153, 156–57, 161, 164–65, 186n3, 187n3
Wind in the Willows, The, 123
Winnie-the-Pooh, 8, 52, 54, 56–59, 60–61, 182n3, 183n5
Wisconsin, 64, 67, 68, 69, 71, 73, 76, 86, 183n5
Witch Baby, 111, 112, 114, 115, 185n3
work, 6, 13, 18, 22, 25, 27, 31, 34, 37, 47, 48, 57, 59, 61–62, 68, 71, 72, 73, 75–77, 78, 82–83, 84–85, 94, 98, 99, 108, 121, 126, 131, 133, 136, 142, 146, 149, 151, 157, 158, 186n8
World's Fair (1939), 97, 98

Yentsch, Anne, 147

Zetter, Roger, 166

ABOUT THE AUTHORS

Photo credit: Ben Leistensnider

KARA K. KEELING is a past president of the Children's Literature Association and serves as professor of English and the Dr. Tracey Schwarze Professor of Arts and Humanities at Christopher Newport University in Newport News, Virginia, where she teaches courses on children's and young adult literature. She coauthored, with Marsha Sprague, *Discovering Their Voices: Engaging Adolescent Girls with Young Adult Literature* (International Reading Association, 2007), and coedited, with Scott Pollard, *Critical Approaches to Food in Children's Literature* (Routledge, 2009). She and Pollard have written on food in children's literature in texts by a number of children's authors (including Neil Gaiman, Polly Horvath, Beatrix Potter, Pam Muñoz Ryan, Maurice Sendak, and Laura Ingalls Wilder).

SCOTT T. POLLARD is professor of English at Christopher Newport University. With Kara Keeling, he coedited *Critical Approaches to Food in Children's Literature* (Routledge 2009). Together they have written and published articles on food in children's literature in texts by a number of children's authors (including Neil Gaiman, Polly Horvath, Beatrix Potter, Pam Muñoz Ryan, Maurice Sendak, and Laura Ingalls Wilder). Pollard also coedited with Margarita Marinova her translation from the Russian of Mikhail Bulgakov's dramatic adaptation of *Don Quixote* (MLA 2014), and he edited a special volume of *Children's Literature Association Quarterly* on disability in 2013.